COMMUNALISM IN MODERN INDIA

Encyclopaedic History of India Series

COMMUNALISM IN MODERN INDIA

Dr. Mahesh Vikram Singh
Professor, Deptt. of History
Mahatma Gandhi Kashi Vidyapeeth
Varanasi (UP)

Dr. Brij Bhushan Shrivastava
Head of Deptt., Ancient History, Archeology & Culture
SMMTPG College, Ballia (UP)

CENTRUM PRESS
NEW DELHI-110002 (INDIA)

CENTRUM PRESS
H.O.: 4360/4, Ansari Road, Daryaganj,
New Delhi-110002 (India)
Tel: 23278000, 23261597, 23255577, 23286875
B.O.: No. 1015, Ist Main Road, BSK IIIrd Stage,
IIIrd Phase, IIIrd Block, Bangalore-560085 (INDIA)
Tel: 080-41723429
Email: centrumpress@gmail.com
Visit us at: www.centrumpress.com

Communalism in Modern India

First Edition, 2011
ISBN 978-93-80836-91-1

PRINTED IN INDIA

Printed at Mehra Offset Press, Delhi

प्रो. विपिन चंद्रा
अध्यक्ष
Prof. Bipan Chandra
Chairman

नेशनल बुक ट्रस्ट, इंडिया
नेहरू भवन
5 इंस्टीट्यूशनल एरिया, फेज़-II, वसंत कुंज, नई दिल्ली-110 070
फोन/ Phone: 011-26121880 फैक्स/ Fax: 011-26121883

NATIONAL BOOK TRUST, INDIA
Nehru Bhawan
5 Institutional Area, Phase II, Vasant Kunj, New Delhi-110 070
ई-मेल / E-mail: chairman@nbtindia.org.in
वेबसाइट / Website: www.nbtindia.org.in

FOREWORD

The term 'history' is derived from the Greek word 'historia' that means knowledge acquired through investigation. Obviously, this knowledge can be correct if the method of investigation is objective and not vitiated by any kind of bias. In other words, if the study of human past is comprehensive and obtained through scientific inquiry, it can provide perspective on the present day problems and help one plan for the future.

A true historian has to identify the sources that can be most useful in a given context. Documents, coins, archaeology, anthropology, geography, travel accounts, oral traditions, mythology and so on can be useful but they can be used only after their veracity is tested and they are critically examined. They should be checked and counter-checked.

Over the centuries, one finds the study and writing of history vitiated by biases. There are numerous instances in which historical data have been distorted to support or oppose certain preconceived ideas and purposes. Strictly speaking such history is just like fiction to accord with preconceived notions and serve some ulterior purposes.

The study of the past has never been static. Conclusions go on changing because of the discovery of new materials and tools of investigation. To give a concrete example, the carbon 14 or radiocarbon dating test has revolutionized the study of civilizations and settlements, especially of prehistoric times, for which written documents, coins, etc. are seldom available. This method has enabled historians to determine more accurately than before the time period of a particular civilization or settlement. This method was discovered only 70 years ago by American scientists.

In our country, excavations brought to light the Indus Valley Civilization and its various features, hitherto unknown. Similarly, no complete text of Kautilya's Arthashastra was available before it was discovered by Shamasastry, the chief of the Mysore Government Oriental Library in the first decade of the last century. Likewise, people's knowledge of the history of the Buddhist period got extended after excavations at Sarnath and the ruins of the Asokan period at Patna. In the future, if the Harappan inscriptions are deciphered, our knowledge of the Indus Valley Civilization will increase enormously. All these instances underline the fact that our knowledge of history is never static and its frontiers go on extending.

In the light of what has been said above the encyclopedic history is going to be of great help to students interested in Indian history. It is comprehensive and as far as possible free from biases. It includes the latest materials, and objective conclusions.

Prof . Bipan Chandra
Professor Emeritus, JNU
Chairman, National Book Trust, India

Contents

Preface

The people of India have had a continuous civilization since 2500 B.C., when the inhabitants of the Indus River valley developed an urban culture based on commerce and sustained by agricultural trade. This civilization declined around 1500 B.C., probably due to ecological changes. During the second millennium B.C., pastoral, Aryan-speaking tribes migrated from the northwest into the subcontinent. As they settled in the middle Ganges River valley, they adapted to antecedent cultures.

The political map of ancient and medieval India was made up of myriad kingdoms with fluctuating boundaries. In the 4th and 5th centuries A.D., northern India was unified under the Gupta Dynasty. During this period, known as India's Golden Age, Hindu culture and political administration reached new heights. Islam spread across the Indian subcontinent over a period of 500 years. In the 10th and 11th centuries, Turks and Afghans invaded India and established sultanates in Delhi. In the early 16th century, descendants of Genghis Khan swept across the Khyber Pass and established the Mughal (Mogul) Dynasty, which lasted for 200 years. From the 11th to the 15th centuries, southern India was dominated by Hindu Chola and Vijayanagar Dynasties. During this time, the two systems—the prevailing Hindu and Muslim—mingled, leaving lasting cultural influences on each other.

The first British outpost in South Asia was established in 1619 at Surat on the northwestern coast. Later in the century, the East India Company opened permanent trading stations at Madras, Bombay, and Calcutta, each under the protection of native rulers. The British expanded their influence from these footholds until, by the 1850s, they controlled most of present-day India, Pakistan, and Bangladesh. In 1857, a rebellion in north India led by mutinous Indian soldiers caused the British Parliament to transfer all political power from the East India Company to the Crown. Great Britain began administering most of India directly while controlling the rest through treaties with local rulers.

In the late 1800s, the first steps were taken toward self-government in British India with the appointment of Indian councillors to advise the British viceroy and the establishment of provincial councils with Indian members; the British subsequently widened participation in legislative councils. Beginning in 1920, Indian leader Mohandas K. Gandhi transformed the Indian National Congress political party into a mass movement to campaign against British colonial rule.

—Authors

1

Introduction

British colonial rule and the impact of western culture and civilization brought forward several categories of response among educated and concerned Indians. These responses were in evidence from 1860 onwards when British policy in India began to undergo drastic changes. Suspicion, repression, systematic exploitation of existing social distance among communities to foster divisive tendencies for political ends and strict surveillance replaced pre-1858 laxity in these matters. For our purpose, however, we take up these strands of responses from 1885 when the Indian National Congress was formally established for the simple reason that some form of organized politics appeared in support of one or the other category of response.

Various Responses

These responses may be stared as follows:

a) Modernization of politics and social reform on the basis of rational principles of Politics and Religion in Modern India: the Interface the west and through a process of gradual adaptation; loyalist, peaceful and constitutionalist in approach;

b) Radicalization/Spiritualization of politics, its goals and methods; mobilization using Hindu religious symbols and emotive appeals to the virtues of self-reliance and past glory; opposition to British rule; traditional approach to social reform;

c) Loyalist, constitutionalist in political approach; mobilization based on appeal to Muslim religion and protection of Muslim interests;

d) A political outlook in which preference for western principles of government was combined with innovative, peaceful and active methods of protest; mobilization and action; freedom as a primary goal.

In addition, there were attempts by *Scheduled Castes* and *Tribes* to share seats and power in the emerging political order. The Marxian left forces, most prominent in the thirties, also represented an important trend of opinion and action in response to colonial subjection; a significant influence on Indian politics.

Indian Response as Reflected in Organizations and Movements

These trends found early expression in organizations and movements associated with the Brahmo Samaj, Prarthana Samaj, Arya Samaj, the Aligarh College and Sir Syed Ahmed Khan, the Ramakrishna Mission, the Theosophical Society, and Social ' Reform Congress. These organizations and corresponding movements stood for *I* reform and regeneration of society or a particular community through religious or rationalist ideas. The movements were limited in scale, and were not overtly political in character. But they did underline directly or indirectly, the crucial role of religion and tradition in generating popular enthusiasm around a cause. Religion was the subject of discourse or a means of social mobilization. The lesson was not lost on the militaht nationalists and the 'extremists' as they were called in Congress parlance; they represented the second strand of political response of western impact.

Moderates' Response

As long as liberal moderate leaders were in charge of the Congress (1885-1906) the effective emphasis was on western liberal principles of reason, rights, loyalty, freedom from prejudice and discrimination, national unity, gradualism and an element of elitism. Religion was considered a matter of personal concern. The liberals were democratic in their principles, but their politics never came down to the level of the people nor did they ever feel the necessity to deliberately blend religion and politics to advance political causes. As some of the Congress leaders (Tilak in Maharashtra and Aurobindo Ghosh, Surendranath Banerjee, Bipin Pal in Bengal and Lala Lajpat Rai in Punjab) entered the era of mass politics, though on a limited scale, and virtually without the approval of the liberal leadership, soon after the government proposed to partition the province of Bengal on grounds of administrative convenience in 1903, the politics of extremists and the militant nationalists could be said to have arrived on the scene.

Militant Nationalists

It was a new brand of politics-active and impatient-growing out of accumulated grievances, new developments in India, as well as a sense of disgust with the existing state of affairs. There was a new found confidence among India's industrial entrepreneurs which prompted them to demand more room for expansion. Growing volume of educated unemployment, the economic distress of the people, the combined effect of Dadabhai Naoroji's 'Poverty and the British Rule in India', R.C.Dutt's 'Economic History of British India', and William Digby's 'Prosperous British India' all contributed to increasing militancy.

Most of the militants of Bengal could be divided into strands: There were believer; in the mother cult; that is, those who extolled shakti which according to them symbolized India of the past, present and future. The other group was called Vedantists who followed the preaching of Swami Vivekananda and the message of Lord Krishna. Both groups believed in the use of force or violence though it cannot be said that was their only programme of action. An interesting comment on both these groups comes from Lajpat Rai. He said

"They are neither nihilist nor anarchist. They are patriots who have raised their patriotism to the pitch of a religion. Their religion remarkably fits in with their patriotism and makes the latter indescribably intense and alive."

Again in the words of K.S. Shelvankar, Indian nationalism in the first decade of the 20th century was "romantic, mystical, aggressive riddled with fallacies but sound enough to restore the self-respect of the middle classes." It was "a self-confident militancy fortified by all that was heroic and splendid in India's past."

Tilak and Aurobindo were of the belief that a quasi-religious appeal would strengthen Indian nationalism. In the second and third decades of the century, militants in Bengal broadly followed two types of activities. One was concerned with bomb throwing terrorization and destabilization through creating scare among officials. The other group concentrated on organized rebellion, infiltration into the army and creating the grounds for revolt and guerilla warfare. They did not believe in individual assassinations or looting.

Tilak represented another and an earlier strand of radical nationalism in Maharashtra concentrating on the systematic use of scriptural interpretations, religious festivals and festivals celebrating the heroic historical figures of the past, like Shivaji to arouse consciousness among people and to ensure enthusiastic participation in the cause of the struggle for freedom from colonial subjection and helplessness. In the words of Aurobindo

"Mr. Tilak was the first political leader to break through the routine of its (Congress) somewhat academical methods, to bridge the gulf between the present and the past and to restore continuity to the political life of the nation.... he used methods which Indianized the movement and brought it to the masses."

Muslim Communal Separatism

Many authors have pointed out that nationalism of the Maharashtra and Bengal school antagonized the Muslims of India and was a potent cause behind the rise of Muslim communal separatism. It should be pointed out here that neither of these two schools of aggressive, popular and uncompromisingly anticolonial nationalism was by intent directly against the Muslim interest or meant to hurt their sentiments. As a matter of fact, in the early stages of militant nationalism in Bengal Muslims could be found in the ranks of the militants though not in large numbers. They were also appreciative of the uncompromising hostility towards British rule and did not oppose the swadeshi movement at its inception.

It is true, however, that the intense religious symbolism of both the schools was bolstered by references to Shivaji who fought against Muslim rule as well as by Bankim Chandra's novel 'Ananda Math' which hinted at a revolt and the missionary zeal which the author of the novel lent to this effort did provide grounds for uneasiness and a sense of alienation in the minds of the Muslims. Of equal importance was certainly the desperate and Political and Relldon on concerted efforts on the part of the British Indian

Government to bring about a rift-Modern India: the Interftee in the nationalist forces, by pulling back sixty two million Muslims from the fold of nationalism. Under the instructions of Lord Morley who was the Viceroy, and Minto and egged on by the bureaucracy, a representative delegation of the Muslim upper classes was invited to be entertained by the Viceroy in his garden at Simla on October 1, 1906 to press on him the urgent need to protect the interests of the Muslim community, ostensibly against the possible onslaught of the Hindu majority.

The Muslim upper classes who were to a large extent dependent on the colonial government readily obliged. The Viceroy sympathized with the claims made by the delegation for state patronage. Referring to the event, an official wrote to the Viceroy that it was "A work of statesmanship that will affect India and Indian history for many a long year."

Similar views were expressed by both Morley and Minto. The same year on December 30 the All India Muslim League was founded to promote feelings of loyalty to the British government and to protect the political and other rights of Indian Muslims. In 1908 and in the following year, the League demanded the extension of representation on communal basis. In the year 1909, the Morley-Minto Reforms brought forward the divisive doctrine of minority representation on the basis of religion.

The efforts of the British to divide Indians and to use one against another was given another expression through the doctrine of communal representation. It was designed to strengthen communalism, introduce political discrimination and create endless complications, especially for the Congress and the nationalist forces engaged in the struggle to free India from colonial 'subjection. The Congress promptly protested against the principle of communal representation as well as disproportionate representation given to the Muslims. The Congress also pointed out in its Lahore session of 1909 that the distinctions to be brought about were "unjust, invidious, and humiliating."

In the analysis of this highly regrettable and regressive development in the struggle for freedom, proper weightage should be given to the religious symbolism of militant nationalism, the role of the Muslim upper class as well as the malicious and mischievous policies of the British government.

Main Trends of Muslim Political Thinking

If we analyse Muslim political thinking of the first two decades of the twentieth century, it will be seen that the main trends in their thinking during this period were:

a) that the Congress does not adequately represent all the nationalities and races of India;

b) that the Muslims are backward educationally and in economic standing, and constitute a minority compared to the Hindus. Therefore, in any future system of representative government and administration in India the Muslim will be swamped by type Hindus;

c) that the Muslims are different from the Hindus in their culture, moral code, social organisation, religion and therefore constitute a separate entity or nationality.

In addition to the above, there were other trends of thought each of which had its asceridance and decline among the Muslims, e.g., it is the duty of Muslims to be loyal to the government, seek protection including political rights. Another trend stood for joining the fight against the British government. There was a small, though occasionally influential, nationalist group which held the opinion that the two communities should co-operate in as many spheres of action as possible including the nationalist struggle and that Hindus should show more enerosity to the requirements and sentiments of the minority community. Apart from these trends of thinking, the pan-Islamic sensitivity always played an important role in prompting the Indian Muslims to unite their ranks for action.

It will be seen that as India's political struggle unfolded, the Muslim League, which claimed to represent the entirecommunity, and succeeded in substantially establishing its claim only after 1937, pitched its political demand on the basis of one or more of the trends of thought listed above. Sir Syed Ahmed Khan's plea for considering the Muslims as a distinct and separate nationality on grounds of "race, culture, religion, physique, social organisation, moral code, political outlook and historical associations" was a substantive formulation on which M.A. Jinnah based his 'Two Nation Theory' and the demand for partition of India in 1940. Loyalty to and dependence on the British colonial government for special favours and protection of Muslim interests resulted in separate electorates, job reservation and demand for parity of status with the majority community in political representation. From the assumed incompatibility of Muslim interests with those of the Hindus, possible intolerance and communal flare-ups that compromised the temper and strength of the anti-colonial struggle of Gandhian Congress and the Marxist parties appears to be a logical development. Similarly, pan-Islamic sentiment and religious affinity with the Muslim cause everywhere, of which Iqbal theorized so eloquently, rallied the Indian Muslims for Khilafat Non-Co-operation struggle against the government by the All India Khilafat Committee and the Indian National Congress during 1920-22. The nationalist trend of thought among the Muslims saw its ascendancy in years of the First World War. It was a trend subscribe to by some of the eminent scholars and professional men like M.A.N. Hydari, R.M. Sayani, Mohammad Ali, M.A. Ansari, Maulana Abul Kalam Azad and M.A. Jinnah. From what has been said above, it should be evident that in the thought pattern of the Muslims, the desire for peace, amity and cooperative action was present and attained temporary dominance at different periods of the anti-colonial struggle in India. But it could not become the effective pattern for the entire period under consideration. In the following passages, we take a look at Hindu religion based political thinking as well as nationalist discourse in an attempt to ascertain the-nature of the problem that existed.

Religious Imagery and Symbolism

The frequent recourse to religious Imagery and symbolism to explain social and economic conditions of a people or to bring into focus political ideas and goals could come about as a result of the high degree of religious orientation of a person or a community, or more deliberately to get quick political results by motivating a people to action on the basis of emotive fervour, a sense of mission, and allegiance to a cause. To individuals or communities having such orientation, no other frame of reference except that which is based on one's religion is valid for understanding and evaluation of larger reality. This is so because to them religion is the only source of relevant knowledge. It is obvious that political discourse based on such frameworks of reference gives rise to channels of communication that are exclusive to a set of believers among whom each word/symbol having a religious connotation assumes a meaning which is unfamiliar to others. It follows that in a country with a social composition such as India's, the use of religious symbolism is bound to be seen as relevant for only one community of co-religionists. For others, it will be alienating.. Such alienation is independent of secular, nationalist intentions of those who speak, write and act to produce a nationalist discourse. That is why in colonial India whenever religious ideas were linked with an essentially political discourse it resulted in Hindu or Muslim nationalism.

Dayananda, Vivekananda and Savarkar were three persons whose ideas on religion, culture and politics had significantly strengthened the foundation of revivalist nationalist politics in India.

Dayananda Saraswati

Dayananda Saraswati, a monotheist Hindu reformer of the 19th century exercised considerable influence as a revivalist nationalist. Dayananda was one of the first to-assert that foreign rule constitutes an aggression on India's culture (the essence of India) which is defined by vedic religion and social organization of the Hindus. Dryanand believed that the vedic religion contained the supreme truths from which Indus have stayed far. He gave an inspired critique of the Hindu religion as it was practised in his time and advocated return to the polity and society of vedic times. Although, not many considered his suggested panacea as workable, large number of Hindus were deeply moved by his uncompromising opposition to foreign rule and his militant reformism as typified in the Arya Samaj, the organization Dayananda had established to implement his ideas.

Swami Vivekananda

Swami Vivekananda, vedantist and an 'extraordinary monk' of the late 19th century India, prote and talked extensively on the idea of spiritual freedom, which according to him is tied up with religious norms, and the subsequent degeneration of freedom into rights that have material power as their-basis. Vivekananda discoursed that India lost her freedom because of the prevalence of the doctrine of rights. Under the influence of material culture and the doctrine of rights individual human beings loose their sociality, and society gets structured into an elaborate system of specific roles. This has weakened India's urge for freedom. Vivekananda warned that unless India underwent a cultural revolution, the promise of freedom which was a part of the legacy of the ancient culture will never be redeemed. Consequently, Vivekananda's message of revolution, for the realization of freedom despite its unmistakable universality coincided with and energized the Hindu revivalist current of nationalism which projected its message of political freedom through religious-cultural symbolism.

V.D. Savarkar

Like Dayananda; Savarkar also stressed the role of race, religion and nationhood. But Savarkar's formulation was different and challenging. For him, people of different religions sharing a feeling of belonging to a common territory (e.g. the geographical entity called India) can equally share common racial and religious ethos. This, he called. 'Hindutva' which farmed the basis of India's nationhood. In the make up of Hindutva, Hindu culture has a greater role to play than religiosity while Savarkar's conceptualization permits a composite nationhood in India. His stand against pan-Islamism and his emphasis on Hindu culture were resented by religious minorities. Note: i) Use the space given below for your answer.

Some Aspects of Hindu-Muslim Problem

From this brief resume of three thinkers from whose ideas Hindu revivalist nationalism drew sustenance at different times, it becomes clear that one aspect of the Hindu-Muslim problem was the language of communication (including the use of religious or cultural symbols).

A second aspect of the same problem has been obliquely referred to by Jawaharlal Nehru in his autobiography. Nehru says that the petty-bourgeois leadership of the Congress sought those remedies that suited its interests and outlooks. What Nehru said about Congress leadership was equally applicable to the leadership of the Muslim League. The Muslim League leadership was composed of rich landlords and the middle class which was scared of competition from Hindu petty-bourgeois counterparts. It has been pointed out that one of the biggest mistakes of the Congress leadership was that Congress approached only the Muslim leadership and ' not the Muslim people. Another fact of the Hindu-Muslim problem comes into focus, when we consider the developments from 1920 onwards. Between 1914 and 1922 Hindu-Muslim relationship appeared to have touched a peak insofar as cordiality is concerned. International political developments, and the misery of the common people at home in India, because of high prices and famines affected Muslim and Hindu feelings alike. The Lucknow Pact between the Congress and the League in 1916, and the joint participation of the Hindus and Muslims in the Khilafat Non-Co-operation Movement during 1919-22 appeared to be a real breakthrough. In retrospect, however, all this would appear to be nothing but a chance coordination of ideas, with no basic understanding.

The Bardoli directive by Gandhi suspending the movement quickly laid bare the lack of mutual confidence. There was an almost immediate and sharp deterioration in the communal situation which continued until 1928. The-widespread sense of insult following the announcement of the all white Simon Commission (1927), the prospects of another dose of constitutional reforms, and perhaps the failure of the post-Bardoli phase of politics of both sides promoted relatively simple proposals from nationalist Muslims for a more viable unity of purpose and action between the two communities, These proposals fell through because of various objections from ' the Congress representatives in the All Parties Committee which was deliberating them to frame a constitution which would be acceptable to all.

In the civil disobedience movements of 1930-32, Muslim participation was not as much as it was in the Khilafat Non-Co-operation Movement. Any hope of communal amity that this may have generated quickly evaporated in the Second Round Table Conference of 1931 which Gandhi attended. The Conference deliberations did not go well for Gandhi and the Congress. The conservatives, the sectarians of both sides, encouraged by the government representatives, took charge of the proceedings at the Second Round Table Conference. Separate electorates could not be prevented, nor could the Congress prevent the fragmentation of the political community it so desired for the nationalist movement and for a free India of the future. For the Congress, Gandhi, and perhaps also Nehru, this was perhaps the point where the hope of Hindu-Muslim unity was given up. There appeared to be a somewhat unexpected reluctance or a lack of enthusiasm on the part of Congress to carry on dialogues with Muslim leaders for any length of time. After the 1937 elections to provincial legislatures, the League's request for a coalition ministry in U.P. was not accepted by the Congress. At about the same time, the Muslim Mass Contact resolution of the Congress which had the important support of Gandhi and Nehru also languished for want of zealous implementation which such a proposal deserved. Soon after the demand for partition was heard, and a formal resolution demanding partition was accepted by the League in 1940.

Why this apparent resignation on the part of the Congress? Why this extreme demand for partitioning the country on the part of the League? Too often the Congress is blamed directly or indirectly for this failure. What appears to be more probable is that there was a mutual lack of trust which resulted in either trivial objections or demand for too many guarantees. Neither was likely to succeed in bringing about unity of purpose and action.

Syed Ahmed Khan

Sir Syed Ahmed Khan, KCSI (also Sayyid Ahmad Khan) (October 17, 1817 – March 27, 1898), commonly known as Sir Syed (although this is technically incorrect; the would have properly been called "Sir Ahmed" as Sayyid is itself a title in this case), was an Indian educator and politician, and an Islamic reformer and modernist. Sir Syed pioneered modern education for the Muslim community in India by founding the Muhammedan Anglo-Oriental College, which later developed into the Aligarh Muslim University. His work gave rise to a new generation of Muslim intellectuals and politicians who composed the Aligarh movement to secure the political future of Muslims in India.

In 1842, Emperor Bahadur Zafar revived upon Syed Ahmad Khan the title of Javad-ud Daulah, conferred upon Syed Ahmad's grandfather Syed Hadi by Emperor Shah Alam II in about the middle of the eighteenth century. The Emperor added to it the additional title of Arif Jang. The conferment of these titles was symbolic of Syed Ahmad Khan's incorporation into the nobility of Delhi.

Born into Mughal nobility, Sir Syed earned a reputation as a distinguished scholar while working as a jurist for the British East India Company. During the Indian Rebellion of 1857 he remained loyal to the British and was noted for his actions in saving European lives. After the rebellion he penned the booklet *Asbab-e-Baghawat-e-Hind* (*The Causes of the Indian Mutiny*) — a daring critique, at the time, of British policies that he blamed for causing the revolt. Believing that the future of Muslims was threatened by the rigidity of their orthodox outlook, Sir Syed began promoting Western-style scientific education by founding modern schools and journals and organising Muslim intellectuals. Towards this goal, Sir Syed founded the Muhammedan Anglo-Oriental College in 1875 with the aim of promoting social and economic development of Indian Muslims.

One of the most influential Muslim politicians of his time, Sir Syed was suspicious of the Indian independence movement and called upon Muslims to loyally serve the British Raj. He denounced nationalist organisations such as the Indian National Congress, instead forming organisations to promote Muslim unity and pro-British attitudes and activities. Sir Syed promoted the adoption of Urdu as the *lingua franca* of all Indian Muslims, and mentored a rising generation of Muslim politicians and intellectuals. Although hailed as a great Muslim leader and social reformer, Sir Syed remains the subject of controversy for his views on Hindu-Muslim issues.

Do not show the face of Islam to others; instead show your face as the follower of true Islam representing character, knowledge, tolerance and piety. —Sir Syed Ahmed Khan

Early Life

Syed Ahmed Khan Bahadur was born in Delhi, then the capital of the Mughal Empire. His family is said to have migrated from Herat (now in Afghanistan) in the time of emperor Akbar, although by other accounts his family descended from Arabia. Many generations of his family had since been highly connected with the Mughal administration. His maternal grandfather Khwaja Fariduddin served as *wazir* in the court of Akbar Shah II. His paternal grandfather Syed Hadi held a *mansab*, a high-ranking administrative position and honorary name of Jawwad Ali Khan in the court of Alamgir II. Sir Syed's father Mir Muhammad Muttaqi was personally close to Akbar Shah II and served as his personal adviser. However, Sir Syed was born at a time when rebellious governors, regional insurrections and the British colonialism had diminished the extent and power of the Mughal state, reducing its monarch to a figurehead status. With his elder brother Syed Muhammad Khan, Sir Syed was raised in a large house in a wealthy area of the city. They were raised in strict accordance with Mughal noble traditions and exposed to politics. Their mother Azis-un-Nisa played a formative role in Sir Syed's life, raising him with rigid discipline with a strong emphasis on education. Sir Syed was taught to read and understand the Qur'an by a female tutor, which was unusual at the time. He received an education traditional to Muslim nobility in Delhi. Under the charge of Maulvi Hamiduddin, Sir Syed was trained in Persian, Arabic, Urdu and religious subjects. He read the works of Muslim scholars and writers such as Sahbai, Rumi and Ghalib. Other tutors instructed him in mathematics, astronomy and Islamic jurisprudence. Sir Syed was also adept at swimming, wrestling and other sports. He took an active part in the Mughal court's cultural activities. His elder brother founded the city's first printing press in the Urdu language along with the journal *Sayyad-ul-Akbar*. Sir Syed pursued the study of medicine for several years, but did not complete the prescribed course of study. Until the death of his father in 1838, Sir Syed had lived a life customary for an affluent young Muslim noble. Upon his father's death, he inherited the titles of his grandfather and father and was awarded the title of *Arif Jung* by the emperor Bahadur Shah Zafar. Financial difficulties put an end to Sir Syed's formal education, although he continued to study in private, using books on a variety of subjects. Sir Syed assumed editorship of his brother's journal and rejected offers of employment from the Mughal court. Having recognised the steady decline in Mughal political power, Sir Syed entered the British East India Company's civil service. He was appointed *serestadar* at the courts of law in Agra, responsible for record-keeping and managing court affairs. In 1840, he was promoted to the title of *munshi*.

Sir Syed Ahmed Khan lived the last two decades of his life in Aligarh, regarded widely as the mentor of 19th-and 20th century Muslim intellectuals and politicians. He remained the most influential Muslim politician in India, with his opinions guiding the convictions of a large majority of Muslims. Battling illnesses and old age, Sir Syed died on March 27, 1898. He was buried besides Sir Syed Masjid inside the campus of the Aligarh university. His funeral was attended by thousands of students, Muslim leaders and British officials. Sir Syed is widely commemorated across South Asia as a great Muslim reformer and visionary.

At the same time, Sir Syed sought to politically ally Muslims to the British government. An avowed loyalist of the British Empire, Sir Syed was nominated as a member of the Civil Service Commission in 1887 by Lord Dufferin. In 1888, he established the United Patriotic Association at Aligarh to promote political cooperation with the British and Muslim participation in the government. Syed Ahmed Khan was knighted by the British government in 1888 and in the following year he received an LL.D. *honoris causa* from the Edinburgh University.

The university he founded remains one of India's most prominent institutions. Prominent alumni of Aligarh include Muslim political leaders Maulana Mohammad Ali, Abdur Rab Nishtar, Maulana Shaukat Ali and Maulvi Abdul Haq, who is hailed in Pakistan as *Baba-e-Urdu* (*Father of Urdu*). The first two Prime Ministers of Pakistan, Liaquat Ali Khan and Khawaja Nazimuddin, as well as the late Indian President Dr. Zakir Hussain, are amongst Aligarh's most famous graduates. In India, Sir Syed is commemorated as a pioneer who worked for the socio-political upliftment of Indian Muslims, Sir Syed is also hailed as a founding father of Pakistan for his role in developing a Muslim political class independent of Hindu-majority organisations. The Sir Syed University of Engineering and Technology was established in honour of Sir Syed in Karachi and is a leading technical institution in Pakistan. Furthermore, Sir Syed Government Girls College in Karachi, Pakistan is also named in the honour of Sir Syed Ahmed Khan. Today he has family living in Denmark and UK.

Criticism

He is criticized for supporting British Imperialists during the War of Independence (1857) in which Indian masses rose up against the foreign rule. He also worked as government's spy and was indirectly responsible for the hangings of several freedom fighters.

Supporters of Sir Syed contend that his political vision gave an independent political expression to the Muslim community, which aided its goal of securing political power in India. His philosophy guided the creation of the All India Muslim League in 1906, as a political party separate from the Congress. Sir Syed's ideas inspired both the liberal, pro-British politicians of the Muslim League and the religious ideologues of the Khilafat struggle. The Muslim League remained at odds with the Congress and continued to advocate the boycott of the Indian independence movement. In the 1940s, the student body of Aligarh committed itself to the establishment of Pakistan and contributed in large measure to the activities of the Muslim League. Sir Syed's patronage of Urdu led to its widespread use amongst Indian Muslim communities and following the Partition of India its adoption as the official language of Pakistan, even though Bengali and Punjabi were more prevalent at the time.

Fundamentalism, Communalism and Secularism

I and secularism. We then explain up each of these basic concepts and expand on them. We take up first the concept of fundamentalism and describe it. Next we turn to communalism and note down the reasons for communal riots and examine their economic aid social dimensions. This is followed by an analysis of inter-community dynamics.

Finally we turn to secularism which is seen, in some ways, as a panacea to fundamentalism and communalism. We examine somedifferent views on secularism, including Gandhiji's viewpoint.

Fundamentalism is the first of our three concepts and it stresses the infallibility of and doctrine. The believe accept it as a literal historical record. The result is that a militant stand is taken by the followers; often preceded or followed by a desire for a separate homeland. At times, this too is taken as a prophecy in the-scriptures. However, society, by its various arms (the police, army and so on), attempts to suppress or eliminate the fundamentalists. This is especially so when they begin acting outside of the law. Communalism is associated with eruption of violence and riots, these conflagrations may not have any particular aim or goal (apart from communal ascendancy or, supremacy). Fundamentalism however is an organised all encompassing movement which aims at promotion of societal goals specifically in the light of religious enshrinements. Operational strategy includes peaceful as well as war-life uses and movements.

Communalism

While discussing the nature of politics in the new states of Africa and Asia, Clifford Geertz, an American anthropologist (1963: 105-157), wrote, "When we speak of communalism in India we refer to religious contrasts, when we speak of it in Malaya we are mainly concerned with racial ones, and in the Congo with tribal ones". Here the significant link is between communal and political loyalties. Thus when we talk of India we are talking mainly of religion based oppositions. Communalism has been described as a sectarian exploitation of social traditions as a medium of political mobilization. This is done to punish the interests of the entrenched groups. Thus communalism is an ideology used to fulfil socio eco-politico hopes of a community or social @ups. It requires proposals and programmes to ensure its very existence. These become active in phases of social change. Communalism arose in India during its colonial phase. Communal politics it strategies on religion and tradition. The interpretation of history is for purposes of mobilisation. Communal organisations have little room for democracy. Secondly they may also involve racist contrasts and perpetrate the same. They consider egalitarianism as abnormal and support patriarchy as a familial and social norm Communalism is therefore a

i) belief system

ii) social phenomenon.

Communalism arises out of a belief system, and assumes great solidarity within a community which is not always true. We find that there are often inter community quarrels. Further, the protagonists of communalism hold a particular view of history and take care to point out that a community has been identified with common sufferings and goals as a whole. The exclusiveness of the community is stressed vis a vis other communities, and it is therefore considered logical to fight for one's rights in a literal way.

Communalism in India has, as noted earlier, a colonial legacy wherein the rulers (Britishers) used religious contrasts, existing among the different communities to their advantage by giving them prominence.

After Independence economic modernization of India expanded economic opportunities but not enough to curb unhealthy competitiveness. Job sharing among the different communities from as smaller pool of opportunities in causing much heartburn. Independence from the colonical power unleashed a horrendous communal holocaust, caused by the partition of the country into two parts on the eve of Independence in 1947.

Secularism

The conceptual construct of secularism is adopted in India by way of a solution to the problems, posed by fundamentalism and communalism. Ideally spealung, it denotes a situation where there is a clear distinction of religion from such spheres of life as political and economic systems. Each religion is to be respected and practiced in private. In ideological terms it is not a system of beliefs and practices that is to be mixed with political ideology, with a view to wooing any particular community into the voting booth. By and large, secularism separates relation and polity. It endorses the view that there should be provided equal opportunities by the state to all the communities. Further, for secularists all religious beliefs are to be approached rationally and finally social life is to be approached in an equalitarian manner. Further the term secularism refers to the ideas opposed to religious education. It has been linked to the process of secularization. This is the process by which various sectors of society are removed from the domination of religious symbols and also the domination of religious' institutions. Finally the idea of secularism has been transferred from 'the dialectic of modem science and Protestantism' in the west to South Asian societies. This transference is full of problems and cannot be conceived in terms of a smooth process.

Aspects of Fundamentalism

Fundamentalism as a concept was first used in 19 10-19 15 when anonymous authors published 12 volumes of literature called them 'The Fundamentals'. In the early 20s the print media used this word with reference to conservative protestant groups in North America. These groups were concerned about liberal interpretations of the Bible. Alarmed by this the conservatives insisted on some "fundamentals" of faith. These included belief in the virgin birth, divinity, the physical resurrection of Jesus were published in 12 pamphlets called *The Fundamentals* between 19 10-19 1 5. Thus began the specialised usage of the concept of "fundamentalism". Thus a fundamental movement is one which takes infallibility of a scripture as a basic issue and as a guide to life. Some fundamentalists add that there is no need to even interpret the scripture as meaning in it is self-evident. *This ojlen amounts to intolerance of any form of disagreement or dissent. Thus there is an apprehension that fundamentalists are narrow minded, and bigoted.* T.N. Madan *(1993)* has pointed out that the word Fundamentalism has gained wide currency in the contemporary world. According to him it refers to a variety of norms, values, attitudes which either judge the fundamentalists or condemn them outright. This world is sometimes erroneously used in place of communalism. In fact the word fundamentalism has become a blanket term. That is to say that various fundamental movements across the world 'are actually not identical but differ in various ways. But they are linked by a 'family' resemblance. Fundamentalist movements are of a collective character. They are ofteri led by charismatic leaders who are usually men. Thus the 1979 Iranian movement was led by Ayatollah Khomeini, and the recent Sikh fundamentalist upsurge by Sant Bhindranwale (Madan, ibid). Fundamentalism leaders need not be religious leaders. Thus Maulana Maududi, founder of the Jamati Islami in India was a journalist. K.B. Hedgewar, founder of the Rashtriya Sewak Sangh was a physician.

The fundamentalists are a practical people and try to purge the way of life of all impurities (religiously speaking). They reject all corrupt lifestyles. An example of this is Dayanands critique of the traditional, superstition filled way of life. Thus Maududi characterised the present Muslim way of life as 'ignorant' and Bhindranwale talked of the 'fallen' Sikhs who shave off their beards, cut their hair and do not observe the traditional Sikh way of life. Thus fundamental movements are not only about religious beliefs and practices, but lifestyles generally.

Thus fundamentalist movement are reactive and a response to what the persons involved-the leaders and participants, consider a crisis. The crisis calls for urgent remedies. The basic programme is presented as a return to the original tradition. That is to say to the contemporarily redefined fundamentals, which cover the present-day needs. This usually involves a selective retrieval of tradition. It may even be an invention of tradition.

The case of Dayananda illustrates this very well. He tried to evolve a sanitized Hinduism in response to the challenge for conversion by Christian missionaries. He claimed that the Vedas were the only true form of Hinduism and his call was back to the Vedas. In Iran Khomeini developed an Islamic state based on the guardianship of the jurists. Again Bhindranwale gave a selective emphasis to Guru Gobind Singh's teaching rather than those of his immediate successors. Assertion of spiritual authority and criticising the culture are two aspects of fundamentalism. A third crucial element is that of the pursuit of political power.

The pursuit of political power is very important to fundamentalism, for without it we would be presented with a case for revivalism. The Arya Samajis were ardent nationalists in North India, and the movement had its political overtones. Again the RSS which has been described as a cultural organisation has had close links with political parties, and contemporarily with the Sangh Parivar. This covers both cultural and political aspects of Hindu nationalism. This explains why fundamentalist movements often turn violent, and the ideology of secularism is rejected. They are totalitarian and do not tolerate dissent. However these movements also perform a particular role in modem society which cannot be ignored.

Thus an objective intellectual analysis should consider fundamentalism as a distinctive category. It is not theocracy or backward communalism.

Communalism in India

'The ideology of communalism in India was, and still is, that the different communities in India cannot co-exist to their mutual benefit, that the minorities will become victims of Hindu subjugation and that the historically created situation nor culture will allow cooperation.

Communalism took deep roots in Indian polity during the later phase of the national movement and this was encouraged by the colonial rulers. This process was a continuation of the weakness and inadequacy of secularism as conceived and practised during the anticolonial struggle.

Impact in all the theories has been the assumption that the growth of Hindu-Muslim tension was not the natural and inevitable outcome of changes taking place in the Indian society. Partition was the culmination of the conflict which could and should have been avoided. Further this line of reasoning states that nation building essentially mens obliteration of communal moulds and creation of a common identity which decries the existence of differentiated groups based on religion, caste or language. Communal forces are therefore viewed as division and a sign of political underdevelopment. *Communalism arises when one or two characteristics of an ethnic identity e.g. religious beliefs are taken and emotionally surcharged. Communal movements are often brief and exist in a dyad, comprising an opposing force or ideology which has to be countered. Unlike imdamentalism,* communalism can only exist dyadically.

Hindu-Muslims riots reflected the religious fears and socioeconomic aspirations of the Hindus and Muslims. Sometimes these riots occur for very minor reasons such as quarrels between Muslim and Hindu shopkeepers (Ghosh, 1981: 93-94). The important point is that these are not isolated acts but often deliberate mechanizations of various socio-religious organisations. Recurrent collisions were engineered on festivals by stopping them and various religious occasions by interfering in their process. This was done to inflame communal passions and bitterness. According to Ghosh (1981) the acme of communal rioting was reached in August 1946 in Calcutta when the Muslim League observed a 'Direct Action Day'. Bombay did the same in the following month. Thus Independence was erected on the corpses of many thousands of people. With Mahatma Gandhi's assassination the riots abated awhile, and this situation was basically sustained by Nehru. Again the passing away of Nehru in 1964 and the deteriorating socioeconomic circumstances led to the resurrection of communal violence.

Recent Communal Riots

Thus during the late 60s and 1970s there was large scale communal rioting in Ahmedabad, Baroda, Ranohi, Jamshedpur etc. Communal configurations in towns such as Ranchi cast a shadow over predictions and beliefs in the future of workers unity. Again in Bhiwandi where there was a carnage in 1969, it was a shock for the leftists. The grassroots movement among the handloom workers fostered by committed communists was unable to stem the on rush of communal violence. In 1969 itself a communal riot occurred in Ahmedabad. The inflammatory factors were insults to holy scriptures and sacred cows. It was suspected however that these riots were politically motivated.

These riots indicated clearly that there were various political factors behind the surface level factors of religion based tensions and confrontations. In the mid seventies the communal riots abated a bit both due to the Emergency and the Janata Regime. The first exercised iron control and discipline the second aroused the hopes of both Hindus and Muslims. The first ix years of the eighties once more created an upward incline in the riot-graph. Patel (1990) keels that Communal violence is backed by religious arguments and backing. He feels that those resorting to it are neither true Hindus or true Muslims. Religion does not preach enmity. However the causes which are often given for communal violence are hurt religious sentiments. The causes are flimsy such as playing music before a mosque insulting the Prophet or the Holy Quran. This is sufficient to provoke violence along some ' of the Muslims. So also disturbing by Muslims of a religious yam is enough to rouse Hindu ire.

Reasons for Communal Riots

In the context of our section of recent-communal riots we turn now to some further reasons for the same. As Ghosh (1981) points out the several arguments have been forwarded for the existence and continuation of communal riots. These are: riots ark part of progress in an under developed country. The class struggle is converted into a communal struggle weakening the solidarity of the proletariat class. Further the middle and backward classes have acquired greater political and economic strength and influence and these often assert themselves. Economic conflicts lead to riots as in Bihar Sharif and Bhiwandi.

Electoral politics determine the objectives and direction of communal violence e.g. Delhi 1986.

These explanations cannot be binding-they cannot be held to the necessary and sufficient. Often economic reasons emerge after (not before) the rioting has begun. Again in a developing society economic factors where competitive or one lagging behind the other can lead to a riot. The same applies to educationist political causes. The idea of behind-the-scene political manipulation may not be valid.

Economic and Social Dimensions

Regarding gaining economic benefits after the eruption of communal riots we find that in Godhra, Hindu Sindhi refugees from Pakistan gave competition to Hindu merchants. But riots have frequently emerged between Sindhis and Muslims. Again in Punjab while Ramgarhia and other Sikhs have gone beyond the Hindu Khatris in commerce there have been no riots because of this.

Lastlym the Punjab tragedy, the terrorist acts while antagonising the Hindus, are not considered to be the acts of the Sikh community as a whole.

Hindu-Muslim riots in recent times have been confined to medium sized towns and cities. These include areas like Meerut, Aligarh, Moradabad, Pune etc.

Inter-Community Dynamics

Medium sized towns/cities are being divided on communal lines. We find that the workers don't have class consciousness. The educated middle class professional act as a bridge between Hindus and Muslims. During preparation there were Muslim doctors, lawyers etc. who also attracted Hindu clients-Similarly Hindu professionals were patronized by Muslim clients-Thus

i) common bonds developed

ii) there were common networks and patronization.

Again the existence of Muslim professionals administrators etc. created a positive image for the Muslims. Post partition mass migrations saw these advantages vanishing. Many trade and economic activities are run by Hindus and there were no problems so long as the Muslims were not competitive. There was an interdependence between Hindu employers and Muslim artisans. However, in recent time economic Competitiveness come from

Muslims and has turned into a religious threat to Hindus. Again channelling of Arab money into mosque renovation and lavish festival celebrations has resulted in an admixture of economics and religion which creates inter community tensions and eruptions of violence.

Aspects of Secularism

While fundamentalism and communalism are widely held to the problematic and disintegrative, the ideology of secularism is held to be a palliative solution to the above. Although there is no single definition of secularism which could be applied worldwide, yet it was first applied to separate the Church from the King. This was the political dimension. In the social sphere secular meant separating the strangle hold of religion over the individual's life. In the Indian context it proclaims the existence of spiritual values which can be stressed in a variety of ways.

As Madan (ed. 1991 : 394-412) notes these dimensions are:

i) the separation of state from religion.

ii) equal and impartial treatment of all communities by the state.

iii) approaching religious beliefs in a spirit of objective rationality.

iv) ensuring a just standard of living for all people irrespective of community.

Secular Views

Through the judicious use of the philosophy of secularism fundamentalism and communalism can be curbed. On combating fundamentalism and communalism through secularism there are three views that can be presented. These are:

i) An ideological campaign against communalism can be waged to *decommunalize* people at all levels. The logic of this approach is that communalism will die out only if the communal ideology is removed.

ii) Grassroot politics is another approach mooted for the eradication of communalism along with ademocratic rights approach. That is to say there has to be an awakening at the grassroots level. Secondly a new type of activity is required which is politically oriented but not the grassroots type. The problem however is that unless this grassroots approach has an All-India spread and a unity within it we do not find it likely' to do well.

iii) A major issue concerning fundamentalism, communalism and secularism is religion.

How do we approach religion in a secular view ? Firstly we should not dismiss any religions or pronounce them to be false. Second we should try to locate the + democratic &d the secular in the social basis of religion. Thirdly the religion should be exposed and a rational approach taken. As Madan (1983) explains India is defined as a secular republic in the Preamble to the Constitution. Secularism in India does not imply abolition of religion but the separation of state from religion. However the separation of politics from religion is not envisaged. The people are free to form religion based political parties. What then is secularism in a multireligious society such as that which India represents.

Sir Syed Ahmad Khan [1817-1898]

The greatest Muslim reformer and statesman of the 19th Century, Sir Syed Ahmad Khan was born in Delhi on October 17, 1817. His family on the maternal and paternal side had close contacts with the Mughal court. His maternal grandfather, Khwajah Farid was a Wazir in the court of Akbar Shah II. His paternal grandfather Syed Hadi held a mansab and the title of Jawwad Ali Khan in the court of Alamgir II. His father, Mir Muttaqi, had been close to Akbar Shah since the days of his prince-hood. Syed Ahmad's mother, Aziz-un-Nisa, took a great deal of interest in the education and upbringing of her son. She imposed a rigid discipline on him and Sir Syed himself admitted that her supervision counted for much in the formation of his character.

The early years of Sir Syed's life were spent in the atmosphere of the family of a Mughal noble. There was nothing in young Syed's habits or behaviour to suggest that he was different from other boys, though he was distinguished on account of his extraordinary physique. As a boy he learnt swimming and archery, which were favourite sports of the well-to-do class in those days.

Sir Syed received his education under the old system. He learnt to read the Quran under a female teacher at his home. After this, he was put in the charge of Maulvi Hamid-ud-Din, the first of his private tutors. Having completed a course in Persian and Arabic, he took to the study of mathematics, which was a favourite subject of the maternal side of his family. He later became interested in medicine and studied some well-known books on the subject. However, he soon gave it up without completing the full course. At the age of 18 or 19 his formal education came to an end but he continued his studies privately. He started taking a keen interest in the literary gatherings and cultural activities of the city.

The death of his father in 1838 left the family in difficulties. Thus young Syed was compelled at the early age of 21 to look for a career. He decided to enter the service of the East India Company. He started his career as Sarishtedar in a court of law. He became Naib Munshi in 1839 and Munshi in 1841. In 1858 he was promoted and appointed as Sadar-us-Sadur at Muradabad. In 1867 he was promoted and posted as the judge of the Small Causes Court. He retired in 1876. He spent the rest of his life for Aligarh College and the Muslims of South Asia.

Sir Syed's greatest achievement was his Aligarh Movement, which was primarily an educational venture. He established Gulshan School at Muradabad in 1859, Victoria School at Ghazipur in 1863, and a scientific society in 1864. When Sir Syed was posted at Aligarh in 1867, he started the Muhammadan Anglo-Oriental School in the city. Sir Syed got the opportunity to visit England in 1869-70. During his stay, he studied the British educational system and appreciated it. On his return home he decided to make M. A. O. High School on the pattern of British boarding schools. The School later became a college in 1875. The status of University was given to the college after the death of Sir Syed in 1920. M. A. O. High School, College and University played a big role in the awareness of the Muslims of South Asia.

Unlike other Muslim leaders of his time, Sir Syed was of the view that Muslims should have friendship with the British if they want to take their due rights. To achieve this he did a lot to convince the British that Muslims were not against them. On the other hand, he tried his best to convince the Muslims that if they did not befriend the British, they could not achieve their goals. Sir Syed wrote many books and journals to remove the misunderstandings between Muslims and the British. The most significant of his literary works were his pamphlets "Loyal Muhammadans of India" and "Cause of Indian Revolt". He also wrote a commentary on the Bible, in which he attempted to prove that Islam is the closest religion to Christianity.

Sir Syed asked the Muslims of his time not to participate in politics unless and until they got modern education. He was of the view that Muslims could not succeed in the field of western politics without knowing the system. He was invited to attend the first session of the Indian National Congress and to join the organization but he refused to accept the offer. He also asked the Muslims to keep themselves away from the Congress and predicted that the party would prove to be a pure Hindu party in the times to come. By establishing the Muhammadan Educational Conference, he provided Muslims with a platform on which he could discuss their political problems. Sir Syed is known as the founder of Two-Nation Theory in the modern era.

In the beginning of 1898 he started keeping abnormally quiet. For hours he would not utter a word to friends who visited him. Medical aid proved ineffective. His condition became critical on 24th of March. On the morning of March 27, a severe headache further worsened it. He expired the same evening in the house of Haji Ismail Khan, where he had been shifted 10 or 12 days earlier. He was buried the following afternoon in the compound of the Mosque of Aligarh College. He was mourned by a large number of friends and admirers both within and outside South Asia.

Sir Syed Ahmed Khan

Sir Syed Ahmed Khan, born at Delhi, India on 17th October, 1817, Muslim educator, jurist and author, founder of the Anglo-Mohammedan Oriental College at Aligarh, UP, India, and principal motivating force behind the revival of Indian Islam in the late 19th century. His works, in Urdu, include *Essays on the Life of Muhammad (PBUH)* (187) and commentaries on the Bible and on the Quran. In 1888 he was made a Knight Commander of the Star of India.

Syed's family, though progressive, was highly regarded by the dying Mughal dynasty. His father, who received an allowance from the Mughal administration, became something of a religious recluse; his maternal grand father had twice served as prime minister of the Mughal emperor of his time and had also held positions of trust under the East India Company. Syed's brother established one of the first printing press at Delhi and started one of the earlier newspapers in Urdu, the principal language of the Muslims of northern India.

The death of Syed's father left the family in financial difficulties, and after a limited education Syed had to work for his livelihood. Starting as a clerk with the East India Company in 1938, he qualified three years later as a sub-judge and served in the judicial department at various places.

Syed Ahmed had a versatile personality, and his position in the judicial department left him time to be active in many fields. His career as an author (in Urdu) started at the age of 23 with religious tracts. In 1847 he brought out a noteworthy book, *Athar Assandid* ("Monuments of the Great"), on the antiquities of Delhi. Even more important was his pamphlet "The Causes of the Indian Revolt". During the Indian Mutiny of 1857 he had taken the side of the British, but the weakness and errors of the British administration that had led to dissatisfaction and countrywide explosion. Widely read by British officials, it had considerable influence on British Policy.

His interest in religion was also active and lifelong. He began a sympathetic interpretation of the Bible, wrote *Essay on the Life of Muhammad (PBUH)* (translated into English by his son), and founded time to write several volumes of a modernist commentary on the Quran. In these works he sought to harmonise the Islamic faith with scientific and politically progressive ideas of his time.

The supreme interest of Syed's life was, however, education – in its widest sense, He began establishing schools, at Muradabad (1858) and Ghazipur (1863). A more ambitious undertaking was the foundation of the Scientific Society, which published translations of many educational texts and issued a bilingual journal – in Urdu and English

These institutions were for the use of all citizens and were jointly operated by the Hindus and Muslims. In the late 1860s there occurred developments that were alert the course of his activities. In 1867 he has transferred to Benares, a city on the Ganges with great religious significance for Hindus. At about the same time a movement started at Benares to replace Urdu, the language cultivated by the Muslims, with Hindi. This movement and the attempts to substitute Hind for Urdu publications of the Scientific Society convinced Syed that the paths of the Hindus and the Muslims must diverge. Thus, when during a visit to England (1869-70) he prepared plans for a great educational institution, they were "a Muslim Cambridge." On his return he set up a committee for the purpose and also started an influential journal, *Tahdhib al-Akhlaq* "Social Reform"), for the "uplift and reform the Muslim". A Muslim school was established at Aligarh in May 1875, and after his retirement in 1876, Syed devoted himself to enlarging it into a college. In January 1977 the Viceroy laid the foundation stone of the college. In spite of conservation opposition to Syed's projects, the college made rapid progress. In 1886 Syed organised the All-India Muhammadan Educational Conference, which met annually at different places to promote education and to provide the Muslims with a common platform. Until the founding of the Muslim League in 1906, it was the principal national centre of Indian Islam.

Syed advised the Muslims against joining active politics and to concentrate instead on education. Later, when some Muslims joined the Indian National Congress, he came out strongly against that organisation and its objectives, which included the establishment of parliamentary democracy in India. He argued that, in a country where communal divisions were all-important and education and political organisations were confined to a few classes, parliamentary democracy would work only inequitably. Muslims, generally, followed his advice and abstained from politics until several years later when they had established their own political organisation i.e. Muslim League. This great scholar and leader died on 27th March, 1898, at Aligarh, India.

Sir Syed Ahmad Khan

Sir Syed Ahmad Khan, one of the greatest Muslim educationists, writers and reformers, was born at Delhi in 1817. He hailed from a well to-do landed aristocracy of Delhi.

Syed Ahmad had Swami Dayananda Saraswati

Maharishi Dayananda Saraswati (February 12, 1824 – October 31, 1883) was an important Hindu religious scholar, reformer and the founder of the Arya Samaj, "Society of Nobles", a Hindu reform movement, founded in 1875. He was the first man who gave the call for *Swarajya*-"India for Indians" in 1876 which was later furthered by Lokmanya Tilak. Denouncing idolatry and ritualistic worship prevalent in Hinduism at the time, he worked towards reviving Vedic ideologies, subsequently philosopher and President of India, S. Radhakrishnan, later called him one of "makers of Modern India" as did Sri Aurobindo.

One of his notable disciples was Shyamji Krishna Varma who founded *India House* in London and guided other revolutionaries like Madam Cama, Veer Sawarkar, Lala Hardyal, Madan Lal Dhingra, Bhagat Singh and others. His other disciples were Swami Shraddhanand, Lala Lajpat Rai and others who got their inspiration from his writings. His book *Satyarth Prakash* contributed to the Indian independence movementis one of his great contributions. He was a sanyasi (ascetic) from his boyhood, and a scholar, who believed in the infallible authority of the Vedas.

Dayananda advocated the doctrine of karma, skepticism in dogma, and emphasised the ideals of Brahmacharya (celibacy and devotion to God). The Theosophical Society and the Arya Samaj were united from 1878 to 1882, when the former adopted the name Theosophical Society of the Arya Samaj.

Among Maharishi Dayananda's contributions are his promoting of the equal rights of women-such as the right to education and reading of Indian scriptures-and his translation of the Vedas from Sanskrit to Hindi so that the common person may be able to read the Vedas.

Early Life

Dayananda was born on on February 12 in 1824, in the village of Tankara near Morvi (Morbi) in the Kathiawar region (present Rajkot district), Gujarat, into a affluent and devout Brahmin family of Krishna Lal Tiwari and Yashodabai. Since he was born under Mul Nakshatra, he was named *Dayananda Mulshankar* and led a very comfortable early life, studying Sanskrit, the Vedas and other religious books so as to prepare himself for a future as a Hindu priest.

A number of incidents resulted in Dayananda's life questioning traditional beliefs of Hinduism and inquiring about God (Bhagwan) in early childhood. Still a young child on the night of Shivratri (literally: the night for God Shiva) when his family went to a temple for overnight worship, he stayed up waiting for God to appear to accept the offerings made to idol of God Shiva. While his family slept, Dayananda saw a mouse eating the offerings kept for the God. He was utterly surprised and wondered how a God, who cannot even protect his own "offerings," would protect humanity. He argued with his father that they should not be worshipping such a helpless God.

The deaths of his younger sister and his uncle from cholera caused Dayananda to ponder the meaning of life and death and he started asking questions, which worried his parents. He was to be married in his early teens (common in 19th century India), but he decided marriage was not for him and ran away from home in 1846.

Search for Knowledge

He was disillusioned with classical Hinduism and became a wandering monk. He learned Panini's Grammar to understand Sanskrit texts, and learnt from them that GOD can be found. After wandering in search of GOD for over 2 decades, he found Swami Virjananda near Mathura who became his guru. Swami Virjananda told him to throw away all his books, as he wanted Dayananda to start from a clean slate and learn directly from the Vedas, the oldest and foundational books. Dayananda stayed under Swami Virjananda's tutelage for two and a half years. After finishing his education, Virjananda asked him to spread the knowledge of the Vedas in society as his *gurudakshina* (tuition-dues). It is during his mission, Dayananda Saraswati gave the call.

Dayananda's Mission

AUM or OM is considered by the Arya Samaj to be the highest and most proper name of God. Dayananda set about the difficult task with dedication despite attempts on his life. He travelled the country challenging religious scholars and priests of the day to discussions and won repeatedly on the strength of his arguments. He believed that Hinduism has been corrupted by divergence from the founding principles of the Vedas and misled by the priesthood for the priests' self-aggrandisement. Hindu priests discouraged common folk from reading Vedic scriptures and encouraged rituals (such as bathing in the Ganges and feeding of priests on anniversaries) which Dayananda pronounced as superstitions or self-serving.

Far from borrowing concepts from other religions, as Raja Ram Mohan Roy had done, Swami Dayananda was quite critical of Islam and Christianity and also of the other Indian faiths like Jainism, Buddhism and Idol Worshipping in Hinduism-as may be seen in his book *Satyartha Prakash*. He was against what he considered to be the corruption of the pure faith in his own country. Unlike many other reform movements within Hinduism, the Arya Samaj's appeal was addressed not only to the educated few in India, but to the world as a whole as evidenced in the 6th principle of the Arya Samaj.

Arya Samaj allows and encourages converts to Hinduism.

Dayananda's concept of Dharma is succinctly set forth in his *Beliefs and Disbeliefs*. He said, I accept as Dharma whatever is in full conformity with impartial justice, truthfulness and the like; that which is not opposed to the teachings of God as embodied in the Vedas. Whatever is not free from partiality and is unjust, partaking of untruth and the like, and opposed to the teachings of God as embodied in the Vedas-that I hold as adharma.

He had also said, He, who after careful thinking, is ever ready to accept truth and reject falsehood; who counts the happiness of others as he does that of his own self, him I call just.

Dayananda's Vedic message was to emphasize respect and reverence for other human beings, supported by the Vedic notion of the divine nature of the individual-divine because the body was the temple where the human essence (soul or "Atma") could possibly interface with the creator ("ParamAtma"). In the 10 principles of the Arya Samaj, he enshrined the idea that "All actions should be performed with the prime objective of benefitting mankind" as opposed to following dogmatic rituals or revering idols and symbols. In his own life, he interpreted Moksha to be a lower calling (due to its benefit to one individual) than the calling to emancipate others.

Dayananda's "back to the Vedas" message influenced many thinkers. Taking the cue from him, Sri Aurobindo decided to look for hidden psychological meanings in the Vedas. Sri Aurobindo Ashram, Pondicherry. 1972.

Arya Samaj

Swami Dayananda's creation, the Arya Samaj, is a unique contribution in Hinduism. The Arya Samaj unequivocally condemns idol-worship, animal sacrifices, ancestor worship, pilgrimages, priestcraft, offerings made in temples, the caste system, untouchability, child marriages and discrimination against women on the grounds that all these lacked Vedic sanction. The Arya Samaj discourages dogma and symbolism and encourages skepticism in beliefs that run contrary to common sense and logic. To many people, the Arya Samaj aims to be a "universal society" based on the authority of the Vedas..

Death

According to Indian History, in 1883 Dayananda was invited by the Maharaja of Jodhpur, to stay at his palace. The Maharaja was eager to become his disciple and learn his teachings. One day Dayananda went to Maharaja's rest room and saw him with a dance girl. Maharaja loved this low-character dance girl. Dayananda boldly asked Maharaja to forsake that girl and all unethical acts and follow Darma of a true Aryan. Dayananda's suggestion went against to that dance girl and she decided to take revenge of this. Dance girl bribed Dayananda's cook to poison him. One evening when Dayananda was about to go to bed he brought him a glass of milk containing poison and ground glass. Dayananda took the glass of milk and went to sleep only to wake up later with a burning sensation. He realized immediately that he had been poisoned and attempted to purge his digestive system of the poisonous substance, but it was too late. The poison had already entered his blood stream. Dayananda was bedridden and suffered excruciating pain. Many doctors came to treat him but all was in vain. His body was covered all over with large bleeding sores. On seeing Dayananda's suffering the cook was overcome with unbearable guilt and remorse. He confessed his crime to Dayananda. On deathbed, Dayananda forgave him and gave him a bag of money and told him to flee the country lest he be found out and executed by the Maharaja's men.

2

Hindu Revivalism

During the 19th century, Hinduism developed a large number of new religious movements, partly inspired by the European Romanticism, nationalism, scientific racism and esotericism (Theosophy) popular at the time (while conversely and contemporaneously, India had a similar effect on European culture with Orientalism, "Hindu style" architecture, reception of Buddhism in the West and similar). These reform movements are summarized under Hindu revivalism and continue into the present.

- Sahajanand Swami establishes the Swaminarayan Sampraday sect around 1800.
- Brahmo Samaj is a social and religious movement founded in Kolkata in 1828 by Raja Ram Mohan Roy. He was one of the first Indians to visit Europe and was influenced by western thought. He died in Bristol, England. The Brahmo Samaj movement thereafter resulted in the Brahmo religion in 1850 founded by Debendranath Tagore — better known as the father of Rabindranath Tagore.
- Sri Ramakrishna and his pupil Swami Vivekananda led a reform in Hinduism in late 19th century. Their ideals and sayings have inspired numerous Indians as well as non-Indians, Hindus as well as non-Hindus. Among the prominent figures whose ideals were very much influenced by them were Rabindranath Tagore, Gandhi, Subhas Bose, Satyendranath Bose, Megh Nad Saha, and Sister Nivedita.
- Arya Samaj ("Society of Nobles") is a Hindu reform movement in India that was founded by Swami Dayananda in 1875. He was a sannyasin (renouncer) who believed in

the infallible authority of the Vedas. Dayananda advocated the doctrine of karma and reincarnation, and emphasised the ideals of Brahmacharya (chastity) and sanyasa (renunciation). Dayananda claimed to be rejecting all non-Vedic beliefs altogether. Hence the Arya Samaj unequivocally condemned idolatry, animal sacrifices, ancestor worship, pilgrimages, priestcraft, offerings made in temples, the caste system, untouchability and child marriages, on the grounds that all these lacked Vedic sanction. It aimed to be a universal church based on the authority of the Vedas. Dayananda stated that he wanted 'to make the whole world Aryan', i.e. he wanted to develop *missionary* Hinduism based on the universality of the Vedas. To this end, the Arya Samaj started Shuddhi movement in early 20th century to bring back to Hinduism people converted to Islam and Christianity, set up schools and missionary organisations, and extended its activities outside India. It now has branches around the world and has a disproportional number of adherents among people of Indian ancestry in Suriname and the Netherlands, in comparison with India apathy and despondence.

Dayananda Saraswati

The founder of the Arya Samaj. The great sage who sought to restore to Hinduism its natural radiance and wisdom. A fearless reformer. He saved the man who poisoned him-so boundless was his goodness.

This happened about 150 years ago. Saurashtra of the present Gujarat State consisted of several small states. Among them was Morvi. Tankara was a town in this state. There lived a wealthy Brahmin, Karshanji Lalji Tiwari by name; he was also the tahsildar of Tankara. The ruler of Morvi had granted him a small troop of horses (cavalry) both for protection and as a mark of honour.

Karshanji was a good and just man. He was generous in his dealings. He had faith in religious practices that had come down from times immemorial. His wife, Amrithbai, was a beautiful and Virtuous woman. She was like a mother his go to all the villagers. In 1824, a son was born to the couple. They named' him Moolashankar. According to the custom of the place, he was also called Dayaram. This child was to become famous as Maharshi Dayananda.

When he attained the age of five, Moolashankar's education started. At the age of eight, his Upanayana Samskara (being invested with the holy thread) was performed. The boy used to perform religious rites like 'Sandhyavandana' with devotion. He had a very good memory. By the time he was fourteen he had learnt by heart the Yajurveda, the scriptures and the upanishads.

Karshanji wished that his son should follow in his footsteps by becoming a devotee of Shiva. He, therefore, used to describe the greatness of Shiva every now and then. He would advise the boy to worship Lord Shiva and only then eat something on days of festivals.

Moolashankar had an uncle whom he loved very much. His uncle himself was a simple man of great learning with a religious bent of mind. He influenced the boy deeply. Moolashankar had a sharp intellect and an extraordinary memory and so his uncle thought some day his nephew would become a great man.

Shuddhi Movement

The socio-political movement, derived from ancient rite of *shuddhikaran*, or purification was started Arya Samaj, and its founder Swami Dayananda Saraswati and his followers like Swami Shraddhanand, who also worked on the *Sangathan* consolidation aspect of Hinduism, in North India, especially Punjab in early 1900s, though it gradually spread across India. Shuddhi had a social reform agenda behind its belligerent rationale and was aimed at abolishing the practise of untouchability by converting outcasts from other religions to Hinduism and integrating them into the mainstream community by elevating their position, and instilling self-confidence and self-determination in them. The movement strove to reduce the conversions of Hindus to Islam and Christianity, which were underway at the time.

In 1923, Swami Shraddhanand founded the 'Bhartiya Hindu Shuddhi Mahasabha' (Indian Hindu Purification Council) and pushed the agenda of reconversion peacefully, but ultimately created a flashpoint between Hindus and Muslims as it offended Muslim exceptionalists, who argued that Hindus, being dhimmis, do not have any rights to convert others to their faith unlike the

Muslims, who are munim. The main point of contention was the reconversion Malkana Rajputs in western United Province Subsequently the movement became controversial and antagonized the Muslims populace to no end and also led to the martyrdom of the leader of the movement, Swami Shraddhanand in 1926. Gradually the movement faded away especially with the rise of nationalistic fervor during the Civil Disobedience movement of Mahatma Gandhi in the 1930s.

Swami Shraddhanand (1856-1926) was an Indian educationist and a Arya Samaj missionary who propagated the teachings of Swami Dayananda which included the establishment of educational institutions, like the Gurukul Kangri University, and played a key role on the *Sangathan* (consolidation) and the *Shuddhi* (re-conversion) a Hindu reform movement in 1920s.

His death at the hands of a Muslim fanatic caused religious strife in India.

Early Life and Education

He was born on 22 February 1856 in the village of Talwan in the Jalandhar District of the Punjab Province of India, and was the youngest in the family of Lala Nanak Chand, was a policeman in the East India Company administered United Provinces (now Uttar Pradesh). His given name was Brihaspati, but later he was called Munshi Ram by his father, a name that stayed with him till he took Sanyas in 1917, variously as Lala Munshi Ram and Mahatma Munshi Ram.

His school education began at Varanasi and ended at Lahore. His father, His early education was interrupted because of his father's frequent transfer to different locations.

Career

Despite this handicap he started his career as a 'Naib-Tehsildar' and later had a successful career as a lawyer from 1885 to 1892, meanwhile his meeting with Swami Dayananda in 1882 gave a new direction to his life, and he immediately took to the cause of Arya Samaj. In 1892, when Arya Samaj split into two factions over making Vedic education the main stay of the curriculum at the DAV College Lahore, he left the organization and formed Punjab Arya Samaj, and in 1902 established a Gurukul in Kangri near Haridwar which is now a recognized University known as Gurukul Kangri University. Previously in 1897, after the assassination of Lala Lekh Ram, he became his successor, and headed the 'Punjab Arya Pratinidhi Sabha', and started its monthly journal, *Arya Musafir*.

In 1915, upon his return from South Africa, M. K. Gandhi stayed at the university campus and met Swami Shraddhanand, it was during this visit that Swami Shraddhanand gave Gandhi, the title of *Mahatma* (great soul), after that he was best known around the world as Mahatama Gandhi to this day..

In 1917, Swami Shraddhanand, till now know as Mahatma Munshiram took sanyas, left Gurukul to jump full-fledged into Hindu reform movements and the Indian Independence movement, working with Congress, which he invited to hold its session at Amritsar in 1919 when due to Jalianwala tragedy no one in the Congress Committe agreed to have a session at Amritsar. Swami shraddhanand presided that session at Amritsar. He joined the nationwide protest against the Rowlatt Act, in the same year, defiantly protested in front of a posse of Gurkha soldiers, at the Clock Tower in Chandni Chowk, after which he was allowed to proceed. In early 1920s he emerged as important force in the Hindu Sangathan (consolidation) movement which was a by product of the now revitalized IIindu Maha Sabha

Swami Shraddhanand was the only Hindu Sanyasi who addressed a huge Muslim gathering from the minarates of the main Jama Mosque, New Delhi, for national solidarity and Vedic Dharma starting his speech with the recitation of Ved Mantras.

He wrote on religious issues in both Hindi and Urdu. He published newspapers in the two languages as well. He promoted Hindi in the Devanagri script, helped the poor and promoted the education of women. By 1923, he left the social arena and plunged whole-heartedly into his earlier work of the shuddhi movement (re-conversion to Hinduism), which he turned into an important force within Hinduism In late 1923, he became the president of *Bhartiya Hindu Shuddhi Sabha*, created with an aim to reconvert Muslims specially 'Malkana Rajputs' in western United Province, this antagonized the Muslims against him irrevocably and brought him in direct confrontation with Muslim clerics and leaders of the time, and on 23 December 1926 he was assassinated by a Muslim fanatic named Abdul Rashid, who entered his home at Naya Bazar, Delhi, posing as a visitor.. Upon his death, Gandhiji moved a condolence motion at the Guwahati session of the Congress on December 25, 1926

Today, the 'Swami Shraddhanand Kaksha' at the Archeological Museum, Gurukul Kangri University, Haridwar houses a photographic journey of his life modem sciences.

Arya Samaj

Arya Samaj is a Hindu reform movement founded by Swami Dayananda in 10th April 1875.. He was a sannyasi who believed in the infallible authority of the Vedas. Dayananda emphasized the ideals of Brahmacharya (chastity). There are approximately 3-4 million followers of Arya Samaj worldwide.

Founding of the Arya Samaj

Vedic Schools

Between 1869 and 1873, Swami Dayananda, a native of the Princely State of Gujarat, made his first earnest attempt at affecting a substantial and lasting reform in his native India. This attempt took the form of the establishment of several "Vedic Schools" which, in contradiction to other public schools at the time, put a marked emphasis on attempting to impart Vedic values, culture and religion to its students. The first was established at Farrukhabad in 1869 and reported 50 students as being enrolled in its first year. This initial success led to the founding of four additional schools in rapid succession at Mirzapur (1870), Kasganj (1870), Chhalesar (1870) and Varanasi (1873).

The Vedic Schools represented the first practical application of Swami Dayananda's vision of religious and social reform. They enjoyed a mixed reception. On the one hand, students were not allowed to perform traditional idol worship (*murtipuja* in Hindi) at the school, and were instead expected to perform *sandhya* (a form of meditative prayer using mantras from the Vedas) and participate in *agnihotra* twice daily. Also, disciplinary action was swift and not infrequently severe. On the other hand, all meals, lodging, clothing and books were given to the students free of charge, and the study of Sanskrit was opened to non-Brahmins. The most noteworthy feature of the Schools was that only those texts which accepted the authority of the Vedas were to be taught. This was critical for the spiritual and social regeneration of Vedic culture in India.

Due primarily to organizational problems, the Vedic Schools soon ran into many difficulties. Swami Dayananda had considerable trouble finding qualified teachers who agreed with his views on religious reform, and there existed a paucity of textbooks which he considered suitable for instruction in Vedic culture. Funding was sporadic, attendance fluctuated considerably, and tangible results in the way of noteworthy student achievement were not forthcoming. Consequentially, some of the schools were forced to close shortly after opening. As early as 1874, it had become clear to Swami Dayananda that, without a wide and solid base of support among the public, setting up schools with the goal of imparting a Vedic education would prove to be an impossible task. He therefore decided to invest the greater part of his resources in the clear formulation and widespread propagation of his ideology of reform. Deprived of the full attention of Swami Dayananda, the Vedic School system all but collapsed shortly thereafter, and the last of the remaining schools (Farrukhabad) was finally closed down in 1876 due to Muslim takeover.

Adi Brahmo Samaj

While travelling (1872 – 1873), Swami Dayananda came to know of several of the pro-Western Indian intellectuals of the age, including Navin Chandra Roy, Rajnarayan Basu, Debendranath Tagore and Hemendranath Tagore all of whom were actively involved in the Brahmo Samaj. This reform organization, founded in 1828, held few views similar to those of Swami Dayananda in matters both religious (e.g. a belief in monotheism and the eternality of the soul) and social (e.g. the need to abolish the hereditary caste system and uplift the masses through education). Debendranath Tagore had written a book entitled *Brahmo Dharma,* which serves as a comprehensive manual of religion and ethics to the members of that society, and Swami Dayananda had read it while in Calcutta.

Although Swami Dayananda was persuaded on more than one occasion to join the Brahmo Samaj, there existed several points of contention which the Swami simply could not overlook, the most important being the position of the Vedas. Swami Dayananda held the Vedas to be divine revelation, and refused to accept any suggestions to the contrary. Despite this difference of opinion, however, it seems that the members of the Brahmo Samaj parted with Swami Dayananda on good terms, the former having publicly praised the latter's visit to Calcutta in several journals.

The Light of Truth

Swami Dayananda made several changes in his approach to the work of reforming Hindu society after having visited Calcutta. The most significant of these changes was that he began lecturing in Hindi. Prior to his tour of Bengal, the Swami had always held his discourses and debates in Sanskrit. While this gained him a certain degree of respect among both the learned and the common people alike, it prevented him from spreading his message to the broader masses. The change to Hindi allowed him to attract increasingly larger following, and as a result his ideas of reform began to circulate among the lower classes of society as well.

After hearing some of Swami Dayananda's speeches delivered in Hindi at Varanasi, Raj Jaikishen Das, a native government official there, suggested that the Swami publish his ideas in a book so that they might be distributed among the public. Witnessing the slow collapse of the Vedic Schools due to a lack of a clear statement of purpose and the resultant flagging public support, Swami Dayananda recognized the potential contained in Das' suggestion and took immediate action.

From June to September 1874, Swami Dayananda dictated a comprehensive series of lectures to his scribe, Pundit Bhimsen Sharma, which dealt with his views and beliefs regarding a wide range of subjects including God, the Vedas, Dharma, the soul, science, philosophy, childrearing, education, government and the possible future of both India and the world. The resulting manuscript was eventually published under the title Satyarth Prakash or The Light of Meaning of Truth in 1875 at Varanasi. This voluminous work would prove to play a central role in the establishment and later growth of the organization which would come to be known as the Arya Samaj.

First Attempt at a 'New Samaj'

While the manuscript of the Satyarth Prakash was being edited at Varanasi, Swami Dayananda received an invitation to travel to

Bombay in order to conduct a debate with some representatives of the Vallabhacharya sect. The Swami arrived in Bombay on the 20th of October, 1874. The debate, though greatly publicised, never materialized. Despite this, however, two members of the Prarthana Samaj approached Swami Dayananda and invited him to deliver a few lectures at one of their gatherings, which were received with appreciation by all those present. The members of the Prarthana Samaj of Bombay recognized in Swami Dayananda an individual in possession of the knowledge and skills necessary for promoting their aims, the greatest and most comprehensive of which being the general uplift of Hindu society at large and its protection from what they perceived to be the advancing threat of Christian and Muslim efforts to convert Hindus.

After his having spent over a month at Bombay, 60 new-found students of Swami Dayananda – among them, prominent members of the Prarthana Samaj – proposed the notion of founding a 'New Samaj' with the Swami's ideas serving as its spiritual and intellectual basis.

Second Attempt at Ahmedabad

After having received a personal invitation from Gopalrao Hari Deshmukh, Swami Dayananda left Bombay and travelled to Ahmedabad, Gujarat, arriving on the 11th of December, 1874. Once there, he conducted a debate with local pundits on the issue of Vedas, and emerged victorious. It is reported that the formation of a Samaj and the founding of a Vedic School at Ahmedabad was proposed following the widely acknowledged and publicized success of the debate, but it was found that not enough support for such a venture could be mustered.

Initial Success at Rajkot

On an invitation from Hargovind Das Dvarkadas, the secretary of the local Prarthana Samaj, Swami Dayananda decided to travel to Rajkot, Gujarat and arrived on the 31st of December, 1874. However, instead of delivering his standard program of lectures, he allowed members of the audience to choose the topics they would like to have him discourse upon. A total of eight topics were chosen, and Swami Dayananda delivered impromptu lectures on all of them to the overwhelming satisfaction of all present. Gifts were bestowed upon the Swami as tokens of gratitude for his masterly orations, and it was announced that the Rajkot Prarthana Samaj was henceforth dissolved and was ready to be reorganized as a new Samaj under the auspices of Swami Dayananda. The Swami, after much deliberation, chose the name 'Arya Samaj' or 'Society of Nobles'. Swami Dayananda himself drafted a list of 28 rules and regulations for the Rajkot Arya Samaj, which he later had printed for distribution.

Setback at Ahmedabad

On his way back to Bombay, Swami Dayananda stopped off in Ahmedabad and related the news of Rajkot, Gujarat, distributing copies of the rules and regulations to those present. A meeting was held on the 27th of January, 1875 to discuss the proposal of forming an Arya Samaj there, yet no conclusive decision was reached. Unwilling to wait for the deliberations to come to an end, Swami Dayananda continued on his way to Bombay.

While travelling, the Swami received word that the still fragile Rajkot Arya Samaj had involved itself in some political dispute and managed to have a government warning issued against it and its members. Thus, the collapse of the just established society was already looming large.

Lasting Success at Bombay

Swami Dayananda reached Bombay on 29 January 1875, and immediately the appeal to establish an Arya Samaj there was renewed. However, the Swami did not want a protracted debate to ensue as had occurred at Ahmedabad, bringing with it the possibility of endless deliberations. Thus, a membership drive was initiated which would circumvent the need for discussions. Within a short time, 100 individuals enrolled themselves as prospective members.

While the membership drive was underway, Swami Dayananda held a now famous discourse with the congregation at Bombay. Someone in the audience asked the Swami: "Should we set up a new Samaj?" Dayananda responded:

"If you are able to achieve something for the good of mankind by a Samaj, then establish a Samaj; I will not stand in your way. But if you do not organize it properly, there will be a lot of trouble in the future. As for me, I will only instruct you in the same way as I teach others, and this much you should keep clearly in mind: my beliefs are not unique, and I am not omniscient. Therefore, if in the future any error of mine should be discovered after rational examination, then set it right. If you do not act in this way, then this Samaj too will later on become just a sect. That is the way by which so many sectarian divisions have become prevalent in India: by making the guru's word the touchstone of truth and thus fostering deep-seated prejudices which make the people religion-blind, cause quarrels and destroy all right knowledge. That is the way India arrived at her sorry contemporary state, and that is the way this Samaj too would grow to be just another sect. This is my firm opinion: even if there be many different sectarian beliefs prevalent in India, if only they all acknowledge the Vedas, then all those small rivers will reunite in the ocean of Vedic Wisdom, and the unity of *dharma* will come about. From that unity of *dharma* there will result social and economic reform, arts and crafts and other human endeavours will improve as desired, and man's life will find fulfilment: because, by the power of that dharma all values will become accessible to him, economic values as well as psychological ones, and also the supreme value of moksha."

On the 10th of April, 1875, the Bombay Arya Samaj was officially established. The original membership amounted to exactly 100 persons, including Swami Dayananda. The members appealed to the Swami that he should serve as either the President or the Guru of the Samaj, but he kindly refused, and instead requested that he be listed as a regular member.

Principles of Arya Samaj

On the 24th of June, 1877, the second major Arya Samaj was established at Lahore. However, the original list of 28 rules and regulations drafted by Dayananda for the Rajkot Arya Samaj and used for the Bombay Arya Samaj were deemed to be too unwieldy. Therefore, it was proposed that the principles should be reduced and simplified, while the bylaws should be removed to a separate document. Everyone present, including Swami Dayananda, agreed, and the 10 Principles of the Arya Samaj as they are known around the world today came into existence.

All subsequently established branches of the Arya Samaj have been founded upon the ten principles. However, each new branch of the Society has a degree of freedom in determining the exact bylaws under which it shall operate. Everyone who wishes to become a member of the Society must agree to uphold these principles in their entirety. However, nothing beyond these 10 Principles has any binding force on any member of the Arya Samaj. For this reason, the early Samaj proved to be attractive to individuals belonging to various religious communities, and enjoyed a notable degree of converts from segments of the Hindu, Sikh, Christian and Muslim populations of Indian society.

Drawing what are seen to be the logical conclusions from these principles, the Arya Samaj also unequivocally condemns practices such as polytheism, iconolatry, animal sacrifice, ancestor worship, pilgrimage, priestcraft, the belief in avatars or incarnations of God, the hereditary caste system, untouchability and child marriage on the grounds that all these lack Vedic sanction.

The Arya Samaj and the Theosophical Society

There continues to this day a considerable controversy regarding the exact nature of the relationship which existed between the Arya Samaj and the Theosophical Society from 1877 to 1882. What follows is a report of the chain of events as understood by members of the Arya Samaj today.

Initial Relationship

In 1877, a meeting occurred in America between some leading members of the Theosophical Society, founded in 1875, and Mulji Thakarshi, an individual who was present in the establishment of the Bombay Arya Samaj that same year. During the course of the exchange, it became clear that the two societies held many views in common, and efforts were undertaken to bring their respective leaders into closer contact. As a result, correspondence began between Henry Steel Olcott, one of the co-founders of the New York Theosophical Society, and Harish Chandra Chintamani, the acting president of the Bombay Arya Samaj.

At the suggestion of Chintamani, Olcott composed a letter addressed to Swami Dayananda dated the 18th of February, 1878 which is reported to have contained, among other things, the following notable passage: "There exist a number of Americans and others who earnestly seek spiritual knowledge. They place themselves at your feet and pray you [sic] to enlighten them. They are united in the object of gaining wisdom and becoming better. For this purpose they organized themselves into a body called the Theosophical Society three years ago. Finding in Christianity nothing that should satisfy their reason or intention they (...) have turned to the East for light and openly proclaimed themselves foes of Christianity. We come to your feet as children to a parent and say: 'Look at us, our teacher. Tell us what we ought to do. We place ourselves under your instructions.' "

Unwilling to wait for what they were led to believe would be a positive response, the heads of the Theosophical Society decided to go ahead with their plans to recast their organization as a branch of the Arya Samaj. On the 22nd of May, 1878, the Theosophical Society was renamed 'The Theosophical Society of the Arya Samaj of Aryavarta' and Swami Dayananda was announced as its director in chief.

Reconsideration and Reorganization

This unilateral move on the part of the Theosophists, however, eventually proved to be grossly miscalculated. While Olcott's open profession of faith in the Vedas was positively received and publicly praised by Swami Dayananda on more than one occasion, when he came to learn of the details of the tenets held by the Theosophists, including their belief in ghosts, mediumistic abilities, miracles and other occult matters, the Swami, taking up the role of teacher, was quick to admonish Olcott for what he termed 'humbuggery' and 'superstition' unbefitting of a seeker of truth.

The Theosophists, however, were unwilling to give up their faith in these matters, and the gulf which had always existed between the two societies suddenly became apparent to all involved. Therefore, in September 1878, the Theosophical Society was reverted to its former status as an independent organization. However, a second organization was simultaneously formed and given the now familiar name 'The Theosophical Society of the Arya Samaj of Aryavarta'.

It was agreed that membership of the new society, which itself was to remain a common branch of both the Theosophical Society and the Arya Samaj, would be open to any persons who wished to remain associated with both societies.

Irreconcilable Differences

This tentative solution, however, proved incapable of bridging the growing divide. Between 1879 and 1881, the founders of the Theosophical Society, Henry Olcott and Helena Blavatsky, paid Swami Dayananda several visits while touring India. Through the course of their discussions and correspondence, it became clear that the differences between the two societies were not, as previously assumed, limited to relatively minor issues, but in fact extended to what the Swami viewed as central tenets of the Vedic Religion. The main point of contention was in regards to the nature of God. While the Theosophists asserted that the highest Divinity is an impersonal Principle, Swami Dayananda maintained that the Vedas and their allied literature clearly teach that God is a personal Being – in his words, "the Personification of Being, Knowledge and Bliss". Thus, the line dividing the two organizations was clearly identified and neither party saw themselves in need of reconsidering their views. Therefore, on the 28th of March, 1882, Swami Dayananda announced that the Arya Samaj had officially cut off all ties with the Theosophical Society.

It has been stated that many of the difficulties and subsequent hostilities which arose between the Theosophical Society and the Arya Samaj were due to an unfortunate combination of personal intrigue and poor translations. Both parties have claimed to have been misrepresented on several occasions and members of each have accused the other of being responsible for the failure of the undertaking. Regardless, the theological and ideological differences between the Theosophical Society and the Arya Samaj persist to this day.

3

Muslim League

The All-India Muslim League, founded at Dacca (now Dhaka), Bengal, in 1906, was a political party in British India that played a role in the Indian independence movement and developed into the driving force behind the creation of Pakistan as a Muslim state on the Indian subcontinent. After the independence of India and Pakistan, the League continued as a minor party in India, especially in Kerala, where it is often in government within a coalition with others. In Pakistan, the League formed the country's first government, but disintegrated during the 1950s following an army coup. One or more factions of the Muslim League have been in power in most of the civilian governments of Pakistan since 1947. In Bangladesh, the party was revived in 1976 and won 14 seats in 1979 parliamentary election. Since then its importance has reduced, rendering it insignificant in the Pakistani political arena.

Background

Muslim rule was established across northern India between the 8th and the 14th centuries. The Muslim Turkic Mughal Empire ruled most of India from Delhi from the early 16th century, but suffered a major decline in the 18th century. The decline of the Mughal empire and its successor states like Avadh led to a feeling of discontentment among Muslim elites. Muslims represented about 25-30% of the population of British India, and constituted the majority of the population in Baluchistan, East Bengal, Kashmir valley, North-West Frontier Province, West Punjab, and the Sindh region of the Bombay Presidency. In the late 19th century an Indian nationalist movement developed with the Indian National Congress being founded in 1885 as a forum, that became a political party subsequently. The Congress made no conscious efforts to enlist the Muslim community in its struggle for Indian independence. Although some Muslims were active in the Congress, majority of Muslim leaders did not trust the Hindu predominance and most of the Muslims remained reluctant to join the Congress Party.

A turning point came in 1900 when the British administration in the largest Indian state, the United Provinces (now Uttar Pradesh), acceded to Hindu demands and made Hindi, written in the Devanagari script, the official language. This seemed to aggravate Muslim fears that the Hindu majority would seek to suppress Muslim culture and religion in an independent India. A British official, Sir Percival Griffiths, wrote of these perceptions: "the Muslim belief that their interest must be regarded as completely separate from those of the Hindus, and that no fusion of the two communities was possible."

Founding Fathers

Foundation: The Muslim league was founded by the admirers, companions, and followers of Sir Syed Ahmed Khan. The founding meeting of the League was held on 30 December 1906 at the occasion of the annual All India Muhammadan Educational Conference (which was founded by Sir Syed Ahmed Khan), at the Ahsan Manzil Palace, Shahbagh, Dhaka that was hosted by Nawab Sir Khwaja Salimullah. The meeting was attended by three thousand delegates and presided over by Nawab Waqar-ul-Mulk Kamboh. Nawab Mohsin-ul-Mulk, and Syed Ameer Ali were also the founding fathers, who attended this meeting.

Early Years

Sir Aga Khan was appointed the first Honorary President of the Muslim League. The headquarters were established at Lucknow. There were also six vice-presidents, a secretary and two joint secretaries initially appointed for a three-years term, proportionately from different provinces. The principles of the League were espoused in the "Green Book," which included the organisation's constitution, written by Maulana Mohammad Ali. Its goals at this stage did not include establishing an independent Muslim state, but rather concentrated on protecting Muslim liberties and rights, promoting understanding between the Muslim community and other Indians, educating the Muslim and Indian community at large on the actions of the government, and discouraging violence.

The Search for a Solution

Jinnah became disillusioned with politics after the failure of his attempt to form a Hindu-Muslim alliance, and he spent most of the 1920s in Britain. The leadership of the League was taken over by Sir Muhammad Iqbal, who in 1930 first put forward the demand for a separate Muslim state in India. The "Two-Nation Theory," the belief that Hindus and Muslims were two different nations who could not live in one country, gained popularity among Muslims. The two-state solution was rejected by the Congress leaders, who favoured a united India based on composite national identity. Iqbal's policy of uniting the North-West Frontier Province, Baluchistan, Punjab, and Sindh into a new Muslim majority state united the many factions of the League.

The League, however, rejected the proposal that the committee returned (called the Nehru Report), arguing that it gave too little representation (one quarter) to Muslims, established Devanagari as the official language of the colony, and demanded that India turn into a de facto unitary state, with residuary powers resting at the centre – the League had demanded at least one-third representation in the legislature and sizeable autonomy for the Muslim provinces. Jinnah reported a "parting of the ways" after his requests for minor amendments to the proposal were denied outright, and relations between the Congress and the League began to sour.

Campaign for Pakistan

At a League conference in Lahore in 1940, Jinnah said: "Hindus and the Muslims belong to two different religions, philosophies, social customs and literature... It is quite clear that Hindus and Muslims derive their inspiration from different sources of history. They have different epics, different heroes and different episodes... To yoke together two such nations under a single state, one as a numerical minority and the other as a majority, must lead to growing discontent and final destruction of any fabric that may be so built up for the government of such a state." At Lahore the League formally recommitted itself to creating an independent

Muslim state called Pakistan, including Sindh, Punjab, Baluchistan, the North West Frontier Province and Bengal, that would be "wholly autonomous and sovereign." The resolution guaranteed protection for non-Muslim religions. The Lahore Resolution was adopted on March 23, 1940, and its principles formed the foundation for Pakistan's first constitution. Talks between Jinnah and Gandhi in 1944 in Bombay failed to achieve agreement. This was the last attempt to reach a single-state solution.

In the 1940s, Jinnah emerged as a leader of the Indian Muslims and was popularly known as *Quaid-e-Azam* (Great Leader). In the Constituent Assembly elections of 1946, the League won 425 out of 496 seats reserved for Muslims (and about 89.2% of Muslim votes) on a policy of creating an independent state of Pakistan, and with an implied threat of secession if this was not granted. Gandhi, Maulana Azad and Nehru, who with the election of another Labour government in Britain in 1945 saw independence within reach, were adamantly opposed to dividing India.

Khwaja Salimullah

Nawab Sir Khwaja Salimullah Bahadur, GCIE, KCSI (1871-1915) was the fourth Nawab of Dhaka and one of the leading Muslim politicians during the British Raj. He is the founder and pioneer of the All India Muslim League which had been established at the Ahsan Manzil Palace in Dhaka, the official residence of the Dhaka Nawab Family. Sir Salimullah, as he is commonly known, was also a key patron of education for the Muslims of Bengal. He had been one of the founders of the University of Dhaka and the prestigious Ahsanullah School of Engineering (now the Bangladesh University of Engineering and Technology BUET). Sir Salimullah was a staunch supporter of the Partition of Bengal. He was a member of East Bengal and Assam Legislative Council from 1906 to 1907. He was also a member of Bengal Legislative Assembly from 1913 till his death in Calcutta in 1915 at the age of 43. He was the founder President of Bengal Muslim League in 1907.

Personal Life

Khwaja Salimullah was the eldest son of the third Nawab of Dhaka, Sir Khwaja Ahsanullah and grandson of the first Nawab of Dhaka, Sir Khwaja Abdul Ghani. Khawaja Salimullah was born at the Ahsan Manzil Palace on 7 June 1871.

Politics

Salimullah began his career in government service in 1893 as Deputy Magistrate, a position he held until he departed in 1895 to start his business in Mymensingh. In 1901 he inherited the position of Nawab of the Dhaka Nawab Family following his father's death.

In 1903-04, Nawab Salimullah began supporting the partition of Bengal in the face of opposition of the Indian National Congress. On 16 October 1905, the day the Bengal Province was parted, Salimullah presided over a meeting of Muslim leaders from all over East Bengal in Northbrook Hall where a political front called Mohammedan Provincial Union was formed. With others of the front, Salimullah organized meetings around East Bengal in favour of the partition, while the Congress built up a movement to oppose it. On 14 and 15 April 1906, Salimullah organized and was named president at the first convention of East Bengal and Assam Provincial Educational Conference at Shahbag, Dhaka. Later that year, newspapers published a dispatch from Salimullah to various Muslim leaders around India urging to form an all-India political party he called Muslim All India Confederacy, and leaders of the Aligarh Movement requested him to convene the 20th meeting of the All India Mohammedan Educational Conference at his own cost. Over two thousand people including Muslim leaders from all over India gathered at the Nawab's family garden-house in Shahbag for the conference held between 27 to 30 December 1906. On the last day, the assembled formed the All Indian Muslim League, appointing Nawab Salimullah the Vice President and placing him on a committee to craft its constitution. Two years later, in December 1908, Salimullah would speak out for free speech in educational institutes and also rights for Muslims to separate elections.

Throughout these years, Salimullah held positions of authority in several leagues and conferences and continued to speak out on important political issues. In 1907, he became president of the All Bengal Muslim League, newly formed in Kolkata. In 1908, he began secretary of the newly established East Bengal and Assam Provincial Muslim League, becoming president in 1909. He served as chair at the 22nd Convention of the All India Mohammedan Educational Conference at Amritsar in December 1908. In 1909, he led people of wealth in the newly formed province to form the Imperial League of Eastern Bengal and Assam.

In March 1911, at a meeting at the Ahsan Manzil, he presided over a decision to maintain the provincial Muslim League and provincial Educational Conference separate for political and educational activities. On 2 March 1912, Salimullah chaired a meeting at which the two Muslim Leagues of the Bengal were combined into the Presidency Muslim League and the two Muslim Associations were combined into the Bengal Presidency Muslim Association. Salimullah was made president of both organisations.

In August 1911, Salimullah demanded a university for Dhaka at a function at a political function at Curzon Hall, but it was not until after the shock of the annulment of the partition by George V on 12 December 1911 that Salimullah was able to achieve this goal. Within days of the annulment, Salimullah submitted a list of demands to Viceroy Lord Hardinge to protect the interest of Muslims.

In response, a pledge was made to establish a university at Dhaka and to provide for Muslims an education officer, which pledge led to the inclusion of an Islamic Studies Department in Dhaka University. Salimullah continued afterwards to champion this cause, making speeches to counter those who argued against it and, in 1914, organizing a convention on 11-12 April for the Muslim Education Conference of United Bengal.

Along with his continued championing of education, Salimullah's last focuses before withdrawing from active politics in 1914 including situations involving Turkey. In 1912, he raised money from East Bengal to assist Turkish Muslims threatened by the Balkan wars. During World War I, however, he supported the Allied Powers after Turkey aligned with Germany.

Honours:

- Companion of the Order of the Star of India (CSI)-New Year Honours, 1906
- Knight Commander of the Order of the Star of India (KCSI)-New Year Honours, 1909
- Knight Grand Commander of the Order of the Indian Empire (GCIE)-23 December 1911.

Legacy

Sir Salimullah is regarded in both Bangladesh and Pakistan as a great freedom fighter. Several of his descendants have gone onto to become prominent politicians in the later days of the British Raj and in Pakistan. They include one of his sons Khwaja Nasrullah who was the Governor of Calcutta, his grandson Sir Khwaja Nazimuddin who was the second Prime Minister of Pakistan, his great grandson Khwaja Hassan Askari who became a Member of the National Assembly of Pakistan. Other family members also became prominent political figures such as Khwaja Atiqullah, Khwaja Khairuddin, Khwaja Shahbuddin, Khwaja Nuruddin and Lieutenant General Khwaja Wasiuddin (the senior most general of Bangladesh Army). Sir Salimullah's great leadership had transformed the Dhaka Nawab Family into one of the most historic and significant political dynasties in the Indian Subcontinent.

Several places in Bangladesh have been dedicated in Sir Salimullah's name. They include most notably the following-

- Salimullah Muslim Hall, University of Dhaka
- Sir Salimullah Medical College, Dhaka
- Salimullah Orphanage
- Nawab Salimullah Road, Naryanganj.

In 1990 the Pakistani government launched commemorative postage stamps honouring Sir Salimullah as one of the Pioneers of Freedom. In 1993 the Bangladeshi government launched a commemorative postage stamp in honour of Sir Salimullah.

Family Tree

He had five sons and five daughters. Among his sons were Nawab Habibullah, Nawabzada Alimullah, Nawabzada Nasarullah, Nawabzada Hafizullah and Nawabzada Alimullah.

Nawabzada Khwaja Nasarullah

Nawabzada Khwaja Nasarullah (1907-1955) was the Son of Nawab Sir Salimullah and Nawab Begum Raushan Akhtar (of Korotia, Tangail) was born on 11th July 1907. He was educated at St.Pauls School Darjeeling, Taluqdar College Lucknow, MAO College Delhi and Aligarh University. He married his first-cousin

Jahanara Begum, the daughter of Syed Abdul Aziz Chowdhury and Nawabzadi Amena Bano Begum, in 1923. Nawabzada Nasarullah was the Vice Chairman of Dhaka Municipality. He Played a role of Police Commissioner in the first ever film of East Bengal "Last Kiss" ("Shukumari"), which was shot in Dilkusha Gardens, Dhaka. He was also a member of the censor board at that time and was involved in two other films named 'Nazma' and 'Babul'.

Khwaja Nasarullah was appointed the Parliamentary Secretary for Civil Supply under the Muslim League and Krishak Praja Party Coalition Government in Bengal during 1937-1943. In 1943 he was made the Governor of Calcutta. On the insistence of Nawabzada Nasarullah the British Government agreed to hand back the Dariya-e-Noor diamond to the Dhaka Nawab Family in 1948. Nawabzada Nasarullah guarded and accompanied by Indian Army soldiers up till the border with East Pakistan brought back the diamond to Dhaka. Nawabzada Khwaja Nasarullah invited Huseyn Shaheed Suhrawardy and Maulana Abdul Khan Bhashani of his house in Dilkusha Gardens in 1948, where they sat together in a political discussion. He Served as Chief Whip from 1947 to 1953. In 1953, Nawabzada Nasarullah was appointed Pakistan's Deputy High Commissiner in Calcutta. Nawabzada Khwaja Nasarullah died in Calcutta in June 1955, aged 45 years. Nawabzada Nasarullah had five sons namely, Khwaja Reshad Nasarullah, Khwaja Khalid Nasarullah, Khwaja Shoib Nasarullah, Khwaja Zaid Nasarullah, and Khwaja Masood Nasarullah.

Nawab Begum Raushan Akhter

Nawab Begum Raushan Akhtar was born in 1887. Her father was Hafez Mahmud Ali Khan Panni, the Zamindar of Korotia in Tangail district. And her mother came from the Royal Ottoman Family, and was the niece of Sultan Abdul Meccid. Raushan Akhtar was educated at home, and was taught Arabic, Persian, Urdu and English. Raushan Akhtar got married to Nawab Sir Salimullah in 1896. They had three children: Nawabzada Hafizullah, Nawabzada Nasarullah and Nawabzadi Ahmedi Bano Begum. Raushan Akhtar's brother, Wajed Ali Khan Panni worked with and supported Nawab Sir Salimullah for the partition of Bengal, and the formation of Muslim League. In 1913, Wajed Ali Khan Panni held the Muslim Education Conference in Korotia, which Nawab Sir Salimullah chaired. Nawab Begum Raushan Akhtar was widowed in 1915, at the young age of 28, yet never remarried, maintaining a dignified quiet, religious and simple lifestyle, in Purdah.

After Independence of Pakistan in 1947, when Muhammad Ali Jinnah and Miss Fatima Jinnah visited Dhaka, Miss Fatima Jinnah called on Nawab Begum Raushan Akhtar, who was the youngest and only surviving Begum of Nawab Salimullah. Nawab Begum Raushan Akhtar, dressed simply in her usual plain white cotton sari, received Miss Fatima Jinnah in the Durbar Hall of the Ahsan Manzil Palace, where both of them sat on the gold and silver throne-chairs. Muhammad Ali Jinnah was received outside, in the gardens of Ahsan Manzil Palace, by her stepson, Nawab Bahadur Habibullah' (to avoid confusion Nawab Waqar-ul-Mulk Kamboh Nawab Waqar-ul-Mulk Kamboh or Nawab Waqar-ul-Mulq Maulvi also known as Mushtaq Hussain (1841 AD-1917 AD) born in the Meerut in 24 March 1841 was a Muslim politician and one of the founders of All India Muslim League.

Early Life

He came of reputed Kamboh lineage of Shaikh Abdul Momin Kamboh who held the office of *Dewan-e-Tun* in Mughal Emperor, Shah Jahan's reign, and Muslim Kambohs of Meerut. Waqar-ul-Mulk did his engineering from Engineering College, Roorki (Roorkee). He served as a Law Secretary in the Government of Hyderabad State, Deccan for some time and then joined Revenue Department. Later he was appointed Governor of "Wararangle", the newly established State and with his untiring efforts, the state soon became very prosperous. Waqar-ul-Mulk received the title of *Nawab Intezar Jung* from the Government of Hyderabad. Then he was appointed Revenue Secretary with the orders of Nizam of Daccan. He served as Secretary, Personal Secretary & Advisor to the Prime Minister Nawab Bashiral Daulla and eventually he became deputy Prime Minister of Hyderabad..

Aligarh Movement

On December 9, 1890, he was conferred the title of *Nawab Waqar-ul-Mulk*. On October 1892, Nawab Waqar-ul-Mulk joined M.A.O. college in Aligarh, Uttar Pradesh. He was a great admirer of Sir Syed Ahmed Khan. He was one of the most ardent followers of Sir Syed and a very active worker of his camp. For the Scientific

Society he translated a book 'French Revolution and Napoleon'. When the College Fund Committee was formed, he became one of its members and worked ceaselessly for popularizing the movement of Sir Syed. He raised a huge amount of Rs. Seven Lakhs and 50 thousand for the establishment of the M. A. O. College. Nawab Waqar-ul-Mulk also remained a member of Scientific Society since 1866. In 1907, he was appointed Honorary Secretary of M.A.O. College.

Founding of Muslim League

Nawab Waqar-ul-Mulk was one of the founders of the Muslim League. In December 1906, the quartet Nawab Waqar-ul-Mulk, Sir Agha Khan, Sir Shafi of Lahore and Nawab Salimullah Khan of Dhaka organised a All India Muhammadan Educational Conference in Calcutta and on the same occasion, they also launched a new party called *Muslim League* of which Nawab Waqar-ul-Mulk became General Secretary. Thus he was the founding father of Muslim league and Pakistan.

Title of "Nawab

In 1908, the Government of India honoured him with the title of *Nawab.*

Influence

Nawab Waqar-ul-Mulk-has carved a niche for himself in the history of the Aligarh movement as Sir Syed's close confidante and the Secretary of the Board of Trustees of the MAO College from 1907 to 1914, during a very turbulent phase of the history of the institution. He also played a role in shaping far-reaching political developments as one of the founders of the All India Muslim League of which he was the first Joint Secretary.

By all accounts he was a very stern, uncompromising person not given to levity and humor so characteristic of the Muslim elite of the age. Someone writes of him as a person "who commanded respect and fear rather than affection." It was the magnetizing personality of Nawab Waqar-ul-Mulk which had induced *Quaid-e-Azam* (Jinnah) to join the All India Muslim League which fact changed the history of Indian subcontinent. The welcome address given by Nawab Waqar-ul-Mulk on the occasion is an important document for the Muslims.

Last Days

Due to bad health, Nawab Waqar-ul Mulk gave up the Secretaryship of Aligarh in 1912 and after a prolonged illness, he died on January 27, 1917.

Mohsin-ul-Mulk

Nawab Mohsin-ul-Mulk (born 9 December 1837 – 16 October 1907) was a prominent Muslim politician. He was a close friend of Sir Syed Ahmed Khan and was involved in the Aligarh Movement and was one of the founders of the All India Muslim League. His real name was Syed Mehdi Ali.

Family and Early Life

Mohsin-ul-Mulk was the son of Syed Mir Zaamin Ali, and was born in the town of Etawah, a part of the United Provinces. Most of his early education was in and around Etawah. As per the trends and tradition during that period, he was given a thorough basic education in Persian and Arabic.

In 1867, he sat for the Provincial Civil Service examination and topped the list of successful candidates. He was appointed as Deputy Collector in U. P. In 1874, Mehdi Ali proceeded to Hyderabad to enter into the service of the Nizam. For his meritorious services over nearly 20 years, he was conferred the titles of Munir Nawaz Jang and Nawab Mohsin-ud-Daula by the Nizam of Hyderabad.

Relationship with Sir Syed Ahmed Khan

During his posting as Tahsildar in Etawah, Mohsin-ul-Mulk met Sir Syed Ahmad Khan for the first time. This meeting resulted in a long lasting companionship and Nawab Mohsinul Mulk became a staunch supporter of Sir Syed's vision and Mission for the rest of his life. Very few friendships have been as stable and strong as the frienship of these two. Mohsin-ul-Mulk retained a very high level of respect despite difference of opinion for his dear friend. Thereafter Nawab Mohsin-ul-Mulk, became one of the strongest supporters of Sir Syed's mission and Aligarh Movement.

He became member of the Scientific Society from its inception in 1864. He wrote passionate articles in *Tahzeebul Akhlaq* to support Sir Syed's vision and spread his mission and became a spokesperson of Sir Syed's social thoughts and the Aligarh Movement. Regarding Sir Syed Ahmad Khan's visit to England, Nawab Mohsinul Mulk wrote a letter to Honourable Haji Ismail Khan: "Syed Ahmad Khan went to England to see with his own eyes the nation which is respected all over the world, and to see the people in their own homes and in their own country. Whatever he observed, he made known to his own people when he returned. When people go to Britain from this country, they usually go for the sights, the theatres, the parks and the museums. But this great friend of Islamic faith went there and sat down in a library to write the *Khutbat-e-Ahmadiya* and to visit colleges and Universities. He went there for the sake of his people, he stayed there for the sake of his people and he came back for the sake of his people."

When Sir Syed formed the committee of the supporters of the advancement of muslim education, Nawab Mohsin-ul-Mulk was his key companion, and started collecting donations for the cause of the newly formed committee.

Upon retirement from service in 1893 from State of Hyderabad, he came to Aligarh and offered his services to Sir Syed Ahmad Khan to assist him in spreading the message of Aligarh Movement. Upon the death of Sir Syed, he was appointed as the Secretary of the Muslim Educational Conference in 1899.

He also became the successor of Sir Syed Ahmed Khan in all aspects. After Sir Syed's death in 1898, he became Secretary of the MAO College management and took Sir Syed's burden on his own shoulders and is regarded with as much respect as his forerunner. He continued the mission of Sir Syed while giving special attention to bring religious and oriental stream scholars together on one platform, i.e. MAO College so that the students could benefit from the scholars to have a proper understanding of religion alongside modern scientific education. He appointed a committee under the Chairmanship of Maulana Habibur Rahman Khan Sherwani to improve the religious studies courses in MAO College. Maulana Shibli Nomani was also a member of that committee. He played a key role in renewing Allama Shibli Nomani's relationship with Aligarh and as a result Allama Shibli joined Aligarh once again.

Mohsin-ul-Mulk remained the Secretary until his death in 1907. He was thus instrumental in the development of MAO College, which eventually became the Aligarh Muslim University in 1920. In later years, the Aligarh Muslim University (AMU) honoured him by naming a Hall of residence after him. The foundation stone of the Hall was laid by the then Vice Chancellor, Mr. Badruddin Mohsin Tyabji on November 4, 1963. It started with an initial strength of 400 and is now one of the largest residential Halls both in size and strength, having 900 students and six different hostels: Allama Shibli Hostel (Previously this was Sir Ziauddin Hostel), Ameen Hostel, Majaz Hostel, Maulana Hali Hostel, Maulana Mohd. Ali Johar Hostel, and Saifi Hostel.

Political Involvements

Nawab Mohsin-ul-Mulk, being a farsighted and politically conscious leader, carried on correspondence with the private secretary of the Viceroy to give his point-of-view on the necessity of separate representation for the Muslims in all legislatures and local bodies. He presided over the 9th session of Muslim Educational Conference which was held in Aligarh in 1894 where he proposed a resolution to help and support Nadwatul Ulama, the newly formed religious school in Lucknow. His impressive presidential remarks softened the hearts of modern educationists to support the cause of Nadwatul Ulama.

In 1906, he became Secretary of All India Muslim League. Along with Nawab Viqar-ul-Mulk, he was asked to draft the constitution of the Muslim League.

Syed Ameer Ali

Syed Ameer Ali C.I.E. (1849-1928), was an Indian Muslim jurist of Bengali decent, political leader, and author of a number of influential books on Muslim history and the modern development of Islam, who is credited for his contributions to the Law of India, particularly Muslim Personal Law, as well as the development of political philosophy for Muslims, during the British Raj. He was a signatory to the 1906 Quran Petition and founding-member of the All India Muslim League, and a contemporary of Muhammad Iqbal.

Family History

Syed Ameer Ali traced his lineage through the eighth Imam, Ali Al-Raza, to Muhammad. Forefathers of his are known to have held office under Shah Abbas II of Persia and taken part in Nadir

Shah's invasion of India. After the plunder of Delhi, the family line then settled in the Sub-continent and started serving Muhammad Shah. Another of his forefathers fought against Marhattas in the third battle of Panipat. Finally, when his grandfather died, his father Saadat Ali Khan was brought up and educated by Syed's maternal uncle.

He was born on 6 April 1849 at Cuttack in Orissa as the fourth of five sons of Syed Saadat Ali. His father moved the family to Calcutta, and then to Chinsura where they settled more permanently among the ashraf elite. His family took advantage of the educational facilities provided by the British government but otherwise shunned by the Muslim community. With the assistance of his British teachers and supported by several competitive scholarships, he achieved outstanding examination results, graduating from Calcutta University in 1867, and gaining an MA with Honours in History in 1868. The LLB followed quickly in 1869. He then began legal practice in Calcutta. By this point he was already one of the few outstanding Muslim achievers of his generation.

Further History

After moving to London, where he stayed between 1869 and 1873, joined the Inner Temple and made contacts with the elite of the city. He absorbed the influence of contemporary liberalism. He had contacts with almost all the administrators concerned with India and with leading English liberals such as John Bright and the Fewcetts, Henry (1831-1898) and his wife, Millicent Fawcett (1847-1929.)

He resumed his legal practice at Calcutta High Court on his return to India in 1873. The year after, he was elected as a Fellow of Calcutta University as well as being appointed as a lecturer in Islamic Law at the Presidency College, Kolkata. In 1878, he was appointed as the member of the Bengal Legislative Council. He revisited England in 1880 for one year.

In 1883, he was nominated to the membership of the Governor General Council. He became a professor of law in Calcutta University in 1881. In 1890 he was made a judge in the Calcutta High Court. He founded the political organisation, Central National Muhamedan Association, in Calcutta in 1877. This made him the first Muslim leader to put into practice the need for such an organisation due to the belief that efforts directed through an organisation would be more effective than those originating from an individual leader. The Association played an important role in the modernisation of Muslims and in arousing their political consciousness. He was associated with it for over 25 years, and worked for the political advancement of the Muslims.

He established the London Muslim League in 1908. This organisation was an independent body and not a branch of All India Muslim League. In 1909, he became the first Indian to sit as a member of the Judicial Committee of the Privy Council. On appointment to the Privy Council he became entitled to be addressed as The Rt Hon. In 1910, he established the first mosque in London. In doing so he formally co-established the London Mosque Fund, alongside a group of prominent British Muslims, to finance the building of the mosque in the capital. His field of activities was now broadened and he stood for Muslim welfare all over the world. He played an important role in securing separate electorates for the Muslims in South Asia and promoting the cause of the Khilafat Movement.

He retired in 1904 and decided to settle down in England where he was out of the way of the main current of Muslim political life. Through his career in general he became a jurist and well-known Islamic scholar. He died on August 4, 1928 in Sussex.

Ali's record as the only Muslim privy councillor in British history was only broken a century later in June 2009 when Sadiq Khan was appointed as Minister of State for Transport with membership of the Privy Council.

His Personal Beliefs

Syed believed that the Muslims as a downtrodden nation could get more benefit from the loyalty to the British rather than from any opposition to them. For this reason he called upon his followers to devote their energy and attention to popularising English education among the Muslims. This perception and consequent activism have been known as the Aligarh Movement.

Referring to the concept of progressive social laws Syed Ameer Ali wrote: "each age has its own standard. What is suited for one time is not suited for the other".

Opinions of the Man

David Samuel Margoliouth in the preface of his book *Mohammed and the Rise of Islam* wrote:

"The charming and eloquent treatise of Syed Ameer Ali, *The Spirit of Islam*, is probably the best achievement in the way of an apology for Mohammed that is ever likely to be composed in a European language"

A comparison was made between Mahadev Gobind Ranade and Syed Ameer Ali, who both held similar positions economically and socially. However historian Yasser Latif Hamdani commented:

"Syed Ameer Ali's impact, though profound on the Turks, has been marginal on the Muslims of South Asia."

In 2005 he was listed in the top 100 Great Muslim Leader of the twentieth century under the category of Ulema and Jurists.

Aga Khan III

Sultan Mahommed Shah, Aga Khan III, GCSI, GCMG, GCIE, GCVO, PC (November 2, 1877 – July 11, 1957) was the 48th Imam of the Shia Ismaili Muslims. He was one of the founders and the first president of the All-India Muslim League, and served as President of the League of Nations from 1937-38.

Early Life

He was born in Karachi (then under British colonial rule), to Aga Khan II and his third wife, Nawab A'lia Shamsul-Muluk, who was a granddaughter of Fath Ali Shah of Persia (Qajar dynasty).

Under the care of his mother, he was given not only that religious and Oriental education which his position as the religious leader of the Ismailis made indispensable, but a sound European training, a boon denied to his father and paternal grandfather. He also attended Eton and Cambridge University.

Career

In 1885, at the age of seven, he succeeded his father as Imam of the Shi'a Isma'ili Muslims.

The Aga Khan travelled in distant parts of the world to receive the homage of his followers, and with the object either of settling differences or of advancing their welfare by pecuniary help and personal advice and guidance. The distinction of a Knight Commander of the Indian Empire was conferred upon him by Queen Victoria in 1897 (and later Knight Grand Commander in 1902 by Edward VII) and he received like recognition for his public services from the German emperor, the sultan of Turkey, the shah of Persia and other potentates.

In 1906, the Aga Khan was a founding member and first president of the All India Muslim League, a political party which pushed for the creation of an independent Muslim nation in the north west regions of South Asia, then under British colonial rule, and later established the country of Pakistan in 1947.

In 1934, he was made a member of the Privy Council and served as a member of the League of Nations (1934–37), becoming the President of the League of Nations in 1937.

He was made a "Knight of the Indian Empire" by Queen Victoria, a Knight Commander of the Order of the Indian Empire by Edward VII (1902), and a Knight Grand Commander of the Order of the Star of India by George V (1912). He was appointed a GCMG in 1923.

Imamate

Under the leadership of Sir Sultan Muhammad Shah, Aga Khan III, the first half of the twentieth century was a period of significant development for the Ismaili community. Numerous institutions for social and economic development were established in South Asia and in East Africa. Ismailis have marked the Jubilees of their Imams with public celebrations, which are symbolic affirmations of the ties that link the Ismaili Imam and his followers. Although the Jubilees have no religious significance, they serve to reaffirm the Imamat's worldwide commitment to the improvement of the quality of human life, especially in the developing countries.

The Jubilees of Sir Sultan Muhammad Shah, Aga Khan III, are well remembered. During his 72 years of Imamat (1885–1957), the community celebrated his Golden (1937), Diamond (1946) and Platinum (1954) Jubilees. To show their appreciation and affection, the Isma'iliyya weighed their Imam in gold, diamonds and, symbolically, in platinum, respectively, the proceeds of which were used to further develop major social welfare and development institutions in Asia and Africa. In India and later Pakistan, social development institutions were established, in the words of Aga Khan, "for the relief of humanity". They included institutions such as the Diamond Jubilee Trust and the Platinum Jubilee Investments Limited which in turn assisted the growth of various types of cooperative societies. Diamond Jubilee Schools for girls were established throughout the remote Northern Areas of what is now Pakistan. In addition, scholarship programs, established at the time of the Golden Jubilee to give assistance to needy students, were progressively expanded. In East Africa, major social welfare and economic development institutions were established. Those involved in social welfare included the accelerated development of schools and community centres, and a modern, fully-equipped hospital in Nairobi. Among the economic development institutions established in East Africa were companies such as the Diamond Jubilee Investment Trust (now Diamond Trust of Kenya) and the Jubilee Insurance Company, which are quoted on the Nairobi Stock Exchange and have become major players in national development.

Sir Sultan Muhammad Shah also introduced organizational forms that gave Ismaili communities the means to structure and regulate their own affairs. These were built on the Muslim tradition of a communitarian ethic on the one hand, and responsible individual conscience with freedom to negotiate one's own moral commitment and destiny on the other. In 1905 he ordained the first Isma'ili Constitution for the social governance of the community in East Africa. The new administration for the Community's affairs was organized into a hierarchy of councils at the local, national, and regional levels. The constitution also set out rules in such matters as marriage, divorce and inheritance, guidelines for mutual cooperation and support among Isma'ilis, and their interface with other communities. Similar constitutions were promulgated in the South Asia, and all were periodically revised to address emerging needs and circumstances in diverse settings.

Following the Second World War, far-reaching social, economic and political changes profoundly affected a number of areas where Ismailis resided. In 1947, British rule in the South Asia was replaced by the sovereign, independent nations of India, Pakistan and later Bangladesh, resulting in the migration of millions people and significant loss of life and property. In the Middle East, the Suez crisis of 1956 as well as the preceding crisis in Iran, demonstrated the sharp upsurge of nationalism, which was as assertive of the region's social and economic aspirations as of its political independence. Africa was also set on its course to decolonization, swept by what Harold Macmillan, the then British Prime Minister, aptly termed the "wind of change". By the early 1960s, most of East and Central Africa, where the majority of the Ismaili population on the continent resided including Tanganyika, Kenya, Uganda, Malagasy, Rwanda, Burundi and Zaire, had attained their political independence.

Race Horse Owner

He was an owner of thoroughbred racing horses, including a record equalling five winners of the Epsom Derby, and a total of sixteen winners of British Classic Races. He was British flat racing Champion Owner thirteen times. According to Ben Pimlott, biographer of Queen Elizabeth II, the Aga Khan presented Her Majesty with a filly called *Astrakhan,* who won at Hurst Park Racecourse in 1950.

Equestrianism

In 1926, the Aga Khan gave a cup (the Aga Khan Trophy) to be awarded to the winners of an international team show jumping competition held at the annual horse show of the Royal Dublin Society in Dublin, Ireland every first week in August. It attracts competitors from all of the main show jumping nations and is carried live on Irish national television.

Marriages and Children

- He married, on November 2, 1896, in Poona, India, Shahzadi Begum, his first cousin and a granddaughter of Aga Khan I.
- He married, in 1908 (Mutah form of marriage) and 1923 (legally), Cleope Teresa Magliano (1888–1926), a dancer with the Ballet Opera of Monte Carlo. They had two sons: Giuseppe Mahdi Khan (d. February 1911) and Ali Solomone Khan (1911–1960)
- He married, on December 7, 1929 (civil), in Aix-les-Bains, France, and December 13, 1929 (religious), in Bombay,

India, Andrée Joséphine Carron (1898–1976). A co-owner of a dressmaking shop in Paris, she became known as Princess Andrée Aga Khan. She did not convert to Islam. By this marriage, he had one son, Prince Sadruddin Aga Khan, in 1933-2003. The couple were divorced in 1943.

- He married, on October 9, 1944, in Geneva, Switzerland, Yvonne Blanche Labrousse (February 1906-July 1, 2000). According to an interview she gave to an Egyptian journalist, her first name was Yvonne, though she is referred to as Yvette in most published references. The daughter of a tram conductor and a dressmaker, she was working as the Aga Khan's social secretary at the time of their marriage. She had been "Miss Lyon 1929" and "Miss France 1930". She converted to Islam and became known as Umm Habiba (Little Mother of the Beloved). In 1954, her husband named her "Mata Salamat"

Publications

He wrote a number of books and papers two of which are of immense importance namely (1).India in Transition, about the preparation politics of India and (2).World Enough & Time-The Memoirs of Sir Sultan Mohammed Shah, Aga Khan III, his autobiography.

Death and Succession

The Aga Khan was succeeded by his grandson Karim Aga Khan, as 'Aga Khan' and is the present Imam of the Ismaili Muslims. At the time of his death on July 11, 1957, his family members were in Versoix. A solicitor brought the will of the Aga Khan III from London to Geneva and read it before the family:

"Ever since the time of my ancestor Ali, the first Imam, that is to say over a period of thirteen hundred years, it has always been the tradition of our family that each Imam chooses his successor at his absolute and unfettered discretion from amongst any of his descendants, whether they be sons or remote male issue and in these circumstances and in view of the fundamentally altered conditions in the world in very recent years due to the great changes which have taken place including the discoveries of atomic science, I am convinced that it is in the best interest of the Shia Muslim Ismailia Community that I should be succeeded by a young man who has been brought up and developed during recent years and in the midst of the new age and who brings a new outlook on life to his office as Imam. For these reasons, I appoint my grandson Karim, the son of my own son, Aly Salomone Khan to succeed to the title of Aga Khan and to the Imam and Pir of all Shia Ismailian followers."

He is buried in Aswan, Egypt at the Mausoleum of Aga Khan.

Maulana Mohammad Ali

Maulana Mohammad Ali Jouhar was an Indian Muslim leader, activist, scholar, journalist and poet, and was among the leading figures of the Khilafat Movement.

Early Life

Muhammad Ali, (10 December 1878 – 4 January 1931)well-known as Maulana Muhammad Ali Jauhar, was born in 1878 in Rampur in India. He belonged to the family of "Rohilla" of the famous "Yousaf Zai" tribe of Pathans. They later on went to Uttar Pardesh and setteled their partially. Maximum of their relatives still live at their native village. He was the brother of Maulana Shaukat Ali and Maulana Zulfiqar Ali. Despite the early death of his father, the family strived and Ali attended the [Deoband Madaressah] Aligarh Muslim University and Lincoln College, Oxford University in 1898, studying modern history.

Upon his return to India, he served as education director for the Rampur state, and later joined the Baroda civil service. He became a brilliant writer and orator, and wrote for major English and Indian newspapers, in both English and Urdu. He himself launched the Urdu weekly *Hamdard* and English *Comrade* in 1911. He moved to Delhi in 1913.

Mohammad Ali worked hard to expand the AMU, then known as the Mohammedan Anglo-Oriental College, and was one of the co-founders of the Jamia Millia Islamia in 1920, which was later moved to Delhi.

Khilafat and Political Activities

Mohammed Ali had attended the founding meeting of the All India Muslim League in Dhaka in 1906, and served as its president in 1918. He remained active in the League till 1928.

Ali represented the Muslim delegation that travelled to England in 1919 in order to convince the British government to influence the Turkish nationalist Mustafa Kemal not to depose the Sultan of Turkey, who was the Caliph of Islam. British rejection of their demands resulted in the formation of the Khilafat committee which directed Muslims all over India to protest and boycott the government.

Now accorded the respectful title of Maulana, Ali formed in 1921, a broad coalition with Muslim nationalists like Maulana Shaukat Ali, Maulana Azad, Hakim Ajmal Khan, Mukhtar Ahmed Ansari and Indian nationalist leader Mahatma Gandhi, who enlisted the support of the Indian National Congress and many thousands of Hindus, who joined the Muslims in a demonstration of unity. Ali also wholeheartedly supported Gandhi's call for a national civil resistance movement, and inspired many hundreds of protests and strikes all over India. He was arrested by British authorities and imprisoned for two years for what was termed as a seditious speech at the meeting of the Khilafat Conference. He was elected as President of Indian National Congress in 1923.

Muslim Separatism

Maulana Mohammad Ali was however, disillusioned by the failure of the Khilafat movement and Gandhi's suspension of civil disobedience in 1922, owing to the Chauri Chaura incident.

He re-started his weekly *Hamdard*, and left the Congress Party. He opposed the Nehru Report, which was a document proposing constitutional reforms and a dominion status of an independent nation within the British Empire, written by a committee of Hindu and Muslim members of the Congress Party headed by President Motilal Nehru. It was a major protest against the Simon Commission which had arrived in India to propose reforms but containing no Indian nor making any effort to listen to Indian voices.

Mohammad Ali opposed the Nehru Report's rejection of separate electorates for Muslims, and supported the *Fourteen Points* of Muhammad Ali Jinnah and the League. He became a critic of Gandhi, breaking with fellow Muslim leaders like Maulana Azad, Hakim Ajmal Khan and Mukhtar Ahmed Ansari, who continued to support Gandhi and the Indian National Congress. Mohammad Ali said: "Even the most degraded Muhammadan was better than

Mahatma Gandhi." Ali attended the Round Table Conference to show that only the Muslim League spoke for India's Muslims. He died soon after the conference in London, on January 4, 1931 and was buried in Jerusalem according to his own wish.

Legacy

Maulana Muhammad Ali Jauhar is remembered as a fiery leader of many of India's Muslims. He is celebrated as a hero by the Muslims of Pakistan, who claim he inspired the Pakistan movement. But in India, he is remembered for his leadership during Khilafat Movement and the Non-Cooperation Movement (1919-1922) and his leadership in Muslim education.

The famous *Muhammad Ali Road* in south Bombay, India's largest city, is named after him. The Gulistan-e-Jauhar neighbourhood of Karachi, Sindh, Pakistan's largest city. Mohammad Ali Cooperative Housing Society (M.A.C.H.S.) in Karachi are named in honour of Maulana Mohammad Ali Johar. Johar Town, Lahore, Punjab is also named after him.

Ali died at a time when the Pakistan movement had not been formed, and it is a matter of continuing debate if he would have ever supported the idea.

Maualana Muhammad Ali mosque in Singapore is named after him.

Jauhar was not only an upright leader, activist, scholar but also a man of letters. His following Urdu stanza about martyrdom of Hussain ibn Ali has been a slogan for many decades now:

Morley-Minto Reforms, began when John Morley, the Liberal Secretary of State for India, and the Conservative Governor-General of India, The Earl of Minto, believed that cracking down on terrorism in Bengal was necessary but not sufficient for restoring stability to the British Raj after Lord Curzon's partitioning of Bengal. They believed that a dramatic step was required to put heart into loyal elements of the Indian upper classes and the growing Westernised section of the population.

They produced the Indian Councils Act of 1909 (Morley-Minto reforms), these reforms did not go any significant distance toward meeting the Indian National Congress demand for 'the system of government obtaining in Self-Governing British Colonies'.

The Act of 1909 was important for the following reasons:

- It effectively allowed the election of Indians to the various legislative councils in India for the first time. Previously some Indians had been appointed to legislative councils. The majorities of the councils remained British government appointments. Moreover the electorate was limited to specific classes of Indian nationals;
- The introduction of the electoral principle laid the groundwork for a parliamentary system even though this was contrary to the intent of Morley. As stated by Burke and Quraishi-

"To Lord Curzon's apprehension that the new Councils could become 'parliamentary bodies in miniature', Morley vehemently replied that, 'if it could be said that this chapter of reforms led directly or indirectly to the establishment of a parliamentary system in India, I for one would have nothing at all to do with it'. But he had already confessed in a letter to Minto in June 1906 that while it was inconceivable to adapt English political institutions to the 'nations who inhabit India...the spirit of English institutions is a different thing and it is a thing that we cannot escape, even if we wished...because the British constituencies are the masters, and they will assuredly insist...all parties alike...on the spirit of their own political system being applied to India.'

He never got down to explaining how the spirit of the British system of government could be achieved without its body."

- Muslims had expressed serious concern that a 'first past the post' British type of electoral system would leave them permanently subject to Hindu majority rule. The Act of 1909 stipulated, as demanded by the Muslim leadership
- that Indian Muslims be allotted reserved seats in the Municipal and District Boards, in the Provincial Councils and in the Imperial Legislature;
- that the number of reserved seats be in excess of their relative population (25 percent of the Indian population); and,
- that only Muslims should vote for candidates for the Muslim seats (' separate electorates').

These concessions were a constant source of strife 1909-47. British statesmen generally considered reserved seats as regrettable in that they encouraged communal extremism as Muslim candidates did not have to appeal for Hindu votes and vice versa. As further power was shifted from the British to Indian politicians in 1919, 1935 and after, Muslims were ever more determined to hold on to, and if possible expand, reserved seats and their weightage. However, Hindu politicians repeatedly tried to eliminate reserved seats as they considered them to be undemocratic and to hinder the development of a shared Hindu-Muslim Indian national feeling.

Minto-Morley Reforms

In 1906, Lord Morley, the Secretary of State for Indian Affairs, announced in the British parliament that his government wanted to introduce new reforms for India, in which the locals were to be given more powers in legislative affairs. With this, a series of correspondences started between him and Lord Minto, the then Governor General of India. A committee was appointed by the Government of India to propose a scheme of reforms. The committee submitted its report, and after the approval of Lord Minto and Lord Morley, the Act of 1909 was passed by the British parliament. The Act of 1909 is commonly known as the Minto-Morley Reforms. The following were the main features of the Act of 1909:

1. The number of the members of the Legislative Council at the Centre was increased from 16 to 60.
2. The number of the members of the Provincial Legislatives was also increased. It was fixed as 50 in the provinces of Bengal, Madras and Bombay, and for the rest of the provinces it was 30.
3. The member of the Legislative Councils, both at the Centre and in the provinces, were to be of four categories i.e. ex-officio members (Governor General and the members of their Executive Councils), nominated official members (those nominated by the Governor General and were government officials), nominated non-official members (nominated by the Governor General but were not government officials) and elected members (elected by different categories of Indian people).

4. Right of separate electorate was given to the Muslims.
5. At the Centre, official members were to form the majority but in provinces non-official members would be in majority.
6. The members of the Legislative Councils were permitted to discuss the budgets, suggest the amendments and even to vote on them; excluding those items that were included as non-vote items. They were also entitled to ask supplementary questions during the legislative proceedings.
7. The Secretary of State for India was empowered to increase the number of the Executive Councils of Madras and Bombay from two to four.
8. Two Indians were nominated to the Council of the Secretary of State for Indian Affairs.
9. The Governor General was empowered to nominate one Indian member to his Executive Council.

Muhammad Iqbal

Allama Dr. Sir Mohammad Iqbal (November 9, 1877, Sialkot – April 21, 1938, Lahore) was a Persian-and Urdu-language poet, philosopher and politician He is commonly referred to as Allama Iqbal (*Allama* meaning "Scholar").

After studying in Cambridge, Munich and Heidelberg, Iqbal established a law practice, but concentrated primarily on writing scholarly works on politics, economics, ishi history, philosophy and religion. He is best known for his poetic works, including *Asrar-e-Khudi*—for which he was knighted—*Rumuz-e-Bekhudi*, and the *Bang-e-Dara*, with its enduring patriotic song *Tarana-e-Hind*. In India, he is widely regarded for the patriotic song, Saare Jahan Se Achcha. In Afghanistan and Iran, where he is known as *Eghbal-e-Lahoori*, he is highly regarded for his Persian works.

Iqbal was a strong proponent of the political and spiritual revival of Islamic civilisation across the world, but specifically in South Asia; a series of famous lectures he delivered to this effect were published as *The Reconstruction of Religious Thought in Islam*. One of the most prominent leaders of the All India Muslim League, Iqbal encouraged the creation of a "state in northwestern India for Muslims" in his 1930 presidential address. Iqbal encouraged and worked closely with Muhammad Ali Jinnah, and he is known as *Muffakir-e-Pakistan* ("The Thinker of Pakistan"), *Shair-e-Mashriq* ("The Poet of the East"), and *Hakeem-ul-Ummat* ("The Sage of Ummah"). He is officially recognized as the national poet of Pakistan. The anniversary of his birth is on November 9, and is a national holiaay in Pakistan.

Early Life

Allama Iqbal was born in Sialkot, Punjab, British India ; the eldest of five siblings in a Kashmiri family. Iqbal's father Shaikh Nur Muhammad was a prosperous tailor, well-known for his devotion to Islam, and the family raised their children with deep religious grounding. His grand father Sahaj Ram Sapru moved to Sialkot after conversion to Islam.

Iqbal was educated initially by tutors in languages and writing, history, poetry and religion. His potential as a poet and writer was recognised by one of his tutors, Sayyid Mir Hassan, and Iqbal would continue to study under him at the Scotch Mission College in Sialkot. The student became proficient in several languages and the skill of writing prose and poetry, and graduated in 1892. Following custom, at the age of 15 Iqbal's family arranged for him to be married to Karim Bibi, the daughter of an affluent Gujrati physician. The couple had two children: a daughter, Mi'raj Begam (born 1895) and a son, Aftab (born 1899). Iqbal's third son died soon after birth. The husband and wife were unhappy in their marriage and eventually divorced in 1916.

Iqbal entered the Government College in Lahore where he studied philosophy, English literature and Arabic and obtained a Bachelor of Arts degree, graduating *cum laude*. He won a gold medal for topping his examination in philosophy. While studying for his masters degree, Iqbal came under the wing of Sir Thomas Arnold, a scholar of Islam and modern philosophy at the college.

Arnold exposed the young man to Western culture and ideas, and served as a bridge for Iqbal between the ideas of East and West. Iqbal was appointed to a readership in Arabic at the Oriental College in Lahore, and he published his first book in Urdu, *The Science of Economics* in 1903. In 1905 Iqbal published the patriotic song, *Tarana-e-Hind* (*Song of India*).

At Sir Thomas's encouragement, Iqbal travelled to and spent many years studying in Europe. He obtained a Bachelor of Arts degree from Trinity College at Cambridge in 1907, while simultaneously studying law at Lincoln's Inn, from where he qualified as a barrister in 1908. Iqbal also met a Muslim student, Atiyah Faizi in 1907, and had a close relationship with her. In Europe, he started writing his poetry in Persian as well. Throughout his life, Iqbal would prefer writing in Persian as he believed it allowed him to fully express philosophical concepts, and it gave him a wider audience. It was while in England that he first participated in politics. Following the formation of the All-India Muslim League in 1906, Iqbal was elected to the executive committee of its British chapter in 1908. Together with two other politicians, Syed Hassan Bilgrami and Syed Ameer Ali, Iqbal sat on the subcommittee which drafted the constitution of the League. Working under the supervision of Friedrich Hommel, Iqbal published a thesis titled: *The Development of Metaphysics in Persia.*

Photo Gallery

Literary Career: Upon his return to India in 1908, Iqbal took up assistant professorship at the Government College in Lahore, but for financial reasons he relinquished it within a year to practice law. During this period, Iqbal's personal life was in turmoil. He divorced Karim Bibi in 1916, but provided financial support to her and their children for the rest of his life.

While maintaining his legal practice, Iqbal began concentrating on spiritual and religious subjects, and publishing poetry and literary works. He became active in the Anjuman-e-Himayat-e-Islam, a congress of Muslim intellectuals, writers and poets as well as politicians, and in 1919 became the general secretary of the organisation.

Iqbal's thoughts in his work primarily focused on the spiritual direction and development of human society, centred around experiences from his travel and stay in Western Europe and the Middle East. He was profoundly influenced by Western philosophers such as Friedrich Nietzsche, Henri Bergson and Goethe, and soon became a strong critic of Western society's separation of religion from state and what he perceived as its obsession with materialist pursuits.

The poetry and philosophy of Mawlana Rumi bore the deepest influence on Iqbal's mind. Deeply grounded in religion since childhood, Iqbal would begin intensely concentrating on the study of Islam, the culture and history of Islamic civilization and its political future, and embrace Rumi as "his guide." Iqbal would feature Rumi in the role of a guide in many of his poems, and his works focused on reminding his readers of the past glories of Islamic civilization, and delivering a message of a pure, spiritual focus on Islam as a source for socio-political liberation and greatness. Iqbal denounced political divisions within and amongst Muslim nations, and frequently alluded to and spoke in terms of the global Muslim community, or the *Ummah*.

Works in Persian

Iqbal's poetic works are written mostly in Persian rather than Urdu. Among his 12,000 verses of poem, about 7,000 verses are in Persian. In 1915, he published his first collection of poetry, the *Asrar-e-Khudi* (*Secrets of the Self*) in Persian. The poems delve into concepts of ego and emphasise the spirit and self from a religious, spiritual perspective. Many critics have called this Iqbal's finest poetic work. In *Asrar-e-Khudi*, Iqbal has explained his philosophy of "Khudi," or "Self." He proves by various means that the whole universe obeys the will of the "Self." Iqbal condemns self-destruction. For him the aim of life is self-realization and self-knowledge. He charts the stages through which the "Self" has to pass before finally arriving at its point of perfection, enabling the knower of the "Self" to become the viceregent of Allah.

In his *Rumuz-e-Bekhudi* (*Hints of Selflessness*), Iqbal seeks to prove that Islamic way of life is the best code of conduct for a nation's viability. A person must keep his individual characteristics intact but once this is achieved he should sacrifice his personal ambitions for the needs of the nation. Man cannot realise the "Self" out of society. Also in Persian and published in 1917, this group of poems has as its main themes the ideal community, Islamic ethical and social principles and the relationship between the individual and society. Although he is true throughout to Islam, Iqbal recognises also the positive analogous aspects of other religions. The *Rumuz-e-Bekhudi* complements the emphasis on the self in the *Asrar-e-Khudi* and the two collections are often put in the same volume under the title *Asrar-e-Rumuz* (*Hinting Secrets*), and it is addressed to the world's Muslims. Iqbal sees the individual and his community as reflections of each other. The individual needs to be strengthened before he can be integrated into the community, whose development in turn depends on the preservation of the communal ego. It is through contact with others that an ego learns to accept the limitations of its own freedom and the meaning of love. Muslim communities must ensure order in life and must therefore preserve their communal tradition. It is in this context that Iqbal sees the vital role of women, who as mothers are directly responsible for inculcating values in their children.

Iqbal's 1924 publication, the *Payam-e-Mashriq* (*The Message of the East*) is closely connected to the *West-östlicher Diwan* by the famous German poet Goethe. Goethe bemoaned that the West had become too materialistic in outlook and expected that the East would provide a message of hope that would resuscitate spiritual values. Iqbal styles his work as a reminder to the West of the importance of morality, religion and civilization by underlining the need for cultivating feeling, ardour and dynamism. He explains that an individual could never aspire for higher dimensions unless he learns of the nature of spirituality. In his first visit to Afghanistan, he presented his book "Payam-e Mashreq" to King Amanullah Khan in which he admired the liberal movements of Afghanistan against the British Empire. In 1933, he was officially invited to Afghanistan to join the meetings regarding the establishment of Kabul University.

The *Zabur-e-Ajam* (*Persian Psalms*), published in 1927, includes the poems *Gulshan-e-Raz-e-Jadeed* (*Garden of New Secrets*) and *Bandagi Nama* (*Book of Slavery*). In *Gulshan-e-Raz-e-Jadeed,* Iqbal first poses questions, then answers them with the help of ancient and modern insight and shows how it effects and concerns the world of action. *Bandagi Nama* denounces slavery by attempting to explain the spirit behind the fine arts of enslaved societies. Here as in other books, Iqbal insists on remembering the past, doing well in the present and preparing for the future, emphasising love, enthusiasm and energy to fill the ideal life. Iqbal's 1932 work, the *Javed Nama* (*Book of Javed*) is named after and in a manner addressed to his son, who is featured in the poems, and follows the examples of the works of Ibn Arabi and Dante's *The Divine Comedy,* through mystical and exaggerated depiction across time. Iqbal depicts himself as *Zinda Rud* ("A stream full of life") guided by Rumi, "the master," through various heavens and spheres, and has the honour of approaching divinity and coming in contact with divine illuminations. In a passage re-living a historical period, Iqbal condemns the Muslim traitors who were instrumental in the defeat and death of Nawab Siraj-ud-Daula of Bengal and Tipu Sultan of Mysore respectively by betraying them for the benefit of the British colonists, and thus delivering their country to the shackles of slavery. At the end, by addressing his son Javid, he speaks to the young people at large, and provides guidance to the "new generation."

His love to Persian language is evident in his works and poetry. He says in one of his poems:

garche Urdu dar uzûbat shakar ast
lék Parsi-am ze Hindi shirintar ast

Translation:

Even though in sweetness Urdu is sugar-(but) My Persian is sweeter than Hindi**

Works in Urdu

Iqbal's first work published in Urdu, the *Bang-e-Dara* (*The Call of the Marching Bell*) of 1924, was a collection of poetry written by him in three distinct phases of his life. The poems he wrote up to 1905, the year Iqbal left for England imbibe patriotism and imagery of landscape, and includes the *Tarana-e-Hind* (*The Song of India*), popularly known as *Saare Jahan Se Achcha* and another poem *Tarana-e-Milli* (Anthem of the (Muslim) Community), which was composed in the same metre and rhyme scheme as Saare Jahan Se Achcha. The second set of poems date from between 1905 and 1908 when Iqbal studied in Europe and dwell upon the nature of European society, which he emphasized had lost spiritual and religious values. This inspired Iqbal to write poems on the historical and cultural heritage of Islamic culture and Muslim people, not from an Indian but a global perspective. Iqbal urges the global community of Muslims, addressed as the *Ummah* to define personal, social and political existence by the values and teachings of Islam. Poems such as *Tulu'i Islam* (*Dawn of Islam*) and *Khizr-e-Rah* (*Guide of the Path*) are especially acclaimed.

Iqbal preferred to work mainly in Persian for a predominant period of his career, but after 1930, his works were mainly in Urdu. The works of this period were often specifically directed at the Muslim masses of India, with an even stronger emphasis on Islam, and Muslim spiritual and political reawakening. Published in 1935, the *Bal-e-Jibril* (*Wings of Gabriel*) is considered by many critics as the finest of Iqbal's Urdu poetry, and was inspired by his visit to Spain, where he visited the monuments and legacy of the kingdom of the Moors. It consists of ghazals, poems, quatrains, epigrams and carries a strong sense religious passion.

The *Pas Cheh Bayed Kard ai Aqwam-e-Sharq* (*What are we to do, O Nations of the East?*) includes the poem *Musafir* (*Traveller*). Again, Iqbal depicts Rumi as a character and an exposition of the mysteries of Islamic laws and Sufi perceptions is given. Iqbal laments the dissension and disunity among the Indian Muslims as well as Muslim nations.

Musafir is an account of one of Iqbal's journeys to Afghanistan, in which the Pashtun people are counseled to learn the "secret of Islam" and to "build up the self" within themselves. Iqbal's final work was the *Armughan-e-Hijaz* (*The Gift of Hijaz*), published posthumously in 1938. The first part contains quatrains in Persian, and the second part contains some poems and epigrams in Urdu. The Persian quatrains convey the impression as though the poet is travelling through the Hijaz in his imagination. Profundity of ideas and intensity of passion are the salient features of these short poems. The Urdu portion of the book contains some categorical criticism of the intellectual movements and social and political revolutions of the modern age.

Political Career

While dividing his time between law and poetry, Iqbal had remained active in the Muslim League. He supported Indian involvement in World War I, as well as the Khilafat movement and remained in close touch with Muslim political leaders such as Maulana Mohammad Ali and Muhammad Ali Jinnah. He was a critic of the mainstream Indian National Congress, which he regarded as dominated by Hindus and was disappointed with the League when during the 1920s, it was absorbed in factional divides between the pro-British group led by Sir Muhammad Shafi and the centrist group led by Jinnah. In November 1926, with the encouragement of friends and supporters, Iqbal contested for a seat in the Punjab Legislative Assembly from the Muslim district of Lahore, and defeated his opponent by a margin of 3,177 votes. He supported the constitutional proposals presented by Jinnah with the aim of guaranteeing Muslim political rights and influence in a coalition with the Congress, and worked with the Aga Khan and other Muslim leaders to mend the factional divisions and achieve unity in the Muslim League.

Revival of Islamic Polity

Iqbal's second book in English, the *Reconstruction of Religious Thought in Islam*, is a collection of his six lectures which he delivered at Madras, Hyderabad and Aligarh; first published as a collection in Lahore, in 1930. These lectures dwell on the role of Islam as a religion as well as a political and legal philosophy in the modern age. In these lectures Iqbal firmly rejects the political attitudes and conduct of Muslim politicians, whom he saw as morally misguided, attached to power and without any standing with Muslim masses. Iqbal expressed fears that not only would secularism weaken the spiritual foundations of Islam and Muslim society, but that India's Hindu-majority population would crowd out Muslim heritage, culture and political influence. In his travels to Egypt, Afghanistan, Iran and Turkey, he promoted ideas of greater Islamic political cooperation and unity, calling for the shedding of nationalist differences. He also speculated on different political arrangements to guarantee Muslim political power; in a dialogue with Dr. B. R. Ambedkar, Iqbal expressed his desire to see Indian provinces as autonomous units under the direct control of the British government and with no central Indian government. He envisaged autonomous Muslim provinces in India. Under one Indian union he feared for Muslims, who would suffer in many respects especially with regard to their existentially separate entity as Muslims. Sir Muhammad Iqbal was elected president of the Muslim League in 1930 at its session in Allahabad, in the United Provinces as well as for the session in Lahore in 1932. In his presidential address on December 29, 1930, Iqbal outlined a vision of an independent state for Muslim-majority provinces in northwestern India: "I would like to see the Punjab, North-West Frontier Province, Sindh and Baluchistan amalgamated into a single state. Self-government within the British Empire, or without the British Empire, the formation of a consolidated Northwest Indian Muslim state appears to me to be the final destiny of the Muslims, at least of Northwest India."

In his speech, Iqbal emphasised that unlike Christianity, Islam came with "legal concepts" with "civic significance," with its "religious ideals" considered as inseparable from social order: "therefore, the construction of a policy on national lines, if it means a displacement of the Islamic principle of solidarity, is simply unthinkable to a Muslim." Iqbal thus stressed not only the need for the political unity of Muslim communities, but the undesirability of blending the Muslim population into a wider society not based on Islamic principles. He thus became the first politician to articulate what would become known as the *Two-Nation Theory* — that Muslims are a distinct nation and thus deserve political independence from other regions and communities of India. However, he would not elucidate or specify if his ideal Islamic state would construe a theocracy, even as he rejected secularism and nationalism. The latter part of Iqbal's life was concentrated on political activity. He would travel across Europe and West Asia to garner political and financial support for the League, and he reiterated his ideas in his 1932 address, and during the Third Round-Table Conference, he opposed the Congress and proposals for transfer of power without considerable autonomy or independence for Muslim provinces. He would serve as president of the Punjab Muslim League, and would deliver speeches and publish articles in an attempt to rally Muslims across India as a single political entity. Iqbal consistently criticised feudal classes in Punjab as well as Muslim politicians averse to the League.

Patron of The Journal Tolu-e-Islam

He was also the first patron of the historical, political, religious, cultural journal of Muslims of British India and Pakistan. This journal played an important part in the Pakistan movement. The name of this journal is The Journal Tolu-e-Islam. In 1935, according to his instructions, Syed Nazeer Niazi initiated and edited, a journal Tolu-e-Islam named after the famous poem of Sir Muhammad Iqbal, Tulu'i Islam. He also dedicated the first edition of this journal to Sir Muhammad Iqbal. For a long time Sir Muhammad Iqbal wanted a journal to propagate his ideas and the aims and objective of Muslim league. It was Syed Nazeer Niazi, a close friend of him and a regular visitor to him during his last two years, who started this journal. He also made Urdu translation of The Reconstruction of Religious Thought in Islam, by Sir Muhammad Iqbal.

In the first monthly journal of Oct. 1935, an article "Millat Islamia Hind" The Muslim nation of India was published. In this article Syed Nazeer Niazi described the political conditions of British India and the aims and objective of Muslim community. He also discussed the basic principles of Islam which were aims and objective of Sir Muhammad Iqbal' concept of an Islamic State.

The early contributors to this journal were eminent Muslim scholars like Maulana Aslam Jairajpuri, Ghulam Ahmed Pervez, Dr. Zakir Hussain Khan, Syed Naseer Ahmed, Raja Hassan Akhtar, Maulvi Ghulam Yezdani, Ragheb Ahsan, Sheikh Suraj ul Haq, Rafee ud din Peer, Prof. fazal ud din Qureshi, Agha Muhammad Safdar, Asad Multani, Dr. Tasadaq Hussain, Prof. Yusuf Saleem Chisti.

Afterward, this journal was continued by Ghulam Ahmed Pervez,who had already contributed many articles in the early editions of this journal. After the emergence of Pakistan, the mission of the journal Tolu-e-Islam was to propagate the implementation of the principle which had inspired the demand for separate Muslim State according to the Quran. This journal is still published by Idara Tolu-e-Islam, Lahore.

Relationship with Muhammad Ali Jinnah

Ideologically separated from Congress Muslim leaders, Iqbal had also been disillusioned with the politicians of the Muslim League owing to the factional conflict that plagued the League in the 1920s. Discontent with factional leaders like Sir Muhammad Shafi and Sir Fazl-ur-Rahman, Iqbal came to believe that only Muhammad Ali Jinnah was a political leader capable of preserving this unity and fulfilling the League's objectives on Muslim political empowerment. Building a strong, personal correspondence with Jinnah, Iqbal was an influential force on convincing Jinnah to end his self-imposed exile in London, return to India and take charge of the League. Iqbal firmly believed that Jinnah was the only leader capable of drawing Indian Muslims to the League and maintaining party unity before the British and the Congress: "I know you are a busy man but I do hope you won't mind my writing to you often, as you are the only Muslim in India today to whom the community has right to look up for safe guidance through the storm which is coming to North-West India and, perhaps, to the whole of India."

There were significant differences between the two men – while Iqbal believed that Islam was the source of government and society, Jinnah was a believer in secular government and had laid out a secular vision for Pakistan where religion would have "nothing to do with the business of the state." Iqbal had backed the Khilafat struggle; Jinnah had dismissed it as "religious frenzy." And while Iqbal espoused the idea of Muslim-majority provinces in 1930, Jinnah would continue to hold talks with the Congress through the decade and only officially embraced the goal of Pakistan in 1940. Some historians postulate that Jinnah always remained hopeful for an agreement with the Congress and never fully desired the independence of India. Iqbal's close correspondence with Jinnah is speculated by some historians as having been responsible for Jinnah's embrace of the idea of Pakistan. Iqbal elucidated to Jinnah his vision of a separate Muslim state in a letter sent on June 21, 1937:

"A separate federation of Muslim Provinces, reformed on the lines I have suggested above, is the only course by which we can secure a peaceful India and save Muslims from the domination of Non-Muslims. Why should not the Muslims of North-West India and Bengal be considered as nations entitled to self-determination just as other nations in India and outside India are."

Iqbal, serving as president of the Punjab Muslim League, criticised Jinnah's political actions, including a political agreement with Punjabi leader Sir Sikandar Hyat Khan, whom Iqbal saw as a representative of feudal classes and not committed to Islam as the core political philosophy. Nevertheless, Iqbal worked constantly to encourage Muslim leaders and masses to support Jinnah and the League. Speaking about the political future of Muslims in India, Iqbal said: "There is only one way out. Muslims should strengthen Jinnah's hands. They should join the Muslim League. Indian question, as is now being solved, can be countered by our united front against both the Hindus and the English. Without it, our demands are not going to be accepted. People say our demands smack of communalism. This is sheer propaganda. These demands relate to the defence of our national existence.... The united front can be formed under the leadership of the Muslim League. And the Muslim League can succeed only on account of Jinnah. Now none but Jinnah is capable of leading the Muslims."

Death

In 1933, after returning from a trip to Spain and Afghanistan, Iqbal began suffering from a mysterious throat illness. He spent his final years working to establish the Idara Dar-ul-Islam, an institution where studies in classical Islam and contemporary social science would be subsidised, and advocating the demand for an independent Muslim state. Iqbal ceased practising law in 1934 and he was granted pension by the Nawab of Bhopal. After suffering for months from his illness, Iqbal died in Lahore in 1938. His tomb is located in the space between the entrance of the Badshahi Mosque and the Lahore Fort, and official guards are maintained there by the Government of Pakistan.

Iqbal is commemorated widely in Pakistan, where he is regarded as the ideological founder of the state. His *Tarana-e-Hind* is a song that is widely used in India as a patriotic song speaking of communal harmony. His birthday is annually commemorated in Pakistan as Iqbal Day, a national holiday. Iqbal is the namesake of many public institutions, including the Allama Iqbal Medical College, Allama Iqbal Open University and the Allama Iqbal International Airport in Lahore. Government and public organizations have sponsored the establishment of colleges and schools dedicated to Iqbal, and have established the Iqbal Academy to research, teach and preserve the works, literature and philosophy of Iqbal. His son Javid Iqbal has served as a justice on the Supreme Court of Pakistan.

Influence and Legacy

If we are resolved to describe Islam as a system of superior values, we are obliged, first of all, to acknowledge that we are not the true representatives of Islam. —Muhammad Iqbal

Allama Iqbal's poetry has also been translated into several European languages where his works were famous during the early part of the 20th century.

Legacy in India

Iqbal's poem Saare Jahan Se Achcha has remained popular in India for over a century. Mahatma Gandhi is said to have sung it over a hundred times when he was imprisoned at Yerawada Jail in Pune in the 1930s. The poem was set to music in the 1950s by sitar maestro Ravi Shankar and recorded by singer Lata Mangeshkar. Stanzas (1), (3), (4), and (6) of the song became an unofficial national anthem in India, and were also turned into the official quick march of the Indian Armed Forces. Rakesh Sharma, the first Indian cosmonaut, employed the first line of the song in 1984 to describe to then prime minister Indira Gandhi how India appeared from outer space. Current prime minister, Manmohan Singh, quoted the poem at his first press conference.

Choudhary Rahmat Ali

Chaudhary Rahmat Ali (November 16, 1897-February 3, 1951) was an Pakistani Muslim nationalist who was one of the earliest proponents of the creation of the state of Pakistan. He is credited with creating the name "Pakistan" for a separate Muslim homeland in South Asia.

Education and Career

Rehmat Ali was born into a Gujjar family in the town of Balachaur in Hoshiarpur District of Punjab (now Nawanshahr District), India. After graduating from Islamia Madrassa Lahore in 1918, he taught at Aitchison College Lahore before continuing Law studies at Punjab University. In 1930 he moved to England to join Emmanuel College, Cambridge in 1931. In 1933, he published a pamphlet, *Now or Never,* coining the word *Pakistan* for the first time. Subsequently, he obtained a BA degree in 1933 and MA in 1940 from the University of Cambridge. In 1943, he was called to the Bar, Middle Temple Inn, London. Until 1947, he continued publishing various booklets about his vision of the South Asia. The independence process disillusioned him due to the mass killings and mass migrations. He was also dissatisfied with the distribution of areas among the two countries and considered it a major reason for disturbances. He died on 3 February 1951 and was buried on 20 February at Newmarket Road Cemetery, Cambridge, UK.

Conception of 'Pakistan'

He was the Secretary of Pakistan Movement in U.K with Muhammad Aslam Khan Khattak as President, and Dr. Abdur Rahim as Vice President. It was in this organization that the name "PAKISTAN" was first suggested.

There are several accounts to the conceptualization of the name. According to a friend (Abdul Kareem Jabbar) the name came up when Rehmat Ali was walking along the banks of the Thames in 1932 with his friends Pir Ahsan-ud-Din and Khawja Abdul Rahim. According to Rehmat Ali's secretary Miss Frost, he came up with the idea of the name 'Pakistan' while riding on the top of a London bus.

In the early 1930s, Ali began writing about the formation of a Muslim nation in India. On January 28, 1933, he voiced his ideas in the pamphlet entitled *"Now or Never; Are We to Live or Perish Forever?"*. The word 'Pakstan' referred to "the five Northern units of India, Viz: Punjab, (Afghanistan Province), Kashmir, Sindh and Baluchistan "". By the end of 1933, 'Pakistan' become common vocabulary where an i was added to ease pronunciation (as in Afghan-i-stan).

In a subsequent book Rehmat Ali discussed the etymology in further detail.

'Pakistan' is both a Persian and an Urdu word. It is composed of letters taken from the names of all our South Asia homelands; that is, Punjab, Afghania, Kashmir, Sindh and Balochistan. It means the land of the Pure.

Philosophy

Like Allama Iqbal, Ali believed that the Muslims of India had to undergo a reformation politically in order to remain a viable, and independent community there. Ali noted that Hazrat Muhammad had succeeded in uniting fractured Arab tribes and that this example was to again be used by Muslims of India to pool together in order to survive in what he perceived to be an increasingly hostile India.

As such, Chaudhary Rahmat Ali's writings, in addition to those of Iqbal and others were major catalysts for the formation of Pakistan. He offered "Bang-i-Islam" for a Muslim homeland in the Bengal, and "Usmanistan" for a Muslim homeland in the Deccan. He also suggested "Dinia" as a name for a South Asia for various religions.

Ali dedicated a lot of time and energy to the idea of Pakistan, and after its formation in 1947, he argued on its behalf at the United Nations over the issue of occupied-Kashmir.

Post-Independence

While Chaudhary Rahmat Ali was a leading figure for the conception of Pakistan, he lived most of his adult life in England. The Cambridge-based pamphleteer had been voicing his dissatisfaction with the creation of Pakistan ever since his arrival in Lahore on April 6 1948. He was unhappy over a *Smaller Pakistan* than the one he had conceived in his 1933 pamphlet Now Or Never.

Consequently, Rahmat Ali died in 1951, buried in Cambridge City graveyard.

Partition of Bengal (1905)

The decision on the Partition of Bengal was announced on 19 July 1905 by then Viceroy of India, Lord Curzon. The partition took effect on 16 October 1905. Due to the high level of political unrest generated by the partition, the eastern and western parts of Bengal were reunited in 1911.

Origin

The province of Bengal had an area of 489,500 sq. km. and a population of over 80 million. Eastern Bengal was almost isolated from the western part by geography and poor communications. In 1836, the upper provinces were placed under a lieutenant governor, and in 1854 the Governor-General-In-Council was relieved of the direct administration of Bengal. In 1874 Assam, including Sylhet, was severed from Bengal to form a Chief-Commissionership, and the Lushai Hills were added to it in 1898.

Partition

Partitioning Bengal was first considered in 1903. There were also additional proposals to separate Chittagong and the districts of Dhaka and Mymensingh from Bengal and attaching them to the province of Assam. In a similar way, Chhota Nagpur was to be incorporated with the central provinces.

The government officially published the idea in January 1904, and in February, Lord Curzon made an official tour to eastern districts of Bengal to assess public opinion on the partition. He consulted with leading personalities and delivered speeches at Dhaka, Chittagong and Mymensingh explaining the government's stand on partition. The idea was opposed by Henry John Stedman Cotton, Chief Commissioner of Assam 1896-1902.

The Partition of Bengal in 1905 was made on October 16 by then Viceroy of India, Lord Curzon. Partition was promoted for administrative regions; Bengal was as large as France but with a significantly larger population. The eastern region was thought to be neglected and under-governed. By splitting the province, an improved administration could be established in the east where, subsequently, the population would benefit from new schools and employment opportunities. However, other motives lurked behind the partition plan. Bengali Hindus were in the forefront of political agitation for greater participation in governance; their position would be weakened, since Muslims would now dominate in the East. Hindus tended to oppose partition, which was more popular among Muslims. What followed partition, however, stimulated an almost national anti-British movement that involved nonviolent and violent protests, boycotts and even an assassination attempt against the Governor of the new province of West Bengal.

Partition barely lasted half a decade, before it was annulled in 1911. Britain's policy of *divide et impera* which lay behind partition, however, continued to impact on the re-united province. In 1919, separate elections were established for Muslims and Hindus. Before this, many members of both communities had advocated national solidarity of all Bengalis. Now, distinctive communities developed, with their own political agendas. Muslims, too, dominated the Legislature, due to their overall numerical strength of roughly twenty eight to twenty two million. Nationally, Hindus and Muslims began to demand the creation of two independent states, one to be formed in majority Hindu and one in majority Muslim areas with most Bengali Hindus now supporting partitioning Bengal on this basis. The Muslims wanted the whole province to join the Muslim state, Pakistan. In 1947, Bengal was partitioned for the second time, this time specifically on religious grounds. It became East Pakistan. However, in 1971 East Pakistan became the independent state of Bangladesh after a successful war for liberation with the West Pakistani military regime. Partition may sometimes be necessary as a pragmatic strategy to avoid bloodshed but more often than not this leads to new problems that divide even more people.

Almost always, partition produces discontent among minorities on both sides of the border. Both partitions of Bengal saw bloodshed.

The new province would consist of the state of Hill Tripura, the Divisions of Chittagong, Dhaka and Rajshahi (excluding Darjeeling) and the district of Malda incorporated with Assam province. Bengal was to surrender not only these large eastern territories but also to cede to the Central Provinces the five Hindi-speaking states. On the western side it was offered Sambalpur and five minor Oriya-speaking states from the Central Provinces. Bengal would be left with an area of 141,580 sq. miles and population of 54 million, of which 42 million would be Hindus and 9 million Muslims.

The new province was named Eastern Bengal and Assam with Dhaka as its capital and subsidiary headquarters at Chittagong. Its area would be 106,540 sq. miles with a population of 31 million, where 18 million would be Muslims and 12 million Hindus. Administration would consist of a Legislative Council, a Board of Revenue of two members, and the jurisdiction of the Calcutta High Court would be left undisturbed. The government pointed out that Eastern Bengal and Assam would have a clearly demarcated western boundary and well defined geographical, ethnological, linguistic and social characteristics. The government of India promulgatea their final decision in a resolution dated July 19, 1905 and the partition of Bengal was effected on October 16 of same year.

This created a huge political crisis. The Muslims in East Bengal had the impression that a separate region would give them more opportunity for education, employment etc. However, the partition was not liked by the people in West Bengal and a huge amount of nationalist literature was created there during this period. Opposition by Indian National Congress was led by Sir Henry

John Stedman Cotton who had been Chief Commissioner of Assam, but Curzon was not to be moved. Later, Cotton, now Liberal MP for Nottingham East coordinated the successful campaign to oust the first lieutenant-governor of East Bengal, Sir Bampfylde Fuller. In 1906, Rabindranath Tagore wrote *Amar Shonar Bangla* as a rallying cry for proponents of annulment of Partition, which, much later, in 1972, became the national anthem of Bangladesh.

Due to these political protests, the two parts of Bengal were reunited in 1911. A new partition which divided the province on linguistic, rather than religious, grounds followed, with the Hindi, Oriya and Assamese areas separated to form separate administrative units. The administrative capital of British India was moved from Calcutta to New Delhi as well.

However, conflict between Muslims and Hindus resulted in new laws having to be introduced so as to satisfy the political needs of both groups.

Lucknow Pact

Lucknow Pact refers to an agreement between Indian National Congress and Muslim League. In 1916, Muhammed Ali Jinnah, a member of the Muslim League negotiated with the Indian National Congress to reach an agreement to pressure the British Government to have a more liberal approach to India and give Indians more authority to run their country. This was a considerable change of policy for the Muslim League, as it was established that to preserve Muslim interests in India, they needed to support British rule in India. After the unpopular partition of Bengal, the Muslim League was confused about its stand and it was at this time that Jinnah approached the League. Jinnah was the mastermind and architect of the pact.

The Lucknow Pact also marked the establishment of cordial relations between the two prominent groups of the Indian National Congress-the bold, fierce leaders or the *garam dal* led by Bal Gangadhar Tilak, and the moderates or the *naram dal* led by Gopal Krishna Gokhale.

Why was the Lucknow pact made?

When All India Muslim League came into existence, it was a moderate organization with its basic aim to establish friendly relations with the Crown. However, due to the decision of the British Government to annul the partition of Bengal, the Muslim leadership decided to change its stance. In 1913, a new group of Muslim leaders entered the folds of the Muslim League with the aim of bridging the gulf between the Muslims and the Hindus. The most prominent amongst them was Muhammad Ali Jinnah, who was already a member of Indian National Congress. The Muslim League changed its major objective and decided to join hands with the Congress in order to put pressure on the British government. Lord Chelmsford's invitation for suggestions from the Indian politicians for the post World War I reforms further helped in the development of the situation.

Muslim League and Congress

As a result of the hard work of Mr. Jinnah, both the Muslim League and the Congress met for their annual sessions at Bombay in December 1915. The principal leaders of the two political parties assembled at one place for the first time in the history of these organizations. The speeches made from the platform of the two groups were similar in tone and theme. Within a few months of the Bombay meetings, 19 Muslim and Hindu elected members of the Imperial Legislative Council addressed a memorandum to the Viceroy on the subject of reforms in October 1916. Their suggestions did not become news in the British circle, but were discussed, amended and accepted at a subsequent meeting of the Congress and Muslim League leaders at Calcutta in November 1916. This meeting settled the details of an agreement about the composition of the legislatures and the quantum of representation to be allowed to the two communities. The agreement was confirmed by the annual sessions of the Congress and the League in their annual sessions held at Lucknow on December 29 and December 31, 1916 respectively. Sarojini Naidu gave Jinnah, the chief architect of the Lucknow Pact, the title of "the Ambassador of Hindu-Muslim Unity".

Main Clauses of the Lucknow Pact

The main clauses of the Lucknow Pact were as follows:

1. There shall be self-government in India.
2. Muslims should be given one-third representation in the central government.

3. There should be separate electorates for all the communities until a community demanded for joint electorates.
4. System of weightage should be adopted.
5. The number of the members of Central Legislative Council should be increased to 150.
6. At the provincial level, four-fifth of the members of the Legislative Councils should be elected and one-fifth should be nominated.
7. The strength of Provincial legislative should not be less than 125 in the major provinces and from 50 to 75 in the minor provinces.
8. All members, except those nominated, were to be elected directly on the basis of adult franchise.
9. No bill concerning a community should be passed if the bill is opposed by three-fourth of the members of that community in the Legislative Council.
10. Term of the Legislative Council should be five years.
11. Members of Legislative Council should themselves elect their president.
12. Half of the members of Imperial Legislative Council should be Indians.
13. Indian Council must be abolished.
14. The salaries of the Secretary of State for Indian Affairs should be paid by the British Government and not from Indian funds.
15. Out of two Under Secretaries, one should be Indian.
16. The Executive should be separated from the Judiciary.

Although this Hindu Muslim Unity was not able to live for more than eight years, and collapsed after the development of differences between the two communities after the Khilafat Movement, yet it was an important event in the history of the Muslims of South Asia.

It was the first time when Congress recognized the Muslim League as the political party representing the Muslims of the region.

Khilafat Movement

The Khilafat movement (1919-1924) was a political campaign launched mainly by Muslims in British India to influence the British government and to protect the Ottoman Empire during the aftermath of World War I. The position of Caliph after the Armistice of Mudros of October 1918 with the military occupation of Istanbul and Treaty of Versailles (1919) fell into a disambiguation along with the Ottoman Empire's existence. The movement gained force after the Treaty of Sèvres (August 1920) which solidified the partitioning of the Ottoman Empire.

In India, although mainly a Muslim religious movement, the movement became a part of the wider Indian independence movement. The movement was a topic in Conference of London (February 1920).

History

The Caliphate is an Islamic system of governance in which the state rules under Islamic law. Caliph literally means "successor" or "representative" and emphasizes religious authority for the head of state. It was adopted as a title by the Ummayad Caliphs and then by the Abbasid Caliphs, as well as by the Fatimid Caliphs of North Africa, the Almohad Caliphs of North Africa and Spain and the Ottoman Dynasty. Most historical Muslim rulers were sultans or amirs, and gave token obedience to a caliph who often had very little real authority. Moreover, the Muslim clergy, the ulema and the various Sufi orders, exercised more religious influence than the Caliph.

Ottoman Caliphate

Ottoman emperor Abdul Hamid II (1876-1909) had launched his Pan-Islamic program in a bid to protect the Ottoman empire from Western attack and dismemberment, and to crush the Westernizing democratic opposition in Turkey. He sent an emissary, Jamaluddin Afghani, to India in the late 19th century. The cause of the Ottoman monarch evoked religious passion and sympathy amongst Indian Muslims. Being a Caliph, the Ottoman emperor was the supreme religious and political leader of all Sunni Muslims across the world (although this authority was titular in practice). A large number of Muslim religious leaders began working to spread awareness and develop Muslim participation on behalf of the Caliphate. Muslim religious leader Maulana Mehmud Hasan attempted to organise a national war of independence against the British with support from the Ottoman Empire. He was overthrown by a secretive nationalist group called the 'Young Turks.' Abdulhamid was succeeded by his brother Mehmed VI (1844-1918) but real power lay with the nationalists.

Partitioning

The Ottoman empire, having sided with the Central Powers during World War I, suffered a major military defeat. The Treaty of Versailles (1919) reduced its territorial extent and diminished its political influence but the victorious European powers promised to protect the Ottoman emperor's status as the Caliph. However, under the Treaty of Sèvres (1920), territories such as Palestine, Syria, Lebanon, Iraq, Egypt severed from the empire.

Within Turkey, a pro-Western nationalist movement arose, Turkish national movement. During the Turkish War of Independence (1919-1924) led by one of the Turkish revolutionaries, Mustafa Kemal Atatürk, abolished the Treaty of Sèvres with the Treaty of Lausanne (1923). Pursuant to Atatürk's Reforms, the Republic of Turkey abolished the position of Caliphate in 1924 and transferred its powers within Turkey to the Grand National Assembly of Turkey.

Khilafat in South Asia

Although political activities and popular outcry on behalf of the caliphate emerged across the Muslim world, the most prominent activities took place in India. A prominent Muslim cleric and journalist, Maulana Mohammad Ali Jouhar had spent four years in prison for preaching resistance to the British and support for the caliphate. At the onset of the Turkish war of independence, Muslim religious leaders feared for the caliphate, which the European powers were reluctant to protect.

Ali and his brother Maulana Shaukat Ali joined with other Muslim leaders such as Sheikh Shaukat Ali Siddiqui, Dr. Mukhtar Ahmed Ansari, Raees-Ul-Muhajireen Barrister Jan Muhammad Junejo, Hasrat Mohani, Maulana Abul Kalam Azad and Dr. Hakim Ajmal Khan to form the All India Khilafat Committee. The organization was based in Lucknow, India at Hathe Shaukat Ali, the compound of Landlord Shaukat Ali Siddiqui. They aimed to build political unity amongst Muslims and use their influence to protect the caliphate. In 1920, they published the Khilafat Manifesto, which called upon the British to protect the caliphate and for Indian Muslims to unite and hold the British accountable for this purpose.

In 1920 an alliance was made between Khilafat leaders and the Indian National Congress, the largest political party in India and of the nationalist movement. Congress leader Mohandas Gandhi and the Khilafat leaders promised to work and fight together for the causes of Khilafat and *Swaraj*. Seeking to increase pressure on the British, the Khilafatists became a major part of the Non-cooperation movement — a nationwide campaign of mass, peaceful civil disobedience. The support of the Khilafatists helped Gandhi and the Congress ensure Hindu-Muslim unity during the struggle. Khilafat leaders such as Dr. Ansari, Maulana Azad and Hakim Ajmal Khan also grew personally close to Gandhi. These leaders founded the Jamia Millia Islamia in 1920 to promote independent education and social rejuvenation for Muslims.

The non-cooperation campaign was at first successful. Massive protests, strikes and acts of civil disobedience spread across India. Hindus and Muslims collectively offered resistance, which was largely peaceful. Gandhi, the Ali brothers and others were imprisoned by the British. However, the Congress-Khilafat alliance began withering soon. The Khilafat campaign had been opposed by other political parties such as the Muslim League and the Hindu Mahasabha. Many Hindu religious and political leaders identified the Khilafat cause as Islamic fundamentalism based on a pan-Islamic agenda.

Collapse

In wake of these disturbances, the Ali brothers began distancing themselves from Gandhi and the Congress. The Ali brothers criticised Gandhi's commitment to non-violence and severed their ties with them after he suspended all non-cooperation movement after the killing of 22 policemen at Chauri Chaura in 1922. Although holding talks with the British and continuing their activities, the Khilafat struggle weakened as Muslims were divided between working for the Congress, the Khilafat cause and the Muslim League.

The final blow came with the victory of Mustafa Kemal's forces, who overthrew the Ottoman rule to establish a pro-Western, secular republic in independent Turkey. The Khilafat leadership fragmented on different political lines. Leaders such as Dr. Ansari, Maulana Azad and Hakim Ajmal Khan remained strong supporters of Gandhi and the Congress. The Ali brothers joined the Muslim League. They would play a major role in the growth of the League's popular appeal and the subsequent Pakistan movement. There was, however, a Caliphate Conference in Jerusalem in 1931 following Turkey's abolition of the Khilafat, to determine what should be done about the caliphate.

Legacy

The Khilafat struggle evokes controversy and strong opinions. It is regarded as a political agitation based on a pan-Islamic, fundamentalist platform and being largely indifferent to the cause of Indian independence. Critics of the Khilafat see its alliance with the Congress as a marriage of convenience. Proponents of the Khilafat see it as a major milestone in improving Hindu-Muslim relations, while advocates of Pakistan and Muslim separatism see it as a major step towards establishing the separate Muslim state.

The Ali brothers are regarded as founding-fathers of Pakistan, while Azad, Dr. Ansari and Hakim Ajmal Khan are widely celebrated as national heroes in India.

The cause of establishing an Islamic State by reviving the caliphate system has been adopted by organisations such as the Muslim Brotherhood, Jamaat-e-Islami umbrella groups in South Asia, founded in 1941 by Maulana Maududi and most of all Hizb ut Tahrir.

Fourteen Points of Jinnah

The Fourteen Points of Jinnah were proposed by Muhammad Ali Jinnah as a constitutional reform plan to safeguard the political rights of Muslims in a self-governing India. The report was given in a meeting of the council of the All India Muslim League on March 28, 1929.

The Fourteen Points

1. The form of the future constitution should be federal with the residuary powers vested in the provinces.
2. A uniform measure of autonomy shall be granted to all provinces.
3. All legislatures in the country and other elected bodies shall be constituted on the definite principle of adequate and effective representation of minorities in every province without reducing the majority in any province to a minority or even equality.
4. In the Central Legislature, Muslim representation shall not be less than one third.
5. Representation of communal groups shall continue to be by means of separate electorate as at present, provided it shall be open to any community at any time to abandon its separate electorate in favour of a joint electorate.
6. Any territorial distribution that might at any time be necessary shall not in any way affect the Muslim majority in the Punjab, Bengal and the North West Frontier Province.
7. Full religious liberty, i.e. liberty of belief, worship and observance, propaganda, association and education, shall be guaranteed to all communities.
8. No bill or any resolution or any part thereof shall be passed in any legislature or any other elected body if three-fourth of the members of any community in that particular body oppose such a bill resolution or part thereof on the ground that it would be injurious to the interests of that community or in the alternative, such other method is devised as may be found feasible and practicable to deal with such cases.
9. Sindh should be separated from the Bombay Presidency.
10. Reforms should be introduced in the North West Frontier Province (NWFP) and Baluchistan on the same footing as in the other provinces.
11. Provision should be made in the constitution giving Muslims an adequate share, along with the other Indians, in all the services of the state and in local self-governing bodies having due regard to the requirements of efficiency.

12. The constitution should embody adequate safeguards for the protection of Muslim culture and for the protection and promotion of Muslim education, language, religion, personal laws and Muslim charitable institution and for their due share in the grants-in-aid given by the state and by local self-governing bodies.
13. No cabinet, either central or provincial, should be formed without there being a proportion of at least one-third Muslim ministers.
14. No change shall be made in the constitution by the Central Legislature except with the concurrence of the State's contribution of the Indian Federation.

Reactions

One newspaper headline described the 14 points as Muslims' irreducible minimum. These demands were rejected by the Congress Party. He was then invited to attend the round table conferences, where he forwarded the Muslims' point of view.

Importance

A comparison of the Nehru Report (1928) with Jinnah's Fourteen points shows a political gap between the Muslims and the Hindus in India. They motivated Jinnah to revive the Muslim League and give it direction. As a result, these points became the demands of the Muslims and greatly influenced the Muslims thinking for the next two decades till the establishment of Pakistan in 1947

Hence, as a response to the Nehru Report, the Muslims presented their own demands as envisaged in the Quiad-i-Azam's famous Fourteen Points which, in fact, were the counter proposals to Hindu demands as expressed in the Nehru Report. The meeting of Muslims on March 28, 1929 thus resolved that no future constitution for India would be acceptable to Muslims unless the following basic principles put-forth by the Quaid-i-Azam were not incorporated in it which envisaged the following demands:

Quaid-i-Azam's Fourteen Points (1929)

1. *"The form of the future constitution should be federal in structure with residuary powers vested in the provinces;*

2. *A uniform measure of autonomy should be granted to all provinces;*
3. *All legislatures, central and provincial, and other elected bodies in the country should be constituted on the definite principle of adequate and effective representation of minorities in every province without reducing the majority in any province to a minority or even equality;*
4. *In the Central Legislature, Muslim representation should not be less than one-third;*
5. *Representation of communal groups should continue to be based on separate electorates, but the option to abandon separate electorate in favour of a joint electorate at any time, should be given to every community;*
6. *Any territorial redistribution that might at any time be necessary should not in any way affect the Muslim majority in the Punjab, Bengal, and North-West Frontier Provinces;*
7. *Full religious liberty that is, liberty of belief, worship and observance, propaganda, association and education should be guaranteed to all communities;*
8. *No Bill or resolution or any part thereof should be passed in any legislative or any elected body if three-fourths of the members of a community in that particular body opposed such a Bill, resolution or part thereof on the ground that it would be injurious to the interests of that community, or alternatively such other methods should be devised which might practically deal with such cases;*
9. *Sindh should be separated from the Bombay Presidency;*
10. *Reforms should be introduced in the North-West Frontier Province and Balochistan on the same footing as in other provinces;*
11. *Provision should be made in the Constitution giving Muslims an adequate share along with the other Indians in all the services of the state and in local self-governing bodies having due regard to the requirements of efficiency;*
12. *The Constitution should embody adequate safeguards for the protection of Muslim culture and for the promotion of Muslim education, language, religion, personal laws, and Muslim*

charitable institutions and for their due share in the grants-in-aid given by the state and by self-government bodies;

13. *No Cabinet, either Central or Provincial, should be formed without there being at least one-third Muslim ministers;*
14. *No change should be made in the Constitution by the central legislature except with the concurrence of the States constituting the Indian Federation".*

Jinnah's Fourteen Point Formula remained a point of reference in many forthcoming negotiations between the Congress and the Muslim League but it was never accepted by the Congress.

It was in 1929 that the All Parties Muslim Conference held at Delhi under the Chairmanship of the Aga Khan III, of which Allama Muhammad Iqbal was an ardent votary, passed a resolution formulating Muslim demands regarding the future political set-up of the sub-continent. This resolution, said Allama Iqbal, a year later, was wholly inspired by the noble idea of a "Muslim India within India". It envisaged recognition of Muslim majorities in the Punjab and Bengal, separation of Sindh from Bombay as a province, introduction of constitutional reforms in N.W.F.P., and Baluchistan, complete Provincial antonomy, representation through separate electorates and a ban on legislating on any inter-communal matter without the approval of the three-fourth majority of the concerned community.

Political events took an ominous turn in the course of the next few months. These was a three-pronged attack on Muslim interests. On the one hand, the Hindus offered a tough opposition and on the other, the Government of India in the course of its observations on the Simon Commission Report ignored the Muslim demands.

At the end of December 1930, Allama Muhammad Iqbal went to Allahabad and in the course of his Presidential Address at the annual session of the All-India Muslim League said: "The formation of a consolidated North-West Muslim State appears to me to be the final destiny of the Muslims at least of North-West India."

Majlis-e-Ahrar-ul-Islam

Majlis-e-Ahrar-ul-Islam or Majlis-e-Ah'rār-e-Islam or Ahrar was a nationalist Muslim party in South Asia. The Majlis-e-Ahrar-ul-Islam, were a short lived separatist political movement who were former Khilafat movement. They differed with the Indian National Congress over certain issues and afterwards announced the formation of their party in a meeting at Lahore in 1931. Freely funded by the Congress, the Ahrar were also opposed to the policies of the Muslim League.

They declared that their objectives were to guide the Muslims of India on matters of nationalism as well as religion. Majlis-e-Ahrar-ul-Islam spearheaded movement to declare Ahmadiyya community as non-Muslims.

By the early 1930s, the Majlis-i-Ahrar-Islam (hereafter MAI) had become an important political party of Muslims in the Punjab. Its agitation in the princely states, and mobilisation on socio-religious issues, earned it an important position in regional politics. Besides these campaigns, the MAI also participated in the mainstream political developments of British India between 1931 to 1947.

Its political career can be divided into two parts; the MAI's response to political and constitutional issues, and its performance in electoral politics. An examination of its role in these two areas can help in addressing the question as to whether the Majlis was a provincial party or an all-India organisation. Its leadership, political programme and its role in and outside the legislature are vital for this investigation. Such inter-connected issues may help us locate the debate on Indian nationalism, Muslim identity politics and the developments within Punjab, the political heartland of the MAI.

Introduction

The MAI strategy was the mobilization of the Muslim masses through the advocacy of emotional and topical issues. However, it did not miss the opportunity of participating in any movement, or commenting on any issue, that was likely to influence the future of India or that of Indian Muslims.

Their main constituencies were the Sunni Muslims, and particularly those living in Punjab. Constitutional issues did not evoke as much interest in its ranks, as social and religious issues; which meant that the clerics and not the lawyers set the agenda. Theanti-colonial and determinedly pro-Muslim attitudes were reflected in the MAI's reaction to the constitutional issues. Soon after its formation, it aimed at projecting itself as an anti-colonial and pro-Indian National Congress (hereafter INC) party by actively participating in the civil disobedience movement of the 1930s, championed by Mahatma Gandhi.

It supported the Red Shirts Movement led by Khan Abdul Ghaffar Khan, the passing of the India Act of 1935, and efforts for an agreement among different communities in India. The MAI maintained contacts with all the political parties and responded positively to other opposition groups, though its pro-INC leanings remained quite explicit. After its initial political ventures in Kashmir, Kapurthala and Alwar, the MAI turned its attention to its organisational and institutional outreach.

Constitutional Issues

The major contemporary constitutional issues hinged on resolving India's complex political challenges, and coincided with the formation of the MAI. The Ahrar leaders boycotted the Simon Commission in 1927-28, and subsequently rejected its recommendations; which included a federal political system for India, and separate electorates for Muslims.

The All-Parties National Convention held at Calcutta in December 1928, adopted the Nehru Report. The adoption of this Report led to a division of the nationalist Muslims into two groups; one group, to which a majority of the future Ahrar leaders belonged, wanted its acceptance with some amendments; while the other group favoured its unconditional acceptance.

The Nehru Report was still being debated when the INC held its annual session at Lahore in December 1929, and abandoned the Report, while adopting complete independence as its ultimate objective. The independence resolution appealed to the anti-imperialist sentiments of the MAI, and brought it closer to the INC. When the latter launched its civil disobedience movement, after the rejection of its demand by the British government, the MAI shelved its organisational work, and enthusiastically participated in the non-cooperation movement.

Meanwhile, the British Government had convened the Round Table Conference (hereafter RTC) in November 1930, to work out an agreed constitutional formula for India; but the MAI, in line with the INC policy, opposed the RTC. The first RTC reached a consensus on a federal system for India, and after spelling out the principles of the future constitution, set up eight sub-committees. However, the MAI stuck to its original objectives and at its all-India conference in July 1931, reiterated that, "the chief aim and object of the Majlis will be complete independence for India".

The British government realised the futility of framing a constitution without the INC, as did the other political parties that had participated in the first RTC. During the INC-led civil disobedience movement, many of its leaders and activists had been imprisoned.

When the British government realised the importance of associating the INC with the constitutional negotiations, it approached its leadership. Wedgwood Benn, the Secretary of State, wrote to the Viceroy, Lord Irwin, about the desirability of coming to terms with the Congress. In order to call off the civil disobedience movement and attend the second RTC, Gandhi was released unconditionally, and the Viceroy held negotiations with him.

These negotiations climaxed with the signing of the Gandhi-Irwin Pact on 5 March 1933; and consequently, Gandhi decided to attend the second RTC in London. The MAI felt the INC had bypassed it. Maulana Habib-ur-Rahman and Syed Ataullah Shah Bukhari (the leaders of Ahrars) rushed to Bombay to persuade Gandhi not to attend the RTC.

They argued that the nationalist leaders should not engage in constitutional discussions with the colonialists because it would be a 'futile' exercise. However, they failed to convince Gandhi, and his decision to participate in the RTC resulted in the 'parting of ways' between the INC and MAI. The blind faith and trust that the MAI leadership had so far reposed in the INC, was shattered. Henceforth, it did not openly share a common platform with the INC.

The INC's participation in the second RTC made the London Conference more representative, although the participants, failed to evolve an agreed formula to resolve the communal differences, or agree on the future politicalmap of India. Consequently, on 16 August 1932, the British Prime Minister, Ramsay Macdonald, announced a Communal Award on behalf of the British Government, which was to be followed by the India Act of 1935.

Communal Award and the India Act of 1935

The Communal Award not only retained the principle of separate electorates for Muslims, but was extended to other minorities as well. Weightage for minorities was also maintained, which was given equally to the Muslims in Hindu majority provinces, and to Sikhs and Hindus in the Muslim majority provinces of Punjab and Bengal.

Hence, the Muslim representation in Punjab and Bengal was less than their ratio in the population. In Punjab, where the proportion of Muslims, Hindus and Sikhs was 57.10%, 27% and 13% of the total population respectively; they were given 49%, 27% and 18 per cent of the provincial seats in the Assembly. Similarly, in Bengal, where the percentage of Muslims and Hindus was 55 and 43 respectively, they were given 48 and 43 per cent of the total seats in the legislature. The lowering of property qualification for voters increased their numbers, although it was still a far cry from universal suffrage.

Sindh, following a long-standing demand, was separated from Bombay and constituted into a separate province. Non-Muslims in Sindh were given more seats than their number warranted. Similarly, in the constitutional reforms carried out in the NWFP, non-Muslims got heavier weightage, which meant that they could play a critical role in case of division among its Muslim members. The Communal Award, in an emphatic way, widened the gulf between the rural and urban Muslims in the Punjab, by offering more representation to the landlords.

This worked to the greater benefit of the Unionist Party, since it favoured the rural classes, as did its trans-communal composition. The Communal Award was not popular with any of the communities. The Muslim League was displeased, because it did not meet the Muslim demands for 56 per cent representation in the Punjab Assembly, and nor did it provide them with amajority in Bengal. The reaction of the Punjabi Hindus and Sikhs was also negative; and they declared that any system of government in Punjab and Bengal under the Communal Award, would amount to a British-imposed 'Muslim Raj' in these provinces. The

Mahasabha dominated Hindu politics in the Punjab, and was more influential than the Congress.

In fact, the Congress had little support among the Punjabi Hindus, who looked towards the Mahasabha for safeguarding their interests. The Punjab Mahasabha's aggressive advocacy of Hindu interests, embittered communal relations. Their relations sank to an all-time low on the issue of separate electorates.

Sikh agitation against the Communal Award was equally hostile. They had demanded 24 per cent of total representation in the Punjab Assembly, whereas they were only provided 18 per cent seats in the provincial legislature.

They opposed separate electorates, and the provision of a possible Muslim majority in the assembly, they organised demonstrations and set up a council of action to achieve their objectives. On 2 August 1932, the council reportedly gathered more than one hundred thousand Sikhs in Lahore, and demanded treatment similar to that of Muslim minorities in the Hindu majority provinces. Earlier, Hindus, Sikhs and Christians had organised a joint Minority Conference to oppose adult franchise. They demanded division of the Punjab province, in case their demands were not met; which was perceived by the Muslims as a plan to subvert Muslim majority in the province.

The communal division of Punjab seemed pre-ordained. The MAI had tried to mobilise the Muslim masses in support of joint electorates at the time of the Nehru Report, but found it difficult. Their campaign for joint electorates convinced them of the growing demand for a "separate Muslim identity", and they gradually came to accept the importance of the system of separate electorates for Muslims.

Their participation in the Congress-led civil disobedience movement and severance of their links with that party in 1931, brought home the realisation that Muslims constituted a 'political entity separate' from the Sikhs and Hindus. Secondly, the MAI was dissatisfied with the weightage provided for the minorities in the Communal Award, which gave the Muslim community a thin majority in the Punjab legislature. They felt that the Award had not awarded to the Muslims their due share in the Punjab Assembly, and believed that a solution acceptable to all the communities could still be found. They proposed that Hindus, Sikhs and Muslims should sit together, and work out an agreed formula for the representation of various communities in the Punjab; an alternative to the Communal Award.

However, they warned that if any community attempted to solve the communal problem by force, Muslims would be justified in fighting back for the protection of their interests. They also criticised the Communal Award, because it was silent on the long-standing Muslim demand of 33 per cent Muslim share in the central legislature.

The MAI was disappointed by the reaction from Hindus and Sikhs in the Punjab, and began to take an equally communal line. They took out processions and rallies in many towns of the province, in support of their position.

With the passage of time, they adopted a more oppositional attitude, not only towards the British, but also against the Hindus and Sikhs. It was alleged that the Sikhs had enlisted 100,000 men to challenge the Muslims, and that the government was supporting the Sikhs, with the objective of precipitating a conflict between the two communities. The MAI called on the Muslims to carry swords to defend themselves, particularly in those districts where the Sikhs carried kirpans. They set up an action committee in the Punjab, to counteract the activities of a similar body established by the Sikhs.

The MAI made Amritsar the centre of their activities over the issue of Communal Award, and from September to December 1932, it organised several public meetings in the Punjab. At a Provincial Ahrar Conference held on 4-5 December 1932, the MAI formed a sub-committee to suggest a formula for the Communal Award. It was to be discussed at the Allahabad Conference, scheduled for March 1933.

But no agreed formula could be worked out at these sessions, and the MAI was thus left with no option but to accept the Communal Award. The All-India Muslim League Council, in a meeting in Delhi on 2 April 1934, accepted the Communal Award till abetter alternative was found.

The Majlis also formally accepted the Communal Award at an All-India Communal Award Conference in Dacca, on 24 March

1935. B. R. Ambedkar, the leader of the Scheduled Castes, was persuaded by Gandhi to renounce separate electorates for the 'Untouchables'. The response of the three communities in the Punjab to the Communal Award strengthened communal identities, intensified competition among them, and thus proved the last proverbial straw. The British Government issued a White Paper after the third Round Table Conference in March 1933.

The Conference appointed a Joint Select Committee, which finalised its report in November 1934, and was subsequently debated in Parliament. The Report consisted of recommendations for the future government of India. It also discussed the issue of communal representation, and provided a basis for the British government to introduce Communal Award. When the Indian Legislative Assembly debated this report in February 1935, the INC moved a resolution for the total rejection of the report, condemning it as one of the 'usual imperialist devices' "to deprive the Indian people of the power to assume charge of their affairs". M. A. Jinnah, then the leader of the Independent Party, disagreed with the INC, and moved an amendment that was finally accepted. The MAI supported Jinnah's position on the White Paper, and also the report of the Joint Select Committee.

The British Parliament passed the Government of India Act 1935 on 2 August 1935, which provided for a federal political system for the sub-continent. Its important features were that it defined provinces as separate legal entities, and lowered property qualifications for voting, thus enlarging the provincial franchise. The Muslim elite had always been apprehensive of a centralised government dominated by the Hindu majority, and the danger of being turned into a 'permanent minority.

The MAI, like all other Muslim political parties, was concerned about the federal part of the constitution, though it preferred to wait and watch. However, this part did not come into operation, since the required number of states did notaccede to the federation. This similarity of views on constitutional issues was an important factor that brought the MAI closer to the All-India Muslim League (AIML). In 1936, the MAI allied itself with the Muslim League, and its leaders accepted membership of the Central Muslim League Parliamentary Board, although this alliance was also short-lived.

Electoral Politics

The MAI decided to participate in the electoral process in the 1930s, without modifying its ultimate objective of complete independence from the British colonial rule. There were several reasons behind this decision. The MAI wanted to influence the constitution-making and law-making processes; and after the severance of its relations with the INC and the formulation of its own platform and programme, it wanted to prove its own separate and distinct existence.

Its spectacular performance in the agitation against the rulers of the three princely states gave it confidence. The MAI, which was primarily an urban political party, like other Muslim political parties, had supported the Communal Award. As the anti-Communal Award campaign of the Mahasabhites and the Akali Sikhs intensified, the MAI felt that it could counter that pressure by participating in the elections, and asserting its Muslim credentials. They also harboured the dream of leading the Muslim urban lower and middle classes, through a sustained struggle.

The increasing communalism in politics had spawned the creation of a number of political groups jostling to capture the leadership of urban Muslims in Punjab, and MAI was emerging as the most influential voice. The Majlis might have contested the August 1930 elections, but boycotted them as a result of its decision to participate in the INC-sponsored civil disobedience movement. Their first electoral activity was in 1933, in the three bye-elections to the Punjab Legislative Assembly.

Then in 1934, the MAI put up candidates in two constituencies, in the elections to the Central Legislative Assembly; and in 1937, it took part in the elections to the provincial assemblies under the Government ofIndia Act of 1935, and supported candidates for the provincial assemblies of the Punjab, Bihar and Bombay.

Bye-elections of 1933

The working committee of the MAI, in a meeting at Lahore on 12 June, 1933, took the decision to participate in the three bye-elections for the Punjab Assembly. It selected three prominent MAI figures as its candidates to contest these polls. One of its candidates was the patron-in-chief of the MAI, Chaudhry Afzal

Haq, who decided to contest the rural Muslim seat from the Hoshiarpur and Ludhiana districts of East Punjab. He was an experienced political figure of Muslim politics in the Punjab. He had been elected twice to the Punjab legislature; in the 1924-27 and the 1927-30 periods.

The second candidate, Chaudhry Abdur Rahman Khan, was a prominent member of a Rajput family of Jallundhar, who had led the Ahrar agitation in Kapurthala. He was selected to contest the Muslim urban seat from the Sheikhupura, Ludhiana, Gurdaspur and Jallundhar's area.

The third candidate was also a senior Ahrar leader, Maulana Mazhar Ali Azhar, who contested the seat vacated by Sheikh Din Muhammad from Gujranwala. He had also been a member of the Punjab Legislative Council from 1924 to 1930. One of his opponents in this urban Muslim constituency was the prominent lawyer from Lahore, Malik Barkat Ali.

The MAI participated in these bye-elections with a high profile, and aimed at building its image as a formidable political force. Other than demanding independence, its economic, social and political programme promised the welfare of the poor and underprivileged Muslim masses. Like its counterparts in the field, it championed their interests as if it was their only saviour.

The MAI had established its credentials by fighting for the civil rights of the Muslim community in the princely states, and their anti-Qadiani stance, had established them as a sectarian party in Indian politics. With a strong anti-feudal stance, the MAI promised to reform the society in a way that would ensure an equitable social and economic environment for the poor Muslim community of India.

They advocated Muslim nationalist causes, but also supported secular anti-imperialism of the INC. The MAI believed in direct interaction with the masses, and used mosques for their election campaign, converting them into their main centres of publicity; but they also used corner meetings as a method of campaigning. They also organised rallies and public meetings, where their leaders spoke in support of the MAI programme and its candidates. While newspapers, according to Afzal Haq, 'are tools in the hands of the capitalists', the MAI was blessed with orators who were a "source of their propaganda." In addition, all the three candidates were notable and well-established Muslim figures of the Punjab. The result was a resounding Ahrar victory in all the three bye-elections; Afzal Haq secured 1800 votes, Mazhar Ali Azhar obtained 2920 out of 6633 votes, while the third candidate secured more than 1500 votes.

Allahabad Address

Allahabad Address was the Presidential Address by Allama Iqbal to the 25th Session of the All-India Muslim League on 29 December 1930, at Allahabad. Here he presented the idea of a separate homeland for Indian Muslims which was ultimately realised in the form of Pakistan.

"The principle of European democracy cannot be applied to India without recognising the fact of communal groups. The Muslim demand for the creation of a Muslim India within India is, therefore, perfectly justified. The resolution of the All-Parties Muslim Conference at Delhi is, to my mind, wholly inspired by this noble ideal of a harmonious whole which, instead of stifling the respective individualities of its component wholes, affords them chances of fully working out the possibilities that may be latent in them. And I have no doubt that this House will emphatically endorse the Muslim demands embodied in this resolution.

Personally, I would go farther than the demands embodied in it. I would like to see the Punjab, North-West Frontier Province, Sindh and Baluchistan amalgamated into a single State. Self-government within the British Empire, or without the British Empire, the formation of a consolidated North-West Indian Muslim State appears to me to be the final destiny of the Muslims, at least of North-West India.

Hindus should not fear that the creation of autonomous Muslim states will mean the introduction of a kind of religious rule in such states. I have already indicated to you the meaning of the word religion, as applied to Islam. The truth is that Islam is not a Church.

For India, it means security and peace resulting from an internal balance of power; for Islam, an opportunity to rid itself of the stamp that Arabian Imperialism was forced to give it, to mobilise its law, its education, its culture, and to bring them into closer contact with its own original spirit and with the spirit of modern times."

Iqbal's Clarification about his Address

Following is the letter, Allama Iqbal wrote to Prof. Edward John Thompson of Oxford University.

Dr. Sir Mohd Iqbal, M.A., Ph.D. Barrister-at-Law

Lahore 4 March 1934

My Dear Mr. Thompson,

I have just received your review of my book. It is excellent and I am grateful to you for the very kind things you have said of me. But you have made one mistake which I hasten to point as I consider it rather serious. You call me a protagonist of the scheme called "Pakistan". Now Pakistan is not my scheme. The one that I suggested in my address is the creation of a Muslim Province – i.e; a province having an overwhelming population of Muslims in the North-West of India. This new province will be, according to my scheme, a part of the proposed Indian Federation. Pakistan scheme proposes a separate federation of Muslim Provinces directly related to England as a separate dominion. This scheme originated in Cambridge. The authors of this scheme believe that we Muslim Round Tablers have sacrificed the Muslim nation on the altar of Hindu or the so called Indian Nationalism.

4

Iqbal and Pakistan Movement

Although his main interests were scholarly, Iqbal was not unconcerned with the political situation of the, country and the political fortunes of the Muslim community of India. Already in 1908, while in England, he had been chosen as a member of the executive council of the newly-established British branch of the Indian Muslim League.

In 1931 and 1932 he represented the Muslims of India in the Round Table Conferences held in England to discuss the issue of the political future of India. And in a 1930 lecture Iqbal suggested the creation of a separate homeland for the Muslims of India. Iqbal died (1938) before thc creation of Pakistan (1947), but it was his teaching that "spiritually... has been the chief force behind the creation of Pakistan."

Iqbal joined the London branch of the All India Muslim League while he was studying Law and Philosophy in England. It was in London when he had a mystical experience. The ghazal containing those divinations is the only one whose year and month of composition is expressly mentioned. It is March 1907. No other ghazal, before or after it has been given such importance. Some verses of that ghazal are:

Your civilization will commit suicide with its own daggers.

A nest built on a frail bough cannot be durable.

The caravan of feeble ants will take the rose petal for a boat

And inspite of all blasts of waves, it shall cross the river.

I will take out may worn-out caravan in the pitch darkness of night.

My sighs will emit sparks and my breath will *produce flames.*

For Iqbal it was a divinely inspired insight. He disclosed this to his listeners in December 1931, when he was invited to Cambridge to address the students. Iqbal was in London, participating in the Second Round Table Conference in 1931. At Cambridge, he referred to what he had proclaimed in 1906:

I would like to offer a few pieces of advice to the youngmen who are at present studying at Cambridge...... I advise you to guard against atheism and materialism. The biggest blunder made by Europe was the separation of Church and State. This deprived their culture of moral soul and diverted it to the atheistic materialism. I had twenty-five years ago seen through the drawbacks of this civilization and therefore had made some prophecies. They had been delivered by my tongue although I did not quite understand them. This happened in 1907..... After six or seven years, my prophecies came true, word by word. The European war of 1914 was an outcome of the aforesaid mistakes made by the European nations in the separation of the Church and the State.

Building upon Sir Sayyid Ahmed's two-nation theory, absorbing the teaching of Shibli, Ameer Ali, Hasrat Mohani and other great Indian Muslim thinkers and politicians, listening to Hindu and British voices, and watching the fermenting Indian scene closely for approximately 60 years, he knew and ultimately convinced his people and their leaders, particularly Quaid-i-Azam Muhammad Ali Jinnah that:

"We both are exiles in this land. Both longing for *our dear home's sight!"*

"That dear home is Pakistan, on which he harpened like a flute-player, but whose birth he did not witness."

Iqbal and Politics

These thoughts crystallised at Allahabad Session (December, 1930) of the All India Muslim League, when Iqbal in the Presidential Address, forwarded the idea of a Muslim State in India:

I would like to see the Punjab, North-West Frontier Provinces, Sindh and Baluchistan into a single State. Self-Government within the British Empire or without the British Empire. The formation of the consolidated North-West Indian Muslim State appears to be the final destiny of the Muslims, at least of the North-West India.

The seed sown, the idea began to evolve and take root. It soon assumed the shape of Muslim state or states in the western and eastern Muslim majority zones as is obvious from the following lines of Iqbal's letter, of June 21, 1937, to the Quaid-i Azam, only ten months before the former's death:

A separate federation of Muslim Provinces, reformed on the lines I have suggested above, is the only course by which we can secure a peaceful India and save Muslims from the domination of Non-Muslims. Why should not the Muslims of North-West India and Bengal be considered as nations entitled to self-determination just as other nations in India and outside India are.

There are some critics of Allama Iqbal who assume that after delivering the Allahabad Address he had slept over the idea of a Muslim State. Nothing is farther from the truth. The idea remained always alive in his mind. It had naturally to mature and hence, had to take time. He was sure that the Muslims of sub-continent were going to achieve an independent homeland for themselves. On 21st March, 1932, Allama Iqbal delivered the Presidential address at Lahore at the annual session of the All-India Muslim Conference.

In that address too he stressed his view regarding nationalism in India and commented on the plight of the Muslims under the circumstances prevailing in the sub-continent. Having attended the Second Round Table Conference in September, 1931 in London, he was keenly aware of the deep-seated Hindu and Sikh prejudice and unaccommodating attitude. He had observed the mind of the British Government. Hence he reiterated his apprehensions and suggested safeguards in respect of the Indian Muslims:

In so far then as the fundamentals of our policy are concerned, I have got nothing fresh to offer. Regarding these I have already expressed my views in my address to the All India Muslim League. In the present address I propose, among other things, to help you, in the first place, in arriving at a correct view of the situation as it emerged from a rather hesitating behaviour of our delegation the final stages of the Round-Table Conference. In the second place, I shall try, according to my lights to show how far it is desirable to construct a fresh policy now that the Premier's announcement at the last London Conference has again necessitated a careful survey of the whole situation.

It must be kept in mind that since Maulana Muhammad Ali had died in Jan. 1931 and Quaid-i Azam had stayed behind in London, the responsibility of providing a proper lead to the Indian Muslims had fallen on him alone. He had to assume the role of a jealous guardian of his nation till Quaid-i Azam returned to the sub-continent in 1935.

The League and the Muslim Conference had become the play-thing of petty leaders, who would not resign office, even after a vote of non-confidence! And, of course, they had no organization in the provinces and no influence with the masses.

During the Third Round-Table Conference, Iqbal was invited by the London National League where he addressed an audience which included among others, foreign diplomats, members of the House of Commons, Members of the House of Lords and Muslim members of the R.T.C. delegation.

In that gathering he dilated upon the situation of the Indian Muslims. He explained why he wanted the communal settlement first and then the constitutional reforms. He stressed the need for provincial autonomy because autonomy gave the Muslim majority provinces some power to safeguard their rights, cultural traditions and religion. Under the central Government the Muslims were bound to lose their cultural and religious entity at the hands of the overwhelming Hindu majority. He referred to what he had said at Allahabad in 1930 and reiterated his belief that before long people were bound to come round to his viewpoint based on cogent reason.

In his dialogue with Dr. Ambedkar Allama Iqbal expressed his desire to see Indian provinces as autonomous units under the direct control of the British Government and with no central Indian Government. He envisaged autonomous Muslim Provinces in India. Under one Indian union he feared for Muslims, who would suffer in many respects especially with regard to their existentially separate entity as Muslims.

Allama Iqbal's statement explaining the attitude of Muslim delegates to the Round-Table Conference issued in December, 1933 was a rejoinder to Jawahar Lal Nehru's statement. Nehru had said that the attitude of the Muslim delegation was based on "reactionarism." Iqbal concluded his rejoinder with:

In conclusion I must put a straight question to punadi Jawhar Lal, how is India's problem to be solved if the majority community will neither concede the minimum safeguards necessary for the protection of a minority of 80 million people, nor accept the award of a third party; but continue to talk of a kind of nationalism which works out only to its own benefit? This position can admit of only two alternatives. Either the Indian majority community will have to accept for itself the permanent position of an agent of British imperialism in the East, or the country will have to be redistributed on a basis of religious, historical and cultural affinities so as to do away with the question of electorates and the communal problem in its present form.

Allama Iqbal's apprehensions were borne out by the Hindu Congress ministries established in Hindu majority province under the Act of 1935. Muslims in those provinces were given dastardly treatment. This deplorable phenomenon added to Allama Iqbal's misgivings regarding the future of Indian Muslims in case India remained united. In his letters to the Quaid-i Azam written in 1936 and in 1937 he referred to an independent Muslim State comprising North-Western and Eastern Muslim majority zones. Now it was not only the North-Western zones alluded to in the Allahabad Address.

There are some within Pakistan and without, who insist that Allama Iqbal never meant a sovereign Muslim country outside India. Rather he desired a Muslim State within the Indian Union. A State within a State. This is absolutely wrong. What he meant was understood very vividly by his Muslim compatriots as well as the non-Muslims. Why Nehru and others had then tried to show that the idea of Muslim nationalism had no basis at all. Nehru stated:

This idea of a Muslim nation is the figment of a few imaginations only, and, but for the publicity given to it by the Press few people would have heard of it. And even if many people believed in it, it would still vanish at the touch of reality.

Iqbal and the Quaid-i Azam

Who could understand Allama Iqbal better than the Quaid-i Azam himself, who was his awaited "Guide of the Era"? The Quaid-i Azam in the Introduction to Allama Iqbal's letters addressed to him, admitted that he had agreed with Allama Iqbal regarding a State for Indian Muslims before the latters death in April, 1938. The Quaid stated:

His views were substantially in consonance with my own and had finally led me to the same conclusions as a result of careful examination and study of the constitutional problems facing India and found expression in due course in the united will of Muslim India as adumbrated in the Lahore Resolution of the All-India Muslim League popularly known as the "Pakistan Resolution" passed on 23rd March, 1940.

Furthermore, it was Allama Iqbal who called upon Quaid-i Azam Muhammad Ali Jinnah to lead the Muslims of India to their cherished goal. He preferred the Quaid to other more experienced Muslim leaders such as Sir Aga Khan, Maulana Hasrat Mohani, Nawab Muhammad Isma il Khan, Maulana Shaukat Ali, Nawab Hamid Ullah Khan of Bhopal, Sir Ali Imam, Maulvi Tameez ud-Din Khan, Maulana Abul Kalam, Allama al-Mashriqi and others. But Allama Iqbal had his own reasons. He had found his "Khizr-i Rah", the veiled guide in Quaid-i Azam Muhammad Ali Jinnah who was destined to lead the Indian branch of the Muslim *Ummah* to their goal of freedom. Allama Iqbal stated:

I know you are a busy man but I do hope you won't mind my writing to you often, as you are the only Muslim in India today to whom the community has right to look up for safe guidance through the storm which is coming to North-West India, and perhaps to the whole of India.

Similar sentiments were expressed by him about three months before his death. Sayyid Nazir Niazi in his book *Iqbal Ke Huzur*, has stated that the future of the Indian Muslims was being discussed and a tenor of pessimism was visible from what his friends said. At this Allama Iqbal observed:

There is only one way out. Muslim should strengthen Jinnah's hands. They should join the Muslim League. Indian question, as is now being solved, can be countered by our united front against both the Hindus and the English. Without it our demands are not going to be accepted. People say our demands smack of communalism. This is sheer propaganda. These demands relate to the defence of our national existence.

He continued:

The united front can be formed under the leadership of the Muslim League. And the Muslim League can succeed only on account of Jinnah. Now none but Jinnah is capable of leading the Muslims.

Matlub ul-Hasan Sayyid stated that after the Lahore Resolution was passed on March 23, 1940, the Quaid-i Azam said to him:

Iqbal is no more amongst us, but had he been alive he would have been happy to know that we did exactly what he wanted us to do.

But the matter does not end here. Allama Iqbal in his letter of March 29, 1937 to the Quaid-i Azam had said:

While we are ready to cooperate with other progressive parties in the country, we must not ignore the fact that the whole future of Islam as a moral and political force in Asia rests very largely on a complete organization of Indian Muslims.

According to Allama Iqbal the future of Islam as a moral and political force not only in India but in the whole of Asia rested on the organization of the Muslims of India led by the Quaid-i Azam.

The "Guide of the Era" Iqbal had envisaged in 1926, was found in the person of Muhammad Ali Jinnah. The "Guide" organized the Muslims of India under the banner of the Muslim League and offered determined resistance to both the Hindu and the English designs for a united Hindu-dominated India. Through their united efforts under the able guidance of Quaid-I Azam Muslims succeeded in dividing India into Pakistan and Bharat and achieving their independent homeland. As observed above, in Allama Iqbal's view, the organization of Indian Muslims which achieved Pakistan would also have to defend other Muslim societies in Asia. The carvan of the resurgence of Islam has to start and come out of this Valley, far off from the centre of the *ummah*. Let us see how and when, Pakistan prepares itself to shoulder this august responsibility. It is Allama Iqbal's prevision.

Sir Muhammad Iqbal's 1930 Presidential Address

Gentlemen, I am deeply grateful to you for the honour you have conferred upon me in inviting me to preside over the deliberations of the All-India Muslim League at one of the most critical moments in the history of Muslim political thought and activity in India. I have no doubt that in this great assembly there are men whose political experience is far more extensive than mine, and for whose knowledge of affairs I have the highest respect. It will, therefore, be presumptuous on my part to claim to guide an assembly of such men in the political decisions which they are called upon to make today. I lead no party; I follow no leader. I have given the best part of my life to a careful study of Islam, its law and polity, its culture, its history and its literature. This constant contact with the spirit of Islam, as it unfolds itself in time, has, I think, given me a kind of insight into its significance as a world fact. It is in the light of this insight, whatever its value, that, while assuming that the Muslims of India are determined to remain true to the spirit of Islam, I propose not to guide you in your decisions, but to attempt the humbler task of bringing clearly to your consciousness the main principle which, in my opinion, should determine the general character of these decisions.

Islam and Nationalism

It cannot be denied that Islam, regarded as an ethical ideal plus a certain kind of polity – by which expression I mean a social structure regulated by a legal system and animated by a specific ethical ideal – has been the chief formative factor in the life-history of the Muslims of India. It has furnished those basic emotions and loyalties which gradually unify scattered individuals and groups, and finally transform them into a well-defined people, possessing a moral consciousness of their own. Indeed it is not an exaggeration to say that India is perhaps the only country in the world where Islam, as a people-building force, has worked at its best. In India, as elsewhere, the structure of Islam as a society is almost entirely due to the working of Islam as a culture inspired by a specific ethical ideal. What I mean to say is that Muslim society, with its remarkable homogeneity and inner unity, has grown to be what it is, under the pressure of the laws and institutions associated with the culture of Islam.

The ideas set free by European political thinking, however, are now rapidly changing the outlook of the present generation of Muslims both in India and outside India. Our younger men, inspired by these ideas, are anxious to see them as living forces in their own countries, without any critical appreciation of the facts which have determined their evolution in Europe. In Europe Christianity was understood to be a purely monastic order which gradually developed into a vast church organisation. The protest of Luther was directed against this church organisation, not against any system of polity of a secular nature, for the obvious reason that there was no such polity associated with Christianity. And Luther was perfectly justified in rising in revolt against this organisation; though, I think, he did not realise that in the peculiar conditions which obtained in Europe, his revolt would eventually mean the complete displacement of [the] universal ethics of Jesus by the growth of a plurality of national and hence narrower systems of ethics.

Thus the upshot of the intellectual movement initiated by such men as Rousseau and Luther was the break-up of the one into [the] mutually ill-adjusted many, the transformation of a human into a national outlook, requiring a more realistic foundation, such as the notion of country, and finding expression through varying systems of polity evolved on national lines, i.e. on lines which recognise territory as the only principle of political solidarity. If you begin with the conception of religion as complete other-worldliness, then what has happened to Christianity in Europe is perfectly natural. The universal ethics of Jesus is displaced by national systems of ethics and polity. The conclusion to which Europe is consequently driven is that religion is a private affair of the individual and has nothing to do with what is called man's temporal life.

Islam does not bifurcate the unity of man into an irreconcilable duality of spirit and matter. In Islam God and the universe, spirit and matter, Church and State, are organic to each other. Man is not the citizen of a profane world to be renounced in the interest of a world of spirit situated elsewhere. To Islam, matter is spirit realising itself in space and time. Europe uncritically accepted the duality of spirit and matter, probably from Manichaean thought. Her best thinkers are realising this initial mistake today, but her statesmen are indirectly forcing the world to accept it as an unquestionable dogma. It is, then, this mistaken separation of spiritual and temporal which has largely influenced European religious and political thought and has resulted practically in the total exclusion of Christianity from the life of European States. The result is a set of mutually ill-adjusted States dominated by interests not human but national. And these mutually ill-adjusted States, after trampling over the moral and religious convictions of Christianity, are today feeling the need of a federated Europe, i.e. the need of a unity which the Christian church organisation originally gave them, but which, instead of reconstructing it in the light of Christ's vision of human brotherhood, they considered fit to destroy under the inspiration of Luther.

A Luther in the world of Islam, however, is an impossible phenomenon; for here there is no church organisation similar to that of Christianity in the Middle Ages, inviting a destroyer. In the world of Islam we have a universal polity whose fundamentals are believed to have been revealed but whose structure, owing to our legists' [=legal theorists'] want of contact with the modern world, today stands in need of renewed power by fresh adjustments. I do not know what will be the final fate of the national idea in the world of Islam. Whether Islam will assimilate and transform it, as it has before assimilated and transformed many ideas expressive of a different spirit, or allow a radical transformation of its own structure by the force of this idea, is hard to predict. Professor Wensinck of Leiden (Holland) wrote to me the other day: "It seems to me that Islam is entering upon a crisis through which Christianity has been passing for more than a century. The great difficulty is how to save the foundations of religion when many antiquated notions have to be given up. It seems to me scarcely possible to state what the outcome will be for Christianity, still less what it will be for Islam." At the present moment the national idea is racialising the outlook of Muslims, and thus materially counteracting the humanizing work of Islam. And the growth of racial consciousness may mean the growth of standards different [from] and even opposed to the standards of Islam.

I hope you will pardon me for this apparently academic discussion. To address this session of the All-India Muslim League you have selected a man who is [=has] not despaired of Islam as a living force for freeing the outlook of man from its geographical limitations, who believes that religion is a power of the utmost importance in the life of individuals as well as States, and finally who believes that *Islam is itself Destiny and will not suffer a destiny*. Such a man cannot but look at matters from his own point of view. Do not think that the problem I am indicating is a purely theoretical one. It is a very living and practical problem calculated to affect the very fabric of Islam as a system of life and conduct. On a proper solution of it alone depends your future as a distinct cultural unit in India. Never in our history has Islam had to stand a greater trial than the one which confronts it today. It is open to a people to modify, reinterpret or reject the foundational principles of their social structure; but it is absolutely necessary for them to see clearly what they are doing before they undertake to try a fresh experiment. Nor should the way in which I am approaching this important problem lead anybody to think that I intend to quarrel with those who happen to think differently. You are a Muslim assembly and, I suppose, anxious to remain true to the spirit and ideals of Islam. My sole desire, therefore, is to tell you frankly what I honestly believe to be the truth about the present situation. In this way alone it is possible for me to illuminate, according to my light, the avenues of your political action.

The Unity of an Indian Nation

What, then, is the problem and its implications? Is religion a private affair? Would you like to see Islam as a moral and political ideal, meeting the same fate in the world of Islam as Christianity has already met in Europe? Is it possible to retain Islam as an ethical ideal and to reject it as a polity, in favour of national polities in which [the] religious attitude is not permitted to play any part? This question becomes of special importance in India, where the Muslims happen to be a minority. The proposition that religion is a private individual experience is not surprising on the lips of a European. In Europe the conception of Christianity as a monastic order, renouncing the world of matter and fixing its gaze entirely on the world of spirit, led, by a logical process of thought, to the view embodied in this proposition. The nature of the Prophet's religious experience, as disclosed in the Quran, however, is wholly different. It is not mere experience in the sense of a purely biological event, happening inside the experient and necessitating no reactions on its social environment. It is individual experience creative of a social order. Its immediate outcome is the fundamentals of a polity with implicit legal concepts whose civic significance cannot be belittled merely because their origin is revelational.

The religious ideal of Islam, therefore, is organically related to the social order which it has created. The rejection of the one will eventually involve the rejection of the other. Therefore the construction of a polity on national lines, if it means a displacement of the Islamic principle of solidarity, is simply unthinkable to a

Muslim. This is a matter which at the present moment directly concerns the Muslims of India. "Man," says Renan, "is enslaved neither by his race, nor by his religion, nor by the course of rivers, nor by the direction of mountain ranges. A great aggregation of men, sane of mind and warm of heart, creates a moral consciousness which is called a nation." Such a formation is quite possible, though it involves the long and arduous process of practically remaking men and furnishing them with a fresh emotional equipment. It might have been a fact in India if the teaching of Kabir and the Divine Faith of Akbar had seized the imagination of the masses of this country. Experience, however, shows that the various caste units and religious units in India have shown no inclination to sink their respective individualities in a larger whole. Each group is intensely jealous of its collective existence. The formation of the kind of moral consciousness which constitutes the essence of a nation in Renan's sense demands a price which the peoples of India are not prepared to pay.

The unity of an Indian nation, therefore, must be sought not in the negation, but in the mutual harmony and cooperation, of the many. True statesmanship cannot ignore facts, however unpleasant they may be. The only practical course is not to assume the existence of a state of things which does not exist, but to recognise facts as they are, and to exploit them to our greatest advantage. And it is on the discovery of Indian unity in this direction that the fate of India as well as of Asia really depends. India is Asia in miniature. Part of her people have cultural affinities with nations of the east, and part with nations in the middle and west of Asia. If an effective principle of cooperation is discovered in India, it will bring peace and mutual goodwill to this ancient land which has suffered so long, more because of her situation in historic space than because of any inherent incapacity of her people. And it will at the same time solve the entire political problem of Asia.

It is, however, painful to observe that our attempts to discover such a principle of internal harmony have so far failed. Why have they failed? Perhaps we suspect each other's intentions and inwardly aim at dominating each other. Perhaps, in the higher interests of mutual cooperation, we cannot afford to part with the monopolies which circumstances have placed in our hands, and [thus we] conceal our egoism under the cloak of nationalism, outwardly simulating a large-hearted patriotism, but inwardly as narrow-minded as a caste or tribe. Perhaps we are unwilling to recognise that each group has a right to free development according to its own cultural traditions. But whatever may be the causes of our failure, I still feel hopeful. Events seem to be tending in the direction of some sort of internal harmony. And as far as I have been able to read the Muslim mind, I have no hesitation in declaring that if the principle that the Indian Muslim is entitled to full and free development on the lines of his own culture and tradition in his own Indian home-lands is recognized as the basis of a permanent communal settlement, he will be ready to stake his all for the freedom of India.

The principle that each group is entitled to its free development on its own lines is not inspired by any feeling of narrow communalism. There are communalisms and communalisms. A community which is inspired by feelings of ill-will towards other communities is low and ignoble. I entertain the highest respect for the customs, laws, religious and social institutions of other communities. Nay, it is my duty, according to the teaching of the Quran, even to defend their places of worship, if need be. *Yet I love the communal group which is the source of my life and behaviour; and which has formed me what I am by giving me its religion, its literature, its thought, its culture, and thereby recreating its whole past as a living operative factor, in my present consciousness.* Even the authors of the Nehru Report recognise the value of this higher aspect of communalism. While discussing the separation of Sindh they say, "To say from the larger viewpoint of nationalism that no communal provinces should be created, is, in a way, equivalent to saying from the still wider international viewpoint that there should be no separate nations. Both these statements have a measure of truth in them. But the staunchest internationalist recognises that without the fullest national autonomy it is extraordinarily difficult to create the international State. *So also without the fullest cultural autonomy – and communalism in its better aspect is culture – it will be difficult to create a harmonious nation.*"

Muslim India Within India

Communalism in its higher aspect, then, is indispensable to the formation of a harmonious whole in a country like India. The units of Indian society are not territorial as in European countries. India is a continent of human groups belonging to different races, speaking different languages, and professing different religions. Their behaviour is not at all determined by a common race-consciousness. Even the Hindus do not form a homogeneous group. The principle of European democracy cannot be applied to India without recognising the fact of communal groups. The Muslim demand for the creation of a Muslim India within India is, therefore, perfectly justified. The resolution of the All-Parties Muslim Conference at Delhi is, to my mind, wholly inspired by this noble ideal of a harmonious whole which, instead of stifling the respective individualities of its component wholes, affords them chances of fully working out the possibilities that may be latent in them. And I have no doubt that this House will emphatically endorse the Muslim demands embodied in this resolution.

Personally, I would go farther than the demands embodied in it. *I would like to see the Punjab, North-West Frontier Province, Sindh and Baluchistan amalgamated into a single State. Self-government within the British Empire, or without the British Empire, the formation of a consolidated North-West Indian Muslim State appears to me to be the final destiny of the Muslims, at least of North-West India.* The proposal was put forward before the Nehru Committee. They rejected it on the ground that, if carried into effect, it would give a very unwieldy State. This is true in so far as the area is concerned; in point of population, the State contemplated by the proposal would be much less than some of the present Indian provinces. The exclusion of Ambala Division, and perhaps of some districts where non-Muslims predominate, will make it less extensive and more Muslim in population – so that the exclusion suggested will enable this consolidated State to give a more effective protection to non-Muslim minorities within its area. The idea need not alarm the Hindus or the British. India is the greatest Muslim country in the world. The life of Islam as a cultural force in the country very largely depends on its centralisation in a specified territory. This centralisation of the most living portion of the Muslims of India, whose military and police service has, notwithstanding unfair treatment from the British, made the British rule possible in this country, will eventually solve the problem of India as well as of

Asia. It will intensify their sense of responsibility and deepen their patriotic feeling.

Thus, possessing full opportunity of development within the body politic of India, the North-West Indian Muslims will prove the best defenders of India against a foreign invasion, be that invasion one of ideas or of bayonets. The Punjab with 56 percent Muslim population supplies 54 percent of the total combatant troops in the Indian Army, and if the 19,000 Gurkhas recruited from the independent State of Nepal are excluded, the Punjab contingent amounts to 62 percent of the whole Indian Army. This percentage does not take into account nearly 6,000 combatants supplied to the Indian Army by the North-West Frontier Province and Baluchistan. From this you can easily calculate the possibilities of North-West Indian Muslims in regard to the defence of India against foreign aggression. The Right Hon'ble Mr. Srinivasa Shastri thinks that the Muslim demand for the creation of autonomous Muslim states along the northwest border is actuated by a desire "to acquire means of exerting pressure in emergencies on the Government of India." I may frankly tell him that the Muslim demand is not actuated by the kind of motive he imputes to us; it is actuated by a genuine desire for free development which is practically impossible under the type of unitary government contemplated by the nationalist Hindu politicians with a view to secure permanent communal dominance in the whole of India.

Nor should the Hindus fear that the creation of autonomous Muslim states will mean the introduction of a kind of religious rule in such states. I have already indicated to you the meaning of the word religion, as applied to Islam. The truth is that Islam is not a Church. It is a State conceived as a contractual organism long before Rousseau ever thought of such a thing, and animated by an ethical ideal which regards man not as an earth-rooted creature, defined by this or that portion of the earth, but as a spiritual being understood in terms of a social mechanism, and possessing rights and duties as a living factor in that mechanism. The character of a Muslim State can be judged from what the *Times of India* pointed out some time ago in a leader on the Indian Banking Inquiry Committee. "In ancient India," the paper points out, "the State framed laws regulating the rates of interest; but in Muslim times, although Islam clearly forbids the realisation of interest on money loaned, Indian Muslim States imposed no restrictions on such rates." I therefore demand the formation of a consolidated Muslim State in the best interests of India and Islam. For India, it means security and peace resulting from an internal balance of power; for Islam, an opportunity to rid itself of the stamp that Arabian Imperialism was forced to give it, to mobilise its law, its education, its culture, and to bring them into closer contact with its own original spirit and with the spirit of modern times.

Federal States

Thus it is clear that in view of India's infinite variety in climates, races, languages, creeds and social systems, the creation of autonomous States, based on the unity of language, race, history, religion and identity of economic interests, is the only possible way to secure a stable constitutional structure in India. The conception of federation underlying the Simon Report necessitates the abolition of the Central Legislative Assembly as a popular assembly, and makes it an assembly of the representatives of federal States. It further demands a redistribution of territory on the lines which I have indicated. And the Report does recommend both. I give my wholehearted support to this view of the matter, and venture to suggest that the redistribution recommended in the Simon Report must fulfil two conditions. It must precede the introduction of the new constitution, and must be so devised as to finally solve the communal problem. Proper redistribution will make the question of joint and separate electorates automatically disappear from the constitutional controversy of India. It is the present structure of the provinces that is largely responsible for this controversy.

The Hindu thinks that separate electorates are contrary to the spirit of true nationalism, because he understands the word nation to mean a kind of universal amalgamation in which no communal entity ought to retain its private individuality. Such a state of things, however, does not exist. Nor is it desirable that it should exist. India is a land of racial and religious variety. Add to this the general economic inferiority of the Muslims, their enormous debt, especially in the Punjab, and their insufficient majorities in some of the provinces as at present constituted, and you will begin to see clearly the meaning of our anxiety to retain separate electorates. In such a country and in such circumstances territorial electorates cannot secure adequate representation of all interests, and must inevitably lead to the creation of an oligarchy. The Muslims of India can have no objection to purely territorial electorates if provinces are demarcated so as to secure comparatively homogeneous communities possessing linguistic, racial, cultural and religious unity.

Federation As Understood in the Simon Report

But in so far as the question of the powers of the Central Federal State is concerned, there is a subtle difference of motive in the constitutions proposed by the pundits of India and the pundits of England. The pundits of India do not disturb the Central authority as it stands at present. All that they desire is that this authority should become fully responsible to the Central Legislature which they maintain intact and where their majority will become further reinforced on the nominated element ceasing to exist. The pundits of England, on the other hand, realising that democracy in the Centre tends to work contrary to their interests and is likely to absorb the whole power now in their hands, in case a further advance is made towards responsible government, have shifted the experience of democracy from the Centre to the provinces. No doubt, they introduce the principle of Federation and appear to have made a beginning by making certain proposals; yet their evaluation of this principle is determined by considerations wholly different to those which determine its value in the eyes of Muslim India. The Muslims demand federation because it is pre-eminently a solution of India's most difficult problem, i.e. the communal problem. The Royal Commissioners' view of federation, though sound in principle, does not seem to aim at responsible government for federal States. Indeed it does not go beyond providing means of escape from the situation which the introduction of democracy in India has created for the British, and wholly disregards the communal problem by leaving it where it was.

Thus it is clear that, in so far as real federation is concerned, the Simon Report virtually negatives the principle of federation in its true significance. The Nehru Report, realising [a] Hindu majority in the Central Assembly, reaches a unitary form of government because such an institution secures Hindu dominance throughout India; the Simon Report retains the present British dominance behind the thin veneer of an unreal federation, partly because the British are naturally unwilling to part with the power they have so long wielded and partly because it is possible for them, in the absence of an inter-communal understanding in India, to make out a plausible case for the retention of that power in their own hands. To my mind a unitary form of government is simply unthinkable in a self-governing India. What is called "residuary powers" must be left entirely to self-governing States, the Central Federal State exercising only those powers which are expressly vested in it by the free consent of federal States. I would never advise the Muslims of India to agree to a system, whether of British or of Indian origin, which virtually negatives the principle of true federation, or fails to recognise them as a distinct political entity.

Federal Scheme As Discussed in the Round Table Conference

The necessity for a structural change in the Central Government was seen probably long before the British discovered the most effective means for introducing this change. That is why at rather a late stage it was announced that the participation of the Indian Princes in the Round Table Conference was essential. It was a kind of surprise to the people of India, particularly the minorities, to see the Indian Princes dramatically expressing their willingness at the Round Table Conference to join an all-India federation and, as a result of their declaration, Hindu delegates – uncompromising advocates of a unitary form of government – quietly agreeing to the evolution of a federal scheme.

Even Mr. Shastri who only a few days before had severely criticised Sir John Simon for recommending a federal scheme for India, suddenly became a convert and admitted his conversion in the plenary session of the Conference – thus offering the Prime Minister of England an occasion for one of his wittiest observations in his concluding speech.

All this has a meaning both for the British who have sought the participation of the Indian Princes, and for the Hindus who have unhesitatingly accepted the evolution of an all-India federation. The truth is that the participation of the Indian Princes, among whom only a few are Muslims, in a federation scheme serves a double purpose. On the one hand, it serves as an all-important factor in maintaining the British power in India practically as it is; on the other hand, it gives [an] overwhelming majority to the Hindus in an All-India Federal Assembly.

It appears to me that the Hindu-Muslim differences regarding the ultimate form of the Central Government are being cleverly exploited by British politicians through the agency of the Princes who see in the scheme prospects of better security for their despotic rule. If the Muslims silently agree to any such scheme, it will simply hasten their end as a political entity in India. The policy of the Indian federation thus created, will be practically controlled by [the] Hindu Princes forming the largest group in the Central Federal Assembly. They will always lend their support to the Crown in matters of Imperial concern; and in so far as internal administration of the country is concerned, they will help in maintaining and strengthening the supremacy of the Hindus. In other words, the scheme appears to be aiming at a kind of understanding between Hindu India and British Imperialism – you perpetuate me in India, and I in return give you a Hindu oligarchy to keep all other Indian communities in perpetual subjection. If, therefore, the British Indian provinces are not transformed into really autonomous States, the Princes' participation in a scheme of Indian federation will be interpreted only as a dexterous move on the part of British politicians to satisfy, without parting with any real power, all parties concerned – Muslims with the *word* federation; Hindus with a majority in the Centre; the British Imperialists – with the *substance* of real power.

The number of Hindu States in India is far greater than Muslim States; and it remains to be seen how the Muslim demand for 33 percent [of the] seats in the Central Federal Assembly is to be met within a House or Houses constituted of representatives taken from British India as well as Indian States. I hope the Muslim delegates are fully aware of the implications of the federal scheme as discussed in the Round Table Conference. The question of Muslim representation in the proposed all-India federation has not yet been discussed. "The interim report," says Reuters' summary, "contemplates two chambers in the Federal Legislature, each containing representatives both of British India and States, the proportion of which will be a matter of subsequent consideration under the heads which have not yet been referred to the Sub-Committee." In my opinion the question of proportion is of the utmost importance and ought to have been considered simultaneously with the main question of the structure of the Assembly.

The best course, I think, would have been to start with a British Indian Federation only. A federal scheme born of an unholy union between democracy and despotism cannot but keep British India in the same vicious circle of a unitary Central Government. Such a unitary form may be of the greatest advantage to the British, to the majority community in British India, and to the Indian Princes; it can be of no advantage to the Muslims, unless they get majority rights in five out of eleven Indian provinces with full residuary powers, and one-third share of seats in the total House of the Federal Assembly. In so far as the attainment of sovereign powers by the British Indian provinces is concerned, the position of His Highness the Ruler of Bhopal, Sir Akbar Hydari, and Mr. Jinnah is unassailable. In view, however, of the participation of the Princes in the Indian Federation, we must now see our demand for representation in the British Indian Assembly in a new light. The questions is not one of [the] Muslim share in a British Indian Assembly, but one which relates to representation of British Indian Muslims in an All-India Federal Assembly. Our demand for 33 per cent must now be taken as a demand for the same proportion in the All-India Federal Assembly, exclusive of the share allotted to the Muslim states entering the Federation.

The Problem of Defence

The other difficult problem which confronts the successful working of a federal system in India is the problem of India's defence. In their discussion of this problem the Royal Commissioners have marshalled all the deficiencies of India in order to make out a case for Imperial administration of the Army. "India and Britain," say the Commissioners, "are so related that India's defence cannot, *now or in any future which is within sight*, be regarded as a matter of purely Indian concern. The control and direction of such an army must rest in the hands of agents of Imperial Government." Now, does it [not] necessarily follow from this that further progress towards the realisation of responsible government in British India is barred until the work of defence can be adequately discharged without the help of British officers and British troops? *As things are, there is a block on the line of constitutional advance.* All hopes of evolution in the Central Government towards the ultimate goal prescribed in the declaration of 20th August 1917, are in danger of being indefinitely frustrated, if the attitude illustrated by the Nehru Report is maintained, that any future change involves the putting of the administration of the army under the authority of an elected Indian Legislature. Further to fortify their argument they emphasize the fact of competing religions and rival races of widely different capacity, and try to make the problem look insoluble by remarking that "the obvious fact that India is not, in the ordinary and natural sense, a single nation is nowhere made more plain than in considering the difference between the martial races of India and the rest." These features of the question have been emphasised in order to demonstrate that the British are not only keeping India secure from foreign menace but are also the "neutral guardians" of internal security.

However, in federated India, as I understand federation, the problem will have only one aspect, i.e. external defence. Apart from provincial armies necessary for maintaining internal peace, the Indian Federal Congress can maintain, on the northwest frontier, a strong Indian Frontier Army, composed of units recruited from all provinces and officered by efficient and experienced military men taken from all communities. I know that India is not in possession of efficient military officers, and this fact is exploited by the Royal Commissioners in the interest of an argument for Imperial administration. On this point I cannot but quote another passage from the Report which, to my mind, furnishes the best argument against the position taken up by the Commissioners. "At the present moment," says the Report, "no Indian holding the King's Commission is of higher army rank than a captain. There are, we believe, 39 captains of whom 25 are in ordinary regimental employ. Some of them are of an age which would prevent their attaining much higher rank, even if they passed the necessary examination before retirement. Most of these have not been through Sandhurst, but got their Commissions during the Great War." Now, however genuine may be the desire, and however earnest the endeavour to work for this transformation, overriding conditions have been so forcibly expressed by the Skeen Committee (whose members, apart from the Chairman and the Army Secretary, were Indian gentlemen) in these words: Progress...must be contingent upon success being secured at each stage and upon military efficiency being maintained, though it must in any case render such development measured and slow. A higher command cannot be evolved at short notice out of existing cadres of Indian officers, all of junior rank and limited experience. Not until the slender trickle of suitable Indian recruits for the officer class – and we earnestly desire an increase in their numbers – flows in much greater volume, not until sufficient Indians have attained the experience and training requisite to provide all the officers for, at any rate, some Indian regiments, not until such units have stood the only test which can possibly determine their efficiency, and not until Indian officers have qualified by a successful army career for the high command, will it be possible to develop the policy of Indianisation to a point which will bring a completely Indianised army within sight. Even then years must elapse before the process could be completed."

Now I venture to ask: who is responsible for the present state of things? Is it due to some inherent incapacity of our martial races, or to the slowness of the process of military training? The military capacity of our martial races is undeniable. The process of military training may be slow as compared to other processes of human training. I am no military expert to judge this matter. But as a layman I feel that the argument, as stated, assumes the process to be practically endless. This means perpetual bondage for India, and makes it all the more necessary that the Frontier Army, as suggested by the Nehru Report, be entrusted to the charge of a committee of defence, the personnel of which may be settled by mutual understanding.

Again, it is significant that the Simon Report has given extraordinary importance to the question of India's land frontier, but has made only passing references to its naval position. India has doubtless had to face invasions from her land frontier; but it is obvious that her present masters took possession of her on account of her defenceless sea coast. A self-governing and free India will, in these days, have to take greater care of her sea coast than [of her] land frontiers.

I have no doubt that if a Federal Government is established, Muslim federal States will willingly agree, for purposes of India's defence, to the creation of neutral Indian military and naval forces. Such a neutral military force for the defence of India was a reality in the days of Mughal rule. Indeed in the time of Akbar the Indian frontier was, on the whole, defended by armies officered by Hindu generals. I am perfectly sure that the scheme for a neutral Indian army, based on a federated India, will intensify Muslim patriotic feeling, and finally set at rest the suspicion, if any, of Indian Muslims joining Muslims from beyond the frontier in the event of an invasion.

The Alternative

I have thus tried briefly to indicate the way in which the Muslims of India ought, in my opinion, to look at the two most important constitutional problems of India. A redistribution of British India, calculated to secure a permanent solution of the communal problem, is the main demand of the Muslims of India. If, however, the Muslim demand of a territorial solution of the communal problem is ignored, then I support, as emphatically as possible, the Muslim demands repeatedly urged by the All-India Muslim League and the All-India Muslim Conference. The Muslims of India cannot agree to any constitutional changes which affect their majority rights, to be secured by separate electorates in the Punjab and Bengal, or [which] fail to guarantee them 33 percent representation in any Central Legislature. There were two pitfalls into which Muslim political leaders fell. The first was the repudiated Lucknow Pact, which originated in a false view of Indian nationalism and deprived the Muslims of India of chances of acquiring any political power in India. The second is the narrow-visioned sacrifice of Islamic solidarity, in the interests of what may be called Punjab ruralism, resulting in a proposal which virtually reduces the Punjab Muslims to a position of minority. It is the duty of the League to condemn both the Pact and the proposal.

The Simon Report does great injustice to the Muslims in not recommending a statutory majority for the Punjab and Bengal. It would make the Muslims either stick to the Lucknow Pact or agree to a scheme of joint electorates. The despatch of the Government of India on the Simon Report admits that since the publication of that document the Muslim community has not expressed its willingness to accept any of the alternatives proposed by the Report. The despatch recognises that it may be a legitimate grievance to deprive the Muslims in the Punjab and Bengal of representation in the councils in proportion to their population merely because of weightage allowed to Muslim minorities elsewhere. But the despatch of the Government of India fails to correct the injustice of the Simon Report.

In so far as the Punjab is concerned – and this is the most crucial point – it endorses the so-called "carefully balanced scheme" worked out by the official members of the Punjab Government which gives the Punjab Muslims a majority of two over Hindus and Sikhs combined, and a proportion of 49 percent of the House as a whole. It is obvious that the Punjab Muslims cannot be satisfied with less than a clear majority in the total House.

However, Lord Irwin and his Government do recognise that the justification for communal electorates for majority communities would not cease unless and until by the extension of franchise their voting strength more correctly reflects their population; and further unless a two-thirds majority of the Muslim members in a provincial Council unanimously agree to surrender the right of separate representation. I cannot, however, understand why the Government of India, having recognised the legitimacy of the Muslim grievances, have not had the courage to recommend a statutory majority for the Muslims in the Punjab and Bengal.

Nor can the Muslims of India agree to any such changes which fail to create at least Sindh as a separate province and treat the North-West Frontier Province as a province of inferior political status. I see no reason why Sindh should not be united with Baluchistan and turned into a separate province. It has nothing in common with Bombay Presidency. In point of life and civilization the Royal Commissioners find it more akin to Mesopotamia and Arabia than India. The Muslim geographer Mas'udi noticed this kinship long ago when he said: "Sindh is a country *nearer* to the dominions of Islam." The first Omayyad ruler is reported to have said of Egypt: "Egypt has her back towards Africa and face towards Arabia." With necessary alterations the same remark describes the exact situation of Sindh. She has her back towards India and face towards Central Asia. Considering further the nature of her agricultural problems which can invoke no sympathy from the

Bombay Government, and her infinite commercial possibilities, dependent on the inevitable growth of Karachi into a second metropolis of India, it is unwise to keep her attached to a Presidency which, though friendly today, is likely to become a rival at no distant period. Financial difficulties, we are told, stand in the way of separation. I do not know of any definite authoritative pronouncement on the matter. But assuming there are any such difficulties, I see no reason why the Government of India should not give temporary financial help to a promising province in her struggle for independent progress.

As to the North-West Frontier Province, it is painful to note that the Royal Commissioners have practically denied that the people of this province have any right to reform. They fall far short of the Bray Committee, and the Council recommended by them is merely a screen to hide the autocracy of the Chief Commissioner. The inherent right of the Afghan to light a cigarette is curtailed merely because he happens to be living in a powder house.

The Royal Commissioners' epigrammatic argument is pleasant enough, but far from convincing. Political reform is light, not fire; and to light every human being is entitled, whether he happens to live in a powder house or a coal mine. Brave, shrewd, and determined to suffer for his legitimate aspirations, the Afghan is sure to resent any attempt to deprive him of opportunities of full self-development. To keep such a people contented is in the best interest of both England and India. What has recently happened in that unfortunate province is the result of a step-motherly treatment shown to the people since the introduction of the principle of self-government in the rest of India. I only hope that British statesmanship will not obscure its view of the situation by hoodwinking itself into the belief that the present unrest in the province is due to any extraneous causes. The recommendation for the introduction of a measure of reform in the North-West Frontier Province made in the Government of India's despatch is also unsatisfactory. No doubt, the despatch goes farther than the Simon Report in recommending a sort of representative Council and a semi-representative cabinet, but it fails to treat this important Muslim province on [an] equal footing with other Indian provinces. Indeed the Afghan is, by instinct, more fitted for democratic institutions than any other people in India.

The Round Table Conference

I think I am now called upon to make a few observations on the Round Table Conference. Personally I do not feel optimistic as to the results of this Conference. It was hoped that away from the actual scene of communal strife and in a changed atmosphere, better counsels would prevail and a genuine settlement of the differences between the two major communities of India would bring India's freedom within sight. Actual events, however, tell a different tale. Indeed, the discussion of the communal question in London has demonstrated more clearly than ever the essential disparity between the two great cultural units of India. Yet the Prime Minister of England apparently refuses to see that the problem of India is international and not national. He is reported to have said that "his government would find it difficult to submit to Parliament proposals for the maintenance of separate electorates, since joint electorates were much more in accordance with British democratic sentiments." Obviously he does not see that the model of British democracy cannot be of any use in a land of many nations; and that a system of separate electorates is only a poor substitute for a territorial solution of the problem. Nor is the Minorities Sub-Committee likely to reach a satisfactory settlement. The whole question will have to go before the British Parliament; and we can only hope that the keen-sighted representatives of [the] British nation, unlike most of our Indian politicians, will be able to pierce through the surface of things and see clearly the true fundamentals of peace and security in a country like India. To base a constitution on the concept of a homogeneous India, or to apply to India principles dictated by British democratic sentiments, is unwittingly to prepare her for a civil war. As far as I can see, there will be no peace in the country until the various peoples that constitute India are given opportunities of free self-development on modern lines without abruptly breaking with their past.

I am glad to be able to say that our Muslim delegates fully realise the importance of a proper solution of what I call [the] Indian international problem. They are perfectly justified in pressing for a solution of the communal question before the question of responsibility in the Central Government is finally settled. No Muslim politician should be sensitive to the taunt embodied in that propaganda word – communalism – expressly devised to exploit what the Prime Minister calls British democratic sentiments, and to mislead England into assuming a state of things which does not really exist in India. Great interests are at stake. We are 70 millions, and far more homogeneous than any other people in India. Indeed the Muslims of India are the only Indian people who can fitly be described as a nation in the modern sense of the word. The Hindus, though ahead of us in almost all respects, have not yet been able to achieve the kind of homogeneity which is necessary for a nation, and which Islam has given you as a free gift. No doubt they are anxious to become a nation, but the process of becoming a nation is kind of travail, and in the case of Hindu India involves a complete overhauling of her social structure.

Nor should the Muslim leaders and politicians allow themselves to be carried away by the subtle but fallacious argument that Turkey and Persia and other Muslim countries are progressing on national, i.e. territorial, lines. The Muslims of India are differently situated. The countries of Islam outside India are practically wholly Muslim in population. The minorities there belong, in the language of the Quran, to the 'people of the Book'. There are no social barriers between Muslims and the 'people of the Book'. A Jew or a Christian or a Zoroastrian does not pollute the food of a Muslim by touching it, and the law of Islam allows intermarriage with the 'people of the Book'. Indeed the first practical step that Islam took towards the realisation of a final combination of humanity was to call upon peoples possessing practically the same ethical ideal to come forward and combind. The Quran declares: "O people of the Book! Come, let us join together on the 'word' (Unity of God), that is common to us all." The wars of Islam and Christianity, and later, European aggression in its various forms, could not allow the infinite meaning of this verse to work itself out in the world of Islam. Today it is being gradually realised in the countries of Islam in the shape of what is called Muslim Nationalism.

It is hardly necessary for me to add that the sole test of the success of our delegates is the extent to which they are able to get the non-Muslim delegates of the Conference to agree to our demands as embodied in the Delhi Resolution. If these demands are not agreed to, then a question of a very great and far-reaching importance will arise for the community. Then will arrive the moment for independent and concerted political action by the

Muslims of India. If you are at all serious about your ideals and aspirations, you must be ready for such an action. Our leading men have done a good deal of political thinking, and their thought has certainly made us, more or less, sensitive to the forces which are now shaping the destinies of peoples in India and outside India. But, I ask, has this thinking prepared us for the kind of action demanded by the situation which may arise in the near future?

Let me tell you frankly that, at the present moment, the Muslims of India are suffering from two evils. The first is the want of personalities. Sir Malcolm Hailey and Lord Irwin were perfectly correct in their diagnosis when they told the Aligarh University that the community had failed to produce leaders. By leaders I mean men who, by Divine gift or experience, possess a keen perception of the spirit and destiny of Islam, along with an equally keen perception of the trend of modern history. Such men are really the driving forces of a people, but they are God's gift and cannot be made to order.

The second evil from which the Muslims of India are suffering is that the community is fast losing what is called the herd instinct. This [loss] makes it possible for individuals and groups to start independent careers without contributing to the general thought and activity of the community. We are doing today in the domain of politics what we have been doing for centuries in the domain of religion. But sectional bickerings in religion do not do much harm to our solidarity. They at least indicate an interest in what makes the sole principle of our structure as a people. Moreover, the principle is so broadly conceived that it is almost impossible for a group to become rebellious to the extent of wholly detaching itself from the general body of Islam. But diversity in political action, at a moment when concerted action is needed in the best interests of the very life of our people, may prove fatal.

How shall we, then, remedy these two evils? The remedy of the first evil is not in our hands. As to the second evil, I think it is possible to discover a remedy. I have got definite views on the subject; but I think it is proper to postpone their expression till the apprehended situation actually arises. In case it does arise, leading Muslims of all shades of opinion will have to meet together, not to pass resolutions, but finally to determine the Muslim attitude and to show the path to tangible achievement. In this address I mention this alternative only because I wish that you may keep it in mind and give some serious thought to it in the meantime.

The Conclusion

Gentlemen, I have finished. In conclusion I cannot but impress upon you that the present crisis in the history of India demands complete organisation and unity of will and purpose in the Muslim community, both in your own interest as a community, and in the interest of India as a whole. The political bondage of India has been and is a source of infinite misery to the whole of Asia. It has suppressed the spirit of the East and wholly deprived her of that joy of self-expression which once made her the creator of a great and glorious culture. We have a duty towards India where we are destined to live and die. We have a duty towards Asia, especially Muslim Asia. And since 70 millions of Muslims in a single country constitute a far more valuable asset to Islam than all the countries of Muslim Asia put together, we must look at the Indian problem not only from the Muslim point of view, but also from the standpoint of the Indian Muslim as such. Our duty towards Asia and India cannot be loyally performed without an organised will fixed on a definite purpose. In your own interest, as a political entity among other political entities of India, such an equipment is an absolute necessity. Our disorganised condition has already confused political issues vital to the life of the community. I am not hopeless of an intercommunal understanding, but I cannot conceal from you the feeling that in the near future our community may be called upon to adopt an independent line of action to cope with the present crisis. And an independent line of political action, in such a crisis, is possible only to a determined people, possessing a will focalised by a single purpose. Is it possible for you to achieve the organic wholeness of a unified will? Yes, it is. Rise above sectional interests and private ambitions, and learn to determine the value of your individual and collective action, however directed on material ends, in the light of the ideal which you are supposed to represent. Pass from matter to spirit. Matter is diversity; spirit is light, life and unity.

One lesson I have learnt from the history of Muslims. At critical moments in their history it is Islam that has saved Muslims and not vice versa. If today you focus your vision on Islam and seek inspiration from the ever-vitalising idea embodied in it, you will be only reassembling your scattered forces, regaining your lost integrity, and thereby saving yourself from total destruction. One of the profoundest verses in the Holy Quran teaches us that the birth and rebirth of the whole of humanity is like the birth and rebirth of a single individual. Why cannot you who, as a people, can well claim to be the first practical exponents of this superb conception of humanity, live and move and have your being as a single individual? I do not wish to mystify anybody when I say that things in India are not what they appear to be. The meaning of this, however, will dawn upon you only when you have achieved a real collective ego to look at them. In the words of the Quran, "Hold fast to yourself; no one who erreth can hurt you, provided you are well guided

Pakistan Declaration

The Pakistan Declaration (titled Now or Never; Are We to Live or Perish Forever?) was a pamphlet published in January 1933 by Choudhary Rahmat Ali, and was supported by Muhammad Aslam Khan Khattak, Sahibzada Sheikh Mohd Sadiq, Inayat Ullah Khan in which the word Pakistan was used for the first time and was presented in the round table conference in 1933.

The pamphlet asked that the "the five Northern units of India"- Punjab, North-West Frontier Province (Afghan Province), Kashmir, Sindh and Baluchistan (or Pakstan) become a state independent of the proposed Indian Federation.

After the publication of the pamphlet the name of Pakistan grew in popularity and led to the Pakistan Movement, and the creation of Pakistan as an independent state in 1947.

Muhammad Ali Jinnah

Muhammad Ali Jinnah (December 25, 1876 – September 11, 1948), a 20th century politician and statesman, is regarded as the founder of Pakistan. He served as leader of The Muslim League and Pakistan's first Governor-General. He is officially known in Pakistan as Quaid-i-Azam and Baba-e-Qaum ("Father of the Nation"). His birthday is a national holiday in Pakistan. Jinnah rose to prominence in the Indian National Congress initially expounding ideas of Hindu-Muslim unity and helping shape the

1916 Lucknow Pact between the Muslim League and the Indian National Congress; he also became a key leader in the All India Home Rule League. He proposed a fourteen-point constitutional reform plan to safeguard the political rights of Muslims in a self-governing India.

Jinnah, advocating the Two-Nation Theory, embraced the goal of creating a separate state for Muslims as per the Lahore Resolution. The League won most reserved Muslim seats in the elections of 1946. After the British and Congress backed out of the Cabinet Mission Plan Jinnah called for a *Direct Action* Day to achieve the formation of Pakistan. The direct action by the Muslim League and its Volunteer Corps, resulted in massive rioting in Calcutta between Muslims and Hindus/Sikhs. As the Indian National Congress and Muslim League failed to reach a power sharing formula for united India, it prompted both the parties and the British to agree to independence of Pakistan and India. As the first Governor-General of Pakistan, Jinnah led efforts to rehabilitate millions of refugees, and to frame national policies on foreign affairs, security and economic development. He died a year after Pakistan's formation in September 1948.

Jinnah was born Mahomedali Jinnahbhai in, some believe, Wazir Mansion, Karachi District, of lower Sindh. However, this is disputed as old textbooks mention Jhirk as his place of birth. Sindh had earlier been conquered by the British and was subsequently grouped with other conquered territories for administrative reasons to form the Bombay Presidency of British India. Although his earliest school records state that he was born on October 20, 1875, Sarojini Naidu, the author of Jinnah's first biography, gives the date as "December 25, 1876".

Jinnah was the eldest of seven children born to Mithibai and Jinnahbhai Poonja. His father, Jinnahbhai (1857–1901), was a prosperous Gujarati merchant who had moved to Sindh from Kathiawar, Gujarat before Jinnah's birth. His grandfather was Poonja Gokuldas Meghji, a Hindu Bhatia Rajput from Paneli village in Gondal state in Kathiawar. Jinnah's ancestors were Hindu Rajput who converted to Islam. Jinnah's family belonged to the Ismaili Khoja branch of Shi'a Islam, though Jinnah later converted to Twelver Shi'a Islam. The first born Jinnah was soon joined by six siblings, brothers Ahmad Ali, Bunde Ali, and Rahmat Ali, and sisters Maryam, Fatima and Shireen. Their mother tongue was Gujarati, however, in time they also came to speak Kutchi, Sindhi and English. The proper Muslim names of Mr. Jinnah and his siblings, unlike those of his father and grandfather, are the consequence of the family's immigration to the Muslim state of Sindh.

Jinnah was a restless student, he studied at several schools: at the Sindh-Madrasa-tul-Islam in Karachi; briefly at the Gokal Das Tej Primary School in Bombay; and finally at the Christian Missionary Society High School in Karachi, where, at age sixteen, he passed the matriculation examination of the University of Bombay.

In 1892, Jinnah was offered an apprenticeship at the London office of Graham's Shipping and Trading Company, a business that had extensive dealings with Jinnahbhai Poonja's firm in Karachi. However, before he left for England, at his mother's urging he married his distant cousin, Emibai Jinnah, who was two years his junior. The marriage was not to last long as Emibai died a few months later. During his sojourn in England, his mother too would pass away. In London, Jinnah soon left the apprenticeship to study law instead, by joining Lincoln's Inn. It is said that the sole reason of Jinnah's joining Lincoln's Inn is that the welcome board of the Lincoln's Inn had the names of the world's all time top ten magistrates and that this list was led by the name of Muhammad. However, no such board exists, although there is a mural which includes a picture of Muhammad. In three years, at age 19, he became the youngest Indian to be called to the bar in England.

The Western world not only inspired Jinnah in his political life. England had greatly influenced his personal preferences, particularly when it came to dress. Jinnah donned Western style clothing and he pursued the fashion with fervor. It is said he owned over 200 hand-tailored suits which he wore with heavily starched shirts with detachable collars. It is also alleged that he never wore the same silk tie twice. M C Chagla, who was a close friend of Jinnah's, has stated that Jinnah was fond of eating pork, an act which is forbidden is Islam. The historian Stanley Wolpert has also alleged this in a book about Jinnah. The Pakistan government has banned books (including Wolpert's) which have mentioned this alleged dietary preference of Jinnah's.

During the final period of his stay in England, Jinnah came under considerable pressure to return home when his father's business was ruined. In 1896 he returned to India and settled in Bombay. He became a successful lawyer—gaining particular fame for his skilled handling of the "Caucus Case". Jinnah built a house in Malabar Hill, later known as Jinnah House. His reputation as a skilled lawyer prompted Indian leader Bal Gangadhar Tilak to hire him as defence counsel for his sedition trial in 1905. Jinnah argued that it was not sedition for an Indian to demand freedom and self-government in his own country, but Tilak received a rigorous term of imprisonment.

When he returned to India his faith in liberalism and progressive politics was confirmed through his close association with three Indian National Congress stalwarts Gopal Krishna Gokhale, Pherozeshah Mehta and Surendranath Banerjee. These people had an important influence in his early life in England and they would influence his later involvement in Indian politics.

Early Political Career

In 1896, Jinnah joined the Indian National Congress, which was the largest Indian political organisation. Like most of the Congress at the time, Jinnah did not favour outright independence, considering British influences on education, law, culture and industry as beneficial to India. Jinnah became a member on the sixty-member Imperial Legislative Council. The council had no real power or authority, and included a large number of un-elected pro-Raj loyalists and Europeans. Nevertheless, Jinnah was instrumental in the passing of the *Child Marriages Restraint Act*, the legitimization of the Muslim waqf (religious endowments) and was appointed to the Sandhurst committee, which helped establish the Indian Military Academy at Dehra Dun. During World War I, Jinnah joined other Indian moderates in supporting the British war effort, hoping that Indians would be rewarded with political freedoms.

Jinnah had initially avoided joining the All India Muslim League, founded in 1906, regarding it as too Muslim oriented. However he decided to provide leadership to the Muslim minority. Eventually, he joined the league in 1913 and became the president at the 1916 session in Lucknow. Jinnah was the architect of the

1916 Lucknow Pact between the Congress and the League, bringing them together on most issues regarding self-government and presenting a united front to the British. Jinnah also played an important role in the founding of the All India Home Rule League in 1916. Along with political leaders Annie Besant and Tilak, Jinnah demanded "home rule" for India—the status of a self-governing dominion in the Empire similar to Canada, New Zealand and Australia. He headed the League's Bombay Presidency chapter.

In 1918, Jinnah married his second wife Rattanbai Petit ("Ruttie"), twenty-four years his junior. She was the fashionable young daughter of his personal friend Sir Dinshaw Petit, of an elite Parsi family of Mumbai. Unexpectedly there was great opposition to the marriage from Rattanbai's family and Parsi society, as well as orthodox Muslim leaders. Rattanbai defied her family and nominally converted to Islam, adopting (though never using) the name Maryam Jinnah, resulting in a permanent estrangement from her family and Parsi society. The couple resided in Mumbai, and frequently travelled across India and Europe. In 1919 she bore Jinnah his only child, daughter Dina Jinnah.

In 1924 Jinnah reorganized the Muslim League, of which he had been president since 1919, and devoted the next seven years attempting to bring about unity among the disparate ranks of Muslims and to develop a rational formula to effect a Hindu Muslim settlement, which he considered the pre condition for Indian freedom. He attended several unity conferences, wrote the Delhi Muslim Proposals in 1927, pleaded for the incorporation of the basic Muslim demands in the Nehru report, and formulated the "Fourteen Points"

Fourteen Points

Jinnah broke with the Congress in 1920 when the Congress leader, Mohandas Gandhi, launched a law violating Non-Cooperation Movement against the British, which a temperamentally law abiding barrister Jinnah disapproved of. Unlike most Congress leaders, Gandhi did not wear western-style clothes, did his best to use an Indian language instead of English, and was deeply rooted to Indian culture. Gandhi's local style of leadership gained great popularity with the Indian people. Jinnah criticised Gandhi's support of the Khilafat Movement, which he saw as an endorsement of religious zealotry. By 1920, Jinnah resigned from the Congress, with a prophetic warning that Gandhi's method of mass struggle would lead to divisions between Hindus and Muslims and within the two communities. Becoming president of the Muslim League, Jinnah was drawn into a conflict between a pro-Congress faction and a pro-British faction.

In September 1923, Jinnah was elected as Muslim member for Bombay in the new Central Legislative Assembly. He showed great gifts as a parliamentarian, organized many Indian members to work with the Swaraj Party, and continued to press demands for full responsible government. He was so active on a wide range of subjects that in 1925 he was offered a knighthood by Lord Reading when he retired as Viceroy and Governor General. Jinnah replied: "I prefer to be plain Mr. Jinnah".

In 1927, Jinnah entered negotiations with Muslim and Hindu leaders on the issue of a future constitution, during the struggle against the all-British Simon Commission. The League wanted separate electorates while the Nehru Report favoured joint electorates. Jinnah personally opposed separate electorates, but then drafted compromises and put forth demands that he thought would satisfy both. These became known as the 14 points of Mr. Jinnah. However, they were rejected by the Congress and other political parties.

Jinnah's personal life and especially his marriage suffered during this period due to his political work. Although they worked to save their marriage by travelling together to Europe when he was appointed to the Sandhurst committee, the couple separated in 1927. Jinnah was deeply saddened when Rattanbai died in 1929, after a serious illness.

At the Round Table Conferences in London, Jinnah was disillusioned by the breakdown of talks. After the failure of the Round Table Conferences, Jinnah returned to London for a few years. In 1936, he returned to India to re-organize Muslim League and contest the elections held under the provisions of the Act of 1935.

Jinnah would receive personal care and support as he became more ill during this time from his sister Fatima Jinnah. She lived and travelled with him, as well as becoming a close advisor. She helped raise his daughter, who was educated in England and India. Jinnah later became estranged from his daughter, Dina Jinnah, after she decided to marry Parsi-born Christian businessman, Neville Wadia (even though he had faced the same issues when he married Rattanbai in 1918). Jinnah continued to correspond cordially with his daughter, but their personal relationship was strained. Dina continued to live in India with her family.

Leader of the Muslim League

Prominent Muslim leaders like the The Aga Khan, Choudhary Rahmat Ali and Sir Muhammad Iqbal made efforts to convince Jinnah to return from London (Where he had moved to in 1931 and planned on permanently relocating in order to practice in the Privy Council Bar.) to India and take charge of a now-reunited Muslim League. In 1934 Jinnah returned and began to re-organise the party, being closely assisted by Liaquat Ali Khan, who would act as his right-hand man. In the 1937 elections to the Central Legislative Assembly, the League emerged as a competent party, capturing a significant number of seats under the Muslim electorate, but lost in the Muslim-majority Punjab, Sindh and the North-West Frontier Province. Jinnah offered an alliance with the Congress-both bodies would face the British together, but the Congress had to share power, accept separate electorates and the League as the representative of India's Muslims. The latter two terms were unacceptable to the Congress, which had its own national Muslim leaders and membership and adhered to secularism. Even as Jinnah held talks with Congress president Rajendra Prasad, Congress leaders suspected that Jinnah would use his position as a lever for exaggerated demands and obstruct government, and demanded that the League merge with the Congress. The talks failed, and while Jinnah declared the resignation of all Congressmen from provincial and central offices in 1938 as a "Day of Deliverance" from Hindu domination, some historians assert that he remained hopeful for an agreement.

In a speech to the League in 1930, Sir Muhammad Iqbal mooted an independent state for Muslims in "northwest India." Choudhary Rahmat Ali published a pamphlet in 1933 advocating a state called "Pakistan". Following the failure to work with the Congress, Jinnah, who had embraced separate electorates and the exclusive right of the League to represent Muslims, was converted to the idea that Muslims needed a separate state to protect their rights. Jinnah came to believe that Muslims and Hindus were distinct nations, with unbridgeable differences—a view later known as the *Two Nation Theory*. Jinnah declared that a united India would lead to the marginalization of Muslims, and eventually civil war between Hindus and Muslims. This change of view may have occurred through his correspondence with Iqbal, who was close to Jinnah. In the session in Lahore in 1940, the Pakistan resolution was adopted as the main goal of the party. The resolution was rejected outright by the Congress, and criticised by many Muslim leaders like Maulana Abul Kalam Azad, Khan Abdul Ghaffar Khan, Syed Ab'ul Ala Maududi and the Jamaat-e-Islami. On July 26, 1943, Jinnah was stabbed and wounded by a member of the extremist Khaksars in an attempted assassination.

Muhammad Ali Jinnah founded *Dawn* in 1941, a major newspaper that helped him propagate the League's point of views. During the mission of British minister Stafford Cripps, Jinnah demanded parity between the number of Congress and League ministers, the League's exclusive right to appoint Muslims and a right for Muslim-majority provinces to secede, leading to the breakdown of talks. Jinnah supported the British effort in World War II, and opposed the Quit India movement. During this period, the League formed provincial governments and entered the central government. The League's influence increased in the Punjab after the death of Unionist leader Sikander Hyat Khan in 1942. Gandhi held talks fourteen times with Jinnah in Bombay in 1944, about a united front—while talks failed, Gandhi's overtures to Jinnah increased the latter's standing with Muslims.

Founding Pakistan

In the 1946 elections for the Constituent Assembly of India, the Congress won most of the elected seats, while the League won a large majority of Muslim electorate seats. The 1946 British Cabinet Mission to India released a plan on May 16, calling for a united Indian state comprising considerably autonomous provinces, and called for "groups" of provinces formed on the basis of religion. A second plan released on June 16, called for the separation of India along religious lines, with princely states to choose between accession to the dominion of their choice or independence. The

Congress, fearing India's fragmentation, criticised the May 16 proposal and rejected the June 16 plan. Jinnah gave the League's assent to both plans, knowing that power would go only to the party that had supported a plan. After much debate and against Gandhi's advice that both plans were divisive, the Congress accepted the May 16 plan while condemning the grouping principle. Jinnah decried this acceptance as "dishonesty", accused the British negotiators of "treachery", and withdrew the League's approval of both plans. The League boycotted the assembly, leaving the Congress in charge of the government but denying it legitimacy in the eyes of many Muslims.

Jinnah gave a precise definition of the term 'Pakistan' in 1941 at Lahore in which he stated:

Some confusion prevails in the minds of some individuals in regard to the use of the work 'Pakistan'. This word has become synonymous with the Lahore resolution owing to the fact that it is a convenient and compendious method of describing [it].... For this reason the British and Indian newspapers generally have adopted the word 'Pakistan' to describe the Moslem demand as embodied in the Lahore resolution.

Jinnah issued a call for all Muslims to launch "Direct Action" on August 16 to "achieve Pakistan". Strikes and protests were planned, but violence broke out all over India, especially in Calcutta and the district of Noakhali in Bengal, and more than 7,000 people were killed in Bihar. Although viceroy Lord Wavell asserted that there was "no satisfactory evidence to that effect", League politicians were blamed by the Congress and the media for orchestrating the violence. Interim Government portfolios were announced on October 25, 1946. Muslim Leaguers were sworn in on October 26, 1946. The League entered the interim government, but Jinnah refrained from accepting office for himself. This was credited as a major victory for Jinnah, as the League entered government having rejected both plans, and was allowed to appoint an equal number of ministers despite being the minority party. The coalition was unable to work, resulting in a rising feeling within the Congress that independence of Pakistan was the only way of avoiding political chaos and possible civil war. The Congress agreed to the division of Punjab and Bengal along religious lines in late 1946. The new viceroy Lord Mountbatten of Burma and

Indian civil servant V. P. Menon proposed a plan that would create a Muslim dominion in West Punjab, East Bengal, Baluchistan and Sindh. After heated and emotional debate, the Congress approved the plan. The North-West Frontier Province voted to join Pakistan in a referendum in July 1947. Jinnah asserted in a speech in Lahore on October 30, 1947 that the League had accepted independence of Pakistan because "the consequences of any other alternative would have been too disastrous to imagine."

The independent state of Pakistan, created on August 14, 1947, represented the outcome of a campaign on the part of the Indian Muslim community for a Muslim homeland which had been triggered by the British decision to consider transferring power to the people of India.

Views on Statehood

A controversy has raged in Pakistan about whether Jinnah wanted Pakistan to be a secular state or an Islamic state. His views as expressed in his policy speech on 11 August 1947 said:

There is no other solution. Now what shall we do? Now, if we want to make this great State of Pakistan happy and prosperous, we should wholly and solely concentrate on the well-being of the people, and especially of the masses and the poor. If you will work in cooperation, forgetting the past, burying the hatchet, you are bound to succeed. If you change your past and work together in a spirit that everyone of you, no matter to what community he belongs, no matter what relations he had with you in the past, no matter what is his colour, caste or creed, is first, second and last a citizen of this State with equal rights, privileges, and obligations, there will be no end to the progress you will make. I cannot emphasize it too much. We should begin to work in that spirit and in course of time all these angularities of the majority and minority communities, the Hindu community and the Muslim community, because even as regards Muslims you have Pathans, Punjabis, Shias, Sunnis and so on, and among the Hindus you have Brahmins, Vashnavas, Khatris, also Bengalis, Madrasis and so on, will vanish. Indeed if you ask me, this has been the biggest hindrance in the way of India to attain the freedom and independence and but for this we would have been free people long long ago. No power can hold another nation, and specially a nation of 400 million souls in subjection; nobody could have conquered you, and even if it had happened, nobody could have continued its hold on you for any length of time, but for this. Therefore, we must learn a lesson from this. You are free; you are free to go to your temples, you are free to go to your mosques or to any other place or worship in this State of Pakistan. You may belong to any religion or caste or creed that has nothing to do with the business of the State. As you know, history shows that in England, conditions, some time ago, were much worse than those prevailing in India today. The Roman Catholics and the Protestants persecuted each other. Even now there are some States in existence where there are discriminations made and bars imposed against a particular class. Thank God, we are not starting in those days. We are starting in the days where there is no discrimination, no distinction between one community and another, no discrimination between one caste or creed and another. We are starting with this fundamental principle that we are all citizens and equal citizens of one State. The people of England in course of time had to face the realities of the situation and had to discharge the responsibilities and burdens placed upon them by the government of their country and they went through that fire step by step. Today, you might say with justice that Roman Catholics and Protestants do not exist; what exists now is that every man is a citizen, an equal citizen of Great Britain and they are all members of the Nation. Now I think we should keep that in front of us as our ideal and you will find that in course of time Hindus would cease to be Hindus and Muslims would cease to be Muslims, not in the religious sense, because that is the personal faith of each individual, but in the political sense as citizens of the State. *Jinnah, 11th August 1947-presiding over the constituent assembly.*

While this may seem to be an indication that Jinnah wanted a secular state, he also referred to Islam and Islamic principles:

The constitution of Pakistan has yet to be framed by the Pakistan Constituent Assembly. I do not know what the ultimate shape of this constitution is going to be, but I am sure that it will be of a democratic type, embodying the essential principle of Islam. Today, they are as applicable in actual life as they were 1,300 years ago. Islam and its idealism have taught us democracy. It has taught equality of man, justice and fairplay to everybody. We are the inheritors of these glorious traditions and are fully alive to our responsibilities and obligations as framers of the future constitution of Pakistan. In any case Pakistan is not going to be a theocratic State to be ruled by priests with a divine mission. We have many non-Muslims —Hindus, Christians, and Parsis —but they are all Pakistanis. They will enjoy the same rights and privileges as any other citizens and will play their rightful part in the affairs of Pakistan. *Broadcast talk to the people of the United States of America on Pakistan recorded February, 1948.*

It has been argued by many people that in this speech Jinnah wanted to point out that Pakistan would be a secular state as mostly people think that an Islamic state is a theocratic state. This perception, however, is wrong and is misinterpreted; the reason is that a true Islamic state is not a theocratic state, as rightly stated by Jinnah in his speech.

On the opening ceremony of the state bank of Pakistan Jinnah pointed out that the financial setup of the state should be based on Islamic economic system.

We must work our destiny in our own way and present to the world an economic system based on true Islamic concept of equality of manhood and social justice. We will thereby be fulfilling our mission as Muslims and giving to humanity the message of peace which alone can save it and secure the welfare, happiness and prosperity of mankind. *Speech at the opening ceremony of State Bank of Pakistan, Karachi July 1, 1948*

It appears that Jinnah felt the state of Pakistan should stand upon Islamic tradition in culture, civilization and national identity rather than on the principles of Islam as a theocratic state.

In 1937, Jinnah further defended his ideology of equality in his speech to the All-India Muslim League in Lucknow where he stated, "Settlement can only be achieved between equals." He also had a rebuttal to Nehru's statement which argued that the only two parties that mattered in India were the British Raj and INC. Jinnah stated that the Muslim League was the third and "equal partner" within Indian politics.

Governor-General

Along with Liaquat Ali Khan and Abdur Rab Nishtar, Muhammad Ali Jinnah represented the League in the Division

Council to appropriately divide public assets between India and Pakistan. The assembly members from the provinces that would comprise Pakistan formed the new state's constituent assembly, and the Military of British India was divided between Muslim and non-Muslim units and officers. Indian leaders were angered at Jinnah's courting the princes of Jodhpur, Bhopal and Indore to accede to Pakistan-these princely states were not geographically aligned with Pakistan, and each had a Hindu-majority population.

Jinnah became the first Governor-General of Pakistan and president of its constituent assembly. Inaugurating the assembly on August 11, 1947, Jinnah spoke of an inclusive and pluralist democracy promising equal rights for all citizens regardless of religion, caste or creed. This address is a cause of much debate in Pakistan as, on its basis, many claim that Jinnah wanted a secular state while supporters of Islamic Pakistan assert that this speech is being taken out of context when compared to other speeches by him.

On October 11, 1947, in an address to Civil, Naval, Military and Air Force Officers of Pakistan Government, Karachi, he said:

We should have a State in which we could live and breathe as free men and which we could develop according to our own lights and culture and where principles of Islamic social justice could find free play.

On February 21, 1948, in an address to the officers and men of the 5th Heavy Ack Ack and 6th Light Ack Ack Regiments in Malir, Karachi, he said:

You have to stand guard over the development and maintenance of Islamic democracy, Islamic social justice and the equality of manhood in your own native soil. With faith, discipline and selfless devotion to duty, there is nothing worthwhile that you cannot achieve.

The office of Governor-General was ceremonial, but Jinnah also assumed the lead of government. The first months of Pakistan's independence were absorbed in ending the intense violence that had arisen in the wake of acrimony between Hindus and Muslims. Jinnah agreed with Indian leaders to organise a swift and secure exchange of populations in the Punjab and Bengal. He visited the border regions with Indian leaders to calm people and encourage peace, and organised large-scale refugee camps. Despite these efforts, estimates on the death toll vary from around two hundred thousand, to over a million people. The estimated number of refugees in both countries exceeds 15 million. The then capital city of Karachi saw an explosive increase in its population owing to the large encampments of refugees, which personally affected and depressed Jinnah.

In his first visit to East Pakistan, under the advice of local party leaders, Jinnah stressed that Urdu alone should be the national language; a policy that was strongly opposed by the Bengali people of East Pakistan (now Bangladesh). This opposition grew after he controversially described Bengali as the language of Hindus.

Jinnah authorised force to achieve the annexation of the princely state of Kalat and suppress the insurgency in Baluchistan. He controversially accepted the accession of Junagadh—a Hindu-majority state with a Muslim ruler located in the Saurashtra peninsula, some 400 kilometres (250 mi) southeast of Pakistan—but this was annulled by Indian intervention. It is unclear if Jinnah planned or knew of the tribal invasion from Pakistan into the kingdom of Jammu and Kashmir in October 1947, but he did send his private secretary Khurshid Ahmed to observe developments in Kashmir. When informed of Kashmir's accession to India, Jinnah deemed the accession illegitimate and ordered the Pakistani army to enter Kashmir. However, Gen. Auchinleck, the supreme commander of all British officers informed Jinnah that while India had the right to send troops to Kashmir, which had acceded to it, Pakistan did not. If Jinnah persisted, Auchinleck would remove all British officers from both sides. As Pakistan had a greater proportion of Britons holding senior command, Jinnah cancelled his order, but protested to the United Nations to intercede.

Death

Through the 1940s, Jinnah suffered from tuberculosis; only his sister and a few others close to him were aware of his condition. In 1948, Jinnah's health began to falter, hindered further by the heavy workload that had fallen upon him following Pakistan's independence from British Rule. Attempting to recuperate, he spent many months at his official retreat in Ziarat. According to his sister, he suffered a hemorrhage on September 1, 1948; doctors said the altitude was not good for him and that he should be taken to Karachi. Jinnah agreed, but he died in Quetta on September 11,

1948 (just over a year after independence) from a combination of tuberculosis and lung cancer. It is said that when the then Viceroy of India, Lord Louis Mountbatten, learned of Jinnah's ailment he said 'had they known that Jinnah was about to die, they'd have postponed India's independence by a few months as he was being inflexible on Pakistan'.

Mohammed Ali Jinnah was flown back to Karachi from Quetta. He was buried in Karachi. His funeral was followed by the construction of a massive mausoleum—Mazar-e-Quaid—in Karachi to honour him; official and military ceremonies are hosted there on special occasions.

He had two separate Funeral prayers one was held privately at Mohatta Palace in a room of the Governor-General's House at which Yusuf Haroon, Hashim Raza and Aftab Hatim Alvi were present at the Namaz-e-Janaza held according to Shia rituals and was led by Syed Anisul Husnain Rizvi, while Liaquat Ali Khan waited outside. After the Shia ritual, the major public Funeral prayers were led by Allamah Shabbir Ahmad Usmani a renowned mainstream Muslim (Sunni) scholar and attended by masses from all over Pakistan. This funeral was well on record and supported by pictures as well.

Dina Wadia remained in India after independence, before ultimately settling in New York City. Jinnah's grandson, Nusli Wadia, is a prominent industrialist residing in Mumbai. In the 1963–1964 elections, Jinnah's sister Fatima Jinnah, known as *Madar-e-Millat* ("Mother of the Nation"), became the presidential candidate of a coalition of political parties that opposed the rule of President Ayub Khan, but lost the election.

The Jinnah House in Malabar Hill, Bombay, is in the possession of the Government of India but the issue of its ownership has been disputed by the Government of Pakistan. Jinnah had personally requested Indian Prime Minister Jawaharlal Nehru to preserve the house and that one day he could return to Mumbai.

There are proposals for the house be offered to the Government of Pakistan to establish a consulate in the city, as a goodwill gesture, but Dina Wadia has also laid claim to the property. Recently she has been involved in litigation regarding Jinnah House claiming that Hindu Law is applicable to Jinnah as he was a Khoja Shia.

Legacy

'Few individuals significantly alter the course of history. Fewer still modify the map of the world. Hardly anyone can be credited with creating a nation-state. Muhammad Ali Jinnah did all three.'- Stanley Wolpert

In Pakistan, Jinnah is honoured with the official title Quaid-i-Azam, and he is depicted on all Pakistani rupee notes of denominations five and higher, and is the namesake of many Pakistani public institutions. The former *Quaid-i-Azam International Airport*, now called the Jinnah International Airport, in Karachi is Pakistan's busiest.

One of the largest streets in the Turkish capital Ankara — Cinnah Caddesi —is named after him. In Iran, one of the capital Tehran's most important new highways is also named after him, while the government released a stamp commemorating the centennial of Jinnah's birthday. In Chicago, a portion of Devon Avenue was named as "Mohammed Ali Jinnah Way". The Mazar-e-Quaid, Jinnah's mausoleum, is among Karachi's most imposing buildings. In media, Jinnah was portrayed by British actors Richard Lintern (as the young Jinnah) and Christopher Lee (as the elder Jinnah) in the 1998 film *Jinnah*. In Richard Attenborough's film *Gandhi*, Jinnah was portrayed by Alyque Padamsee. In the 1986 televised mini-series *Lord Mountbatten: the Last Viceroy*, Jinnah was played by Polish actor Vladek Sheybal.

Some historians like H M Seervai and Ayesha Jalal assert that Jinnah never wanted partition of India —it was the outcome of the Congress leaders being unwilling to share power with the Muslim League. It is asserted that Jinnah only used the Pakistan demand as a method to mobilise support to obtain significant political rights for Muslims.

Jinnah has gained the admiration of major Indian nationalist politicians like Lal Krishna Advani—whose comments praising Jinnah caused an uproar in his own Bharatiya Janata Party (BJP). Jaswant Singh likewise praised Jinnah for standing up to the Indian National Congress and the British. In August 2009, Singh was expelled from the BJP for writing a controversial book praising Jinnah, and shortly after, the state of Gujarat banned Singh's book because of its negative statements about Vallabhbhai Patel, the first home minister of India. Although Jaswant Singh's book does portray the failure of Jinnah's Ideology of Indian Muslim's forming a separate Kaum (Nation) evident from the separation of Bangladesh in 1971.

Criticism

Some critics allege that Jinnah's courting the princes of Hindu states and his gambit with Junagadh is proof of ill intentions towards India, as he was the proponent of the theory that Hindus and Muslims could not live together, yet being interested in Hindu-majority states. In his book *Patel: A Life,* Rajmohan Gandhi asserts that Jinnah sought to engage the question of Junagadh with an eye on Kashmir—he wanted India to ask for a plebiscite in Junagadh, knowing thus that the principle then would have to be applied to Kashmir, where the Muslim-majority would, he believed, vote for Pakistan.

According to Akbar S. Ahmed, nearly every book about Jinnah outside Pakistan mentions the fact that he drank alcohol. Several sources indicate he gave up alcohol near the end of his life.

Apart from cultural legacies, it seems that Mohammad Ali Jinnah left a legacy as one of the most controversially portrayed figures in contemporary Asian history. From a Hindu nationalist perspective, Jinnah tends to be depicted as a cunning and relentless force that compromised the unity of India to create Pakistan, for a range of religious, cultural, political, and personal motives ;On other hand Jaswant Singh, a former BJP leader, viewed Nehru, not Mohammad Ali Jinnah, as causing the partition of India, mostly referring to his highly centralised policies for an independent India in 1947, which Jinnah opposed in favour of a more decentralised India. The split between the two was among the causes of partition. It is believed that personal animosity between the two leaders led to the partition of India.. Pakistanis tend to view Jinnah as a revered founding father, a man that was dedicated to safeguarding Muslim interests during independence movements in India, whatever the cost. Despite any of a range of biases, it almost impossible to argue that, despite motive and manner, there is any figure during the first half of the twentieth century that had more of an influence on the formation of modern day Pakistan than Jinnah.

Lahore Resolution

The Lahore Resolution, commonly known as the Pakistan Resolution, was a formal political statement adopted by the Muslim League at the occasion of its three-day general session on 22–24 March 1940 that called for greater Muslim autonomy in British India. This has been largely interpreted as a demand for a separate Muslim state, Pakistan. The resolution was presented by A. K. Fazlul Huq.

Although the name "Pakistan" had been proposed by Choudhary Rahmat Ali in his Pakistan Declaration in 1933, Muhammad Ali Jinnah and other leaders had kept firm their belief in Hindu-Muslim unity. However, the volatile political climate and religious hostilities gave the idea stronger backing.

Background

With the beginning of the Second World War in September 1939, the Viceroy of India Lord Linlithgow declared India's entrance into the war without consulting the provincial governments. In this situation, Jinnah called a general session of the All India Muslim League in Lahore to discuss the circumstances and also analyze the reasons for the defeat of Muslim League in the Indian general election of 1937 in some Muslim majority provinces.

Proceedings

The session was held between 22 March and 24 March, 1940, at Manto Park (now Iqbal Park), Lahore. The welcome address was made by Nawab Sir Shah Nawaz Mamdot. In his speech, Jinnah recounted the contemporary situation, stressing that the problem of India was no more of an inter-communal nature, but manifestly an international. He criticised the Congress and the nationalist Muslims, and espoused the Two-Nation Theory and the reasons for the demand for separate Muslim homelands. According to Stanley Wolpert, this was the moment when Jinnah, the former ambassador of Hindu-Muslim unity, totally transformed himself into Pakistan's great leader.

Sikandar Hayat Khan, the Chief Minister of the Punjab, drafted the original Lahore Resolution, which was placed before the Subject Committee of the All India Muslim League for discussion and amendments. The Resolution text unanimously rejected the concept of a United India on the grounds of growing inter-communal violence and recommended the creation of an independent Muslim state.

After the presentation of the annual report by Liaquat Ali Khan, the Resolution was moved in the general session by A.K. Fazlul Huq, the Chief Minister of undivided Bengal and was seconded by Choudhury Khaliquzzaman who explained his views on the causes which led to the demand of a separate state. Subsequently, Maulana Zafar Ali Khan from Punjab, Sardar Aurangzeb from the North-West Frontier Province, Sir Abdullah Haroon from Sindh, and Qazi Esa from Baluchistan, and other leaders announced their support. In the same session, Jinnah also presented a resolution to condemn the Khaksar massacre of 19 March, owing to a clash between the Khaksars and the police, that had resulted in the loss of lives.

The Statement

The principle text of the Lahore Resolution was passed on 24 March. In 1941 it became part of the Muslim League's constitution. In 1946, it formed the basis for the decision of Muslim League to struggle for one state for the Muslims. The statement declared:

No constitutional plan would be workable or acceptable to the Muslims unless geographical contiguous units are demarcated into regions which should be so constituted with such territorial readjustments as may be necessary. That the areas in which the Muslims are numerically in majority as in the North-Western and Eastern zones of India should be grouped to constitute independent states in which the constituent units shall be autonomous and sovereign.

Additionally, it stated: That adequate, effective and mandatory safeguards shall be specifically provided in the constitution for minorities in the units and in the regions for the protection of their religious, cultural, economic, political, administrative and other rights of the minorities, with their consultation. Arrangements thus should be made for the security of Muslims where they were in a minority.

Pakistan Resolution in the Sindh Assembly

The Sindh assembly was the first British Indian legislature to pass the resolution in favour of Pakistan. G. M. Syed, an influential Sindhi activist, revolutionary and Sufi and one of the important leaders to the forefront of the provincial autonomy movement joined the Muslim League in 1938 and presented the Pakistan resolution in the Sindh Assembly. This text was buried under the Minar-e-Pakistan during its building in the Ayub regime.

Commemoration

- To commemorate the event, *Minar-e-Pakistan,* a 60 meters tall distinctive monument in the shape of a minaret has been built at the site in Iqbal Park Lahore, where the resolution was passed.
- 23 March is a national holiday in Pakistan, celebrated as Republic Day to commemorate Lahore Resolution as well as the day in 1956 when the country became the first Islamic Republic.

Khaksars

The Khaksar Tehrik was a social movement based in Lahore, British India, established by Allama Mashriqi in 1930 to free India from foreign rule, to uplift the masses, and to revive the Muslims, who had previously ruled parts of India at different times during a period spanning nearly a thousand years. Although Mashriqi firmly believed that the right to rule India belonged to the Muslims, at the same time, he wanted to create an environment of fairness, justice, and equal rights for non-Muslims as well. For this reason, non-Muslims were allowed to join the Tahrik keeping it free from prejudice against any person, regardless of his/her caste, colour, creed. The word "Khaksar" is derived from the Persian language, *Khak* means *dust,* and *Sar* means *life,* roughly translated as "a humble person." The Khaksar Tehrik worked under a charter that everyone was required to follow, with no exceptions. The charter was created to ensure all were treated fairly; even Allama Mashriqi, founder and leader of the Tehrik, was held accountable for his actions. The Tehrik was also kept free of any membership fee. All Khaksars were required to bear their own expenses and donate their time. The purpose was to develop the spirit of self-reliance and encourag the Khaksars to spend their own money and time for the national cause.

Attire and Spade

The Khaksars all wore the same khaki attire with the word "Ukhuwwat" (brotherhood) written on the sleeve of their shirts. In their hands, they carried a belcha (spade). The attire was chosen specifically, the Khaki colour of their clothing was chosen because it is closest to the colour of the Earth.

The spade represents humility, in the same way that a spade is used to level the ground, the Khaksars used it as a symbol of the "leveling" of society. Most importantly, the Khaki attire and spade was designed to remove the barrier between the rich and the poor. This dress code was created to bring equality among all members of the Khaskars regardless of their economic or social background.

Goals and Functions

1. Reform the nation by laying emphasis on character building.
2. Remove sectarianism and prejudices and bring brotherhood and unity to the people.
3. Impart the spirit of sacrifice for the national cause.
4. Make community service an integral part of every Khaksar. Every Khaksar was required to perform community service for Muslims as well as non-Muslims. The community service included helping the poor, elderly, sick, needy, etc. Khaksars were also required to help keep their respective neighborhoods clean. In the event of a national calamity or disaster, Khaksars were required to render all services to help the affected people. Social service created brotherhood and a spirit of nation building among the Khaksars and set an example for others to follow. The gathering of Khaksars every evening brought them together and gave them a sense of achievement and pride because they were performing a collective duty towards the national cause.
5. Remove distinction between the rich and the poor. Every Khaksar was required to wear Khaki clothes in order to bring equality and a sense of belonging to the Tehrik.
6. Impart discipline in every Khaksar.

7. Impart soldierly and disciplined training in order to ensure the physical and mental health.
8. Produce leaders. To achieve this, a system of ranks was introduced to the Tehrik.
9. Achieve freedom.
10. Finally, bring peace and unite humanity by creating love among the people.

Mashriqi worked to achieve the goals that he had set forth for the Khaksar Tehrik. The ideals of the Tehrik combined with Mashriqi's speeches and writings soon attracted a following, predominantly Muslims. These people came from all walks of life and from every part of the Indian sub-continent. By the late 1930s, the Movement was at its peak and had not only through-out India, but had established offices in other countries as well. Mashriqi's followers, supporters, and sympathizers were now well into the millions.

Growth

The membership of the Khaksar Tehreek was over 4 million. In 1942, *The Eastern Times* reported:

"He [Mashraqi] asserted that 40 lakh [four million] persons had joined his movement and they carried the red badge on their shoulders.".

The veteran journalist Syed Shabbir Hussain wrote in his book titled*Kashmir Aur Allama Mashriqi*:

"In the span of 17 years, four million people showed their inclination towards this movement"..

On 4 October 1939 after the commencement of the Second World War, Mashriqui, who was then in Lucknow jail, offered to increase the size of the organization to help with the war effort. He offered a force of 30,000 well drilled soldiers for the internal defence of India, 10,000 for the police, and 10,000 to provide help for Turkey or to fight on European soil. His offer was not accepted.

Mashraqi was released from Vellore Jail on January 19, 1942, but his movements were restricted to Madras Presidency. He remained interned until December 28, 1942. Mashraqi arrived in New Delhi on January 2, 1942.

Allama Mashriqi disbanded the Khaksar Tehrik on July 4, 1947. Khaksar Tehrik was revived after the death of Allama Mashriqi. It operates in different parts of Pakistan.

After the creation of Pakistan, Allama Mashriqi founded the Islam League. This organization was started in October 1947.

Pakistan Movement

Pakistan Movement or Tehrik-e-Pakistan has its origins in the United Provinces of Agra and Oudh (present day Uttar Pradesh). Muslims there were a minority, yet their Elite had a disproportionate amount of representaion in the civil service and overall influence. The idea of Pakistan began from this part of Northern India, from the Elite of this region to popular following and then onwards to the rest of India. The movement was led by a lawyer named Muhammad Ali Jinnah, along with such leaders as Allama Iqbal, Liaqat Ali Khan, Fatima Jinnah, Huseyn Shaheed Suhrawardy, A.K. Fazlul Huq, and Sardar Abdur Rab Nishtar among the many others.

History of the Movement

Minority Muslims

Muhammad Ali Jinnah desired to build a state on a principle, composed of three parts, "one nation, one culture, one language". Pakistan was to be the homeland of Muslims belonging to British India. Jinnah represented the Muslims of the British Raj, who belonged to the provinces where Muslims were a minority i.e. present-day Uttar Pradesh, Bihar, Gujarat and Maharashtra. Muslims who migrated to Pakistan after the partition are known as Muhajirs in Pakistan today. The replacement of Persian, in 1837, with English and the local languages, of the various provinces of British-ruled India, as official and court languages, resulted in Hindi being given the same status as Urdu as an official language of the United Provinces of Agra and Oudh. This made the Muslim elite wary. Furthermore, the democratization process by the British in the late 1800s, made these Muslims feel that they would lose all of their privileged influence.

In 1909, the British allowed their subjects elect part of their Legislative Councils. This move added further to the fears of marginalization among Muslims as they made up only 20% of the population of British India and, to make matters worse, only a small number of them (20%) even bothered to vote (1881 census). The provinces where the Muslims were a minority were the most alarmed, particularly those belonging to the United Provinces of Agra and Oudh as the Muslim elite there had the most to lose. In the United Provinces, Muslims made up only 13.4% of the population but held 45% of the civil service jobs. An example of the privilege they still enjoyed.

In the late 1800s, the Muslims from the United Provinces assembled under Syed Ahmed Khan. First of all, he wanted to improve education within his community. Toward this goal he founded the Muhammedan Anglo-Oriental College (MAO College) in Aligarh in 1869 which later developed into the Aligarh Muslim University by 1911. MAO College produced the first opponents of the Indian National Congress. Congress claimed to represent all Indians, but Muslims made up only 6.6% of the delegates between 1892 and 1909.

The 1882 local self-government act had already troubled Syed Ahmed Khan. When, in 1906, the British announced their intention to establish Legislative Councils, Muhsin al-Mulk, the secretary of MAO College, hoping to win a separate Legislative Council for Muslims, led a delegation to meet with Viceroy Lord Minto, a deal to which Minto agreed because it followed the British divide and rule strategy. The UP Muslims were over-represented in the delegation, which included only seven Punjabis and one Bengali, totally out of proportion to their numbers.

The role of the graduates from Aligarh in creating the Muslim League and then taking part in the Khilafat movement shows the significance of UP Muslims in the origin of Muslim separatist ideas in India. These Muslims actually had a sense of Muslim identity. Separatist feelings among Muslims developed due to not discrimination but social and economic factors. The Muslim elite of UP saw their influence being challenged by the Hindu elite who benefited from their much more speedy integration into the English medium education system.

Though Muslim separatism was diluted as a result of the irregularity of social dissatisfaction felt by the community, people from present-day Uttar Pradesh, Bihar, Gujarat (Jinnah's native state) and Maharashtra were anxious to distance themselves from the growing Hindu influence. However, the Muslims in majority from Greater Punjab, Greater Bengal, Sindh, and NWFP did not share the same sentiment, as they ruled their own regions: Punjab abd Bengal. Jinnah's task was to convince these Muslims into backing the two-nation theory.

For Jinnah, Islam laid a cultural base for an ideology of ethnic nationalism whose objective was to gather the Muslim community in order to defend the Muslim minorities. Jinnah's representation of minoritarian Muslims was quite apparent in 1928, when in the All-Party Muslim Conference, he was ready to swap the advantages of separate electorates for a quota of 33% of seats at the Centre. He maintained his views at the Round Table Conferences, while the Muslims of Punjab and Bengal were vying for a much more decentralized political setup. Many of their requests were met in the 1935 Government of India Act. Jinnah and Muslim League played a peripheral role at the time and in 1937 could manage to gather only 5% of the Muslim vote. Jinnah refused to back down and went ahead with his separatist plan. He presented the two-nation theory in the now famous Lahore Resolution in March 1940, seeking a separate Muslim state,

The idea of a separate state had first been introduced by Allama Iqbal in his speech in December 1930 as the President of the Muslim League.. The state that he visualized included only Punjab, Sindh, North West Frontier Province (NWFP), and Balochistan. Three years later, the name Pakistan was proposed in a declaration in 1933 by Choudhary Rahmat Ali, a University of Cambridge graduate. Again, Bengal was left out of the proposal.. In the Lahore Resolution of March 1940, the proposed state's name remained unrecognized and its borders so undetermined that it was not clear whether there would be one Muslim state or two. It stated "that the areas in which the Muslims are numerically in a majority, as in the north-western and eastern zones of India should be grouped to constitute independent states in which the constituent units shall be autonomous and sovereign."

Part of Jinnah's strategy to entice the leaders of those provinces who continued to oppose the idea of Pakistan was to present all the provinces as loose groupings of the state. The 1937 election resulted in a major shift in Indian politics; the Congress won in seven provinces and lost in four. The Congress success worried the Muslims. Jinnah grasped this moment and suggested that Muslims would be left to contend with a Hindu government after the withdrawal of the British. He stated that "Hindu Congress" was "putting Islam in danger."

Punjab

This was an effective move by Jinnah, especially in Punjab, where the Muslim League had to fend off not just the Congress, whose support base was Hindus living in the cities, but also the Unionist Party, founded in 1922, by peasant leaders Fazl-e-Hussain (a Muslim) and Chhotu Ram (a Hindu). This party won all the elections between 1923 and 1937. However, Fazl-e-Hussain died in 1936 and in September 1937, the new party leader, Sikandar Hayat Khan (Punjabi politician) agreed to sign a pact with Jinnah. Sikandar Hayat Khan's motives remain unclear, but it is suspected that he hoped to become the leader of Muslim League in his own province, if not its ultimate leader. Whatever be the reason, this helped the Muslim League to carve out a niche in Punjab. In the 1946 election campaign, the Muslim League was able to publicize its views widely. It claimed that Islam was threatened by Congress. "Pirs" and "Sajjada Nashin" helped the Muslim League to attract Muslim voters. It won 75 seats to Union Party's 10.

Sindh

In Sindh, the Muslim League remained at the margins till the mid-1940s. Just as in Punjab, it faced two parties, Congress and the Sindh United Party, which had been founded in 1936 when the Sindh Province came into being. Its inspiration was the Punjab Unionist Party. The Muslim League first gained a foothold in Sindh in the 1930s over the Manzilgarh issue, named after a very controversial site that the Muslim League wanted to officially declare as a mosque.

The Muslim League in Sindh was more interested in defending Sindhi culture than in creating an Islamic state for British Raj Muslims. This was obvious from the behaviour of its leader in the 1940s, G. M. Syed, who left Congress in 1938 to become the leader of the Muslim League in Sindh. He championed the cause of regional self-determination in 1946 at the Cabinet Mission. He had been dismissed from the Muslim League, but the Muslim League in Sindh continued to remain steeped in Sindhi nationalism. Many

Sindhis regarded the formation of Pakistan as a way of freeing their region from British rule.

Bengal

In Bengal, the Muslim League enjoyed more support than in the other majoritarian Provinces. But even here, it gained strength later on. Its popularity was based on its ability to create separatist feelings in East Bengal where the Muslims were mostly concentrated. Here again, the Muslim League had to face off two parties in the 1930s: the Congress and the Krishak Proja Party, a peasant party, founded in 1936 by A.K.Fazlul Haq. This party narrowly ousted the Muslim League by winning 31% of the votes, compared to Muslim League's 27% in the 1937 Elections. However, by 1946, the League had won 104 of the 111 seats, by again branding the Congress as "Hindu" and calling it a "threat-to Islam." However, the success of the two-nation theory depended on the strong regional feelings with the President of the Bengal Muslim League, declaring in 1944, that religion transcends geographical boundaries, but culture does not and so Bengalis are different from people of other provinces of India and the "religious brothers" of Pakistan.

NWFP

In NWFP, the Muslim League faced its hardest challenge yet. It had intense competition from Khan Abdul Ghaffar Khan dubbed as the "Frontier Gandhi" due to his efforts in following in the footsteps of Gandhi. The popularity of the Congress, along with the strong Paktoon identity created by Ghaffar Khan in the cultural and the political arenas made life hard for the Muslim League. With the support of Ghaffar Khan, the Congress was able to contain the Muslim League to the non-Pakhtoon areas, particularly, the Hazara region. The Muslim League could only manage to win 17 seats, against the 30 won by Congress, in the 1946 elections.

Conclusion

In conclusion, Muslim separatism has its origin in the Provinces where the minoritarian Muslims resided as they faced social and political marginalization. In 1946, the Muslim majorities agreed to the idea of Pakistan, as a response to Congress, portrayed as the "Hindu" party by Jinnah, winning in seven out of the 11 provinces. This was a small moment of political unity as the

Muslim League had not completely established itself in the provinces where the Muslims were in a majority. The principal role of the Muslims of UP was clearly visible from their over-representation in the governing body of the Muslim League. Prior to 1938, Bengal with 33 million Muslims had only 10 representatives, less than the United Provinces of Agra and Oudh, which were home to only seven million Muslims. The desire of the Muslim minorities to dominate a nation that was still to be created, or whose creation had to be sustained, became obvious soon after Partition in 1947, when a clause in the Lahore Resolution which stated that "constituent units [of the states to come] shall be autonomous and sovereign" was not respected. This clause was used only to bring on board Muslim majorities. Once Pakistan was born, there was no longer any need to woo Muslims who were in majority in any region.

Migration

Data from the 1951 census suggests that migrants constituted 7 million people in Pakistan with 6.3 million in West Pakistan and 700,000 in East Pakistan, the majority being Punjabis who crossed from East Punjab to West Punjab and hence settled in the same cultural environment. However, there were 100,000 people who went from Bihar to East Bengal and a million from the United Provinces, Bombay Presidency and Hyderabad who migrated to West Pakistan. These groups later on came to be known as Muhajirs in Pakistan. At the time of partition, migrants from the United Provinces of Agra and Oudh made up only 2% of the migrants and 3% of Pakistan's total Population.

Statements and Sayings

Allama Iqbal : "I would like to see the Punjab, North-West Frontier Province, Sindh and Baluchistan amalgamated into a single State. Self-government within the British Empire, or without the British Empire, the formation of a consolidated North-West Indian Muslim State appears to me to be the final destiny of the Muslims, at least of North-West India. "

Choudhary Rahmat Ali

"At this solemn hour in the history of India, when British and Indian statesmen are laying the foundations of a Federal

Constitution for that land, we address this appeal to you, in the name of our common heritage, on behalf of our thirty million Muslim brethren who live in *Pakistan*-by which we mean the five Northern units of India, Viz: Punjab, North-West Frontier Province (Afghan Province), Kashmir, Sindh and Baluchistan-for your sympathy and support in our grim and fateful struggle against political crucifixion and complete annihilation. "

Quaid-e-Azam

"It is extremely difficult to appreciate why our Hindu friends fail to understand the real nature of Islam and Hinduism. They are not religious in the strict sense of the word, but are, in fact, different and distinct social orders, and it is a dream that the Hindus and Muslims can ever evolve a common nationality, and this misconception of one Indian nation has troubles and will lead India to destruction if we fail to revise our notions in time. The Hindus and Muslims belong to two different religious philosophies, social customs, literatures. They neither intermarry nor interdine together and, indeed, they belong to two different civilizations which are based mainly on conflicting ideas and conceptions. Their aspect on life and of life are different. It is quite clear that Hindus and Mussalmans derive their inspiration from different sources of history. They have different epics, different heroes, and different episodes. Very often the hero of one is a foe of the other and, likewise, their victories and defeats overlap. To yoke together two such nations under a single state, one as a numerical minority and the other as a majority, must lead to growing discontent and final

Direct Action Day

Direct Action Day, also known as the Great Calcutta Riot, was on 16 August 1946—a day of widespread riot and manslaughter in the city of Calcutta (now known as Kolkata) in the Bengal province of British India. The day also marked the start of what is known as "The Week of the Long Knives".

The Muslim League and the Indian National Congress were the two largest political parties in the Constituent Assembly of India in the 1940s. The 1946 Cabinet Mission to India for planning of the transfer of power from the British Raj to the Indian leadership proposed an initial plan of composition of the new Dominion of India and its government. However, soon an alternative plan to divide the British Raj into a Hindu-majority India and a Muslim-majority Pakistan was proposed. The Congress rejected the alternative proposal outright. Muslim League planned general strike (*hartal*) on 16 August to protest this rejection, and to assert its demand for a separate Muslim homeland.

The protest triggered massive riots in Calcutta. In Calcutta, within 72 hours, more than 4,000 people lost their lives and 100,000 residents in the city of Calcutta were left homeless. Violence in Calcutta sparked off further religious riots in the surrounding regions of Noakhali, Bihar, United Province (modern Uttar Pradesh), Punjab, and the North Western Frontier Province. These events sowed the seeds for the eventual Partition of India.

Background

In 1946, the Indian independence movement against the British Raj had reached a pivotal stage when the British Prime Minister Clement Attlee sent a three member Cabinet Mission to India aimed at discussing and finalising plans for the transfer of power from the British Raj to the Indian leadership, providing India with independence under Dominion status in the Commonwealth of Nations. After holding talks with the representatives of the Indian National Congress and the All India Muslim League—the two largest political parties in the Constituent Assembly of India—on May 16, 1946, the Mission proposed initial plans of composition of the new Dominion of India and its government. On June 16, under pressure from the Muslim League headed by Muhammad Ali Jinnah, the Mission proposed an alternative plan to arrange for India to be divided into Hindu-majority India and a Muslim-majority Pakistan. The princely states of India would be permitted to accede to either dominion or attain independence.

Muhammad Ali Jinnah, the one time Congressman and Indian Nationalist, and now the leader of the Muslim League, had accepted the Cabinet Mission Plan of 16 June whereas the Congress rejected it outright. On July 10, Jawaharlal Nehru held a press conference in Bombay declaring that the Congress had agreed only to participate in the Constituent Assembly and regarded itself free to change or modify the Cabinet Mission Plan as it thought best.

Fearing *Hindu Domination* in the Constituent Assembly, Jinnah denounced the British Cabinet Mission and decided to boycott the Constituent Assembly to try and put pressure on Congress and the British, by resorting to "Direct Action".

In July 1946, Jinnah held a press conference at his home in Bombay where he declared his intent to create Pakistan. Jinnah proclaimed that the Muslim league was "preparing to launch a struggle" and that they "have chalked a plan". He had decided to boycott the Constituent Assembly. He rejected the British plan for transfer of power to an interim government which would combine both the Muslim League and the Indian National Congress. He said that if the Muslims were not granted Pakistan then he would launch "Direct Action". When asked to specify Jinnah retorted: "Go to the Congress and ask them their plans. When they take you into their confidence I will take you into mine. Why do you expect me alone to sit with folded hands? I also am going to make trouble."

On the next day, Jinnah announced August 16, 1946 would be "Direct Action Day" for the purpose of winning the separate Muslim state and warned congress, "We do not want war, if you want war we accept your offer unhesitatingly. We shall have India divided or we shall have India destroyed." Muslim League Council Meeting held during the period 27 July–29 July 1946 passed a resolution declaring, the Direct Action Day was intended to unfold "direct action for the achievement of Pakistan."

In his book *The Great Divide,* H V Hodson recounted, "The working committee followed up by calling on Muslims throughout India to observe 16th August as direct action day. On that Day meeting would be held all over the country to explain League's resolution. These meetings and processions passed off — as was manifestly the Central league leaders' intention — without more than commonplace and limited disturbance with one vast and tragic exception... what happened was more than anyone could have foreseen."

In *Muslim Societies: Historical and Comparative Aspects,* edited by Sato Tsugitaka, Nakazato Nariaki writes:

"From the viewpoint of institutional politics, the Calcutta disturbances possessed a distinguishing feature in that they broke out in a transitional period which was marked by the power vacuum and systemic breakdown. It is also important to note that they constituted part of a political struggle in which the Congress and the Muslim League competed with each other for the initiative in establishing the new nation-state(s), while the British made an all-out attempt to carry out decolonization at the lowest possible political cost for them. The political rivalry among the major nationalist parties in Bengal took a form different from that in New Delhi, mainly because of the broad mass base those organizations enjoyed and the tradition of flexible political dealing in which they excelled. At the initial stage of the riots, the Congress and the Muslim League appeared to be confident that they could draw on this tradition even if a difficult situation arose out of political showdown. Most probably, Direct Action Day in Calcutta was planned to be a large-scale *hartal* and mass rally which they knew very well how to con. .ol. However, the response from the masses far exceeded any expectations. The political leaders seriously miscalculated the strong emotional response that the word 'nation', as interpreted under the new situation, had evoked. In August 1946 the 'nation' was no longer a mere political slogan. It was rapidly turning into 'reality' both in realpolitik and in people's imaginations. The system to which Bengal political leaders had grown accustomed for decades could not cope with this dynamic change. As we have seen, it quickly and easily broke down on the first day of the disturbances."

Prelude

Following Jinnah's declaration of 16 August as the Direct Action Day, acting on the advice of R.L. Walker, the then chief secretary of Bengal, the Muslim League Chief Minister of Bengal, Huseyn Shaheed Suhrawardy, requested Governor Burrows to declare a public holiday on that day. Governor Burrows agreed. Walker made this proposal with the hope that the risk of conflicts, especially those related to picketing, would be minimized if government offices, commercial houses and shops remained closed throughout Calcutta on the 16th Bengal Congress protested against the declaration of public holiday, arguing that a holiday would enable 'the idle folks' to successfully enforce *hartals* in areas where the Muslim League leadership was uncertain. Congress accused the League government for "indulging in communal policies' for narrow goal". Congress leaders thought that if a public holiday was observed, its own supporters would have no choice but to close down their offices and shops, and thus be compelled against their will to lend a hand in the Muslim League's *hartal*. In addition, there was an element of pride involved in that the monopolistic position that the Congress had hitherto enjoyed in imposing and enforcing hartals, strikes, etc. was being challenged. However, the League went ahead with the declaration, and Muslim newspapers published the program for the day.

The *Star of India*, an influential local Muslim newspaper, published detailed programme for the day. The programme called for complete *hartal* and general strike in all spheres of civic, commercial and industrial life except essential services. The notice proclaimed that processions would start from multiple parts of Calcutta, Howrah, Hooghly, Metiabruz and 24 Parganas, and would converge at the foot of the Ochterlony Monument (now known as Shaheed Minar) where a joint mass rally presided over by Huseyn Shaheed Suhrawardy would be held. The Muslim League branches were advised to depute three workers in every mosque in every ward to explain the League's action plan before *Juma* prayers and to report to the district headquarters about arrangements. Moreover, special prayers were arranged in every mosque on Friday after *Juma* prayers for the freedom of Muslim India.

The notice drew divine inspiration from the Quran, emphasizing on the coincidence of Direct Action Day with the holy month of *Ramzaan*, claiming that the upcoming protests were an allegory of Prophet Muhammad's conflict with heathenism and subsequent conquest of Mecca and establishment of the kingdom of Heaven in Arabia.

Hindu public opinion was mobilised around the *Akhand Hindusthan* (United India) slogan. Certain Congress leaders in Bengal imbibed a strong sense of Hindu identity, especially in view of the perceived threat from the Pakistan movement. Such mobilisation along communal lines was partly successful due to a concerted propaganda campaign which resulted in a 'legitimization of communal solidarities'.

On the other hand, following the protests against the British after INA trials, the British administration decided to give more importance to protests against the government, rather than management of communal violence within the Indian populace, according to their "Emergency Action Scheme". Frederick Burrows, the Governor of Bengal, rationalized the declaration of "public holiday" in his report to Lord Wavell –

"...many of the mischief-makers were people who would have had idle hands anyhow. If shops and markets had been generally open, I believe that there would have been even more looting and murder than there was; the holiday gave the peaceable citizens the chance of staying at home..." —Frederick Burrows, Burrows' Report to Lord Wavell.

Riots and Massacre

Troubles started on the morning of the August 16. Even before 10 o'clock Police Headquarters had reported that there was excitement throughout the city, that shops were being forced to close, and that there were many reports of stabbing and throwing of stones and brickbats. The trouble had assumed the communal character which it was to retain throughout. The League's rally began at Ochterloney Monument. The gathering was considered as the 'largest ever Muslim assembly' at that time.

The meeting began around 4 pm though processions of Muslims from all parts of Calcutta had started assembling since the midday prayers. A large number of the participants were reported to have been armed with iron bars and *lathis* (bamboo sticks). The numbers attending were estimated by a Central Intelligence Officer's reporter (a Hindu) at 30,000 and by a Special Branch Inspector (a Muslim) at 500,000. The latter figure is impossibly high and the (Muslim) *Star of India* reporter put it at about 100,000. The main speakers were Khawaja Nazimuddin and Chief Minister Suhrawardy. Nazimuddin in his speech preached peacefulness and restraint but rather spoilt the effect by asserting that till 11 o'clock that morning all the injured persons were Muslims, and the Muslim community had only retaliated in self-defence. The Chief Minister's speech consisted of both calming and excitatory passages, of which the audience remembered the hot passages more clearly than the cold.

The Special Branch had sent only one Urdu shorthand reporter to the meeting, with the result that no transcript of the Chief Minister's speech is available. But the Central Intelligence Officer and a reporter, who Frederick Burrows believed was reliable, deputed by the military authorities agree on one mischievous statement (not reported at all by the Calcutta Police). The version in the former's report was—"He [the Chief Minister] had seen to police and military arrangements who would not interfere". The version of the latter's was—"He had been able to restrain the military and the police". However, the police did not receive any specific order to "hold back". So, whatever Suhrawardy may have meant to convey by this, the impression of such a statement on a largely uneducated audience must have been that it was an open invitation to disorder indeed, many of the listeners started attacking Hindus and looting Hindu shops as soon as they left the meeting. Subsequently, there were reports of lorries (trucks) that came down Harrison Road in Calcutta, carrying Muslim men armed with brickbats and bottles as weapons and attacking Hindu-owned shops.

Hindus and Sikhs were every bit as fierce as the Muslims in the beginning. Field Marshal Viscount Wavell estimated that appreciably more Muslims than Hindus were killed. Parties of one community would lie in wait, and as soon as they caught one of the other community, they would cut him to pieces. Near military installations, static guards, forces specially trained to protect such installation, took over from police guards and a party of troops under Major Littleboy, the Assistant Provost-Marshal, did valuable work in the rescue operation for displaced and needy persons. Outside the military areas, the situation worsened hourly. Buses and taxis were charging about loaded with Sikhs and Hindus armed with swords, iron bars and firearms. In later interviews some of the Hindu participants recounted —

"... I heard that two goalas (milkmen) had been killed in Beliaghata and riots have started in Boubazar ...;it was a very critical time for the country; the country had to be saved. If we become a part of Pakistan, we will be oppressed… so I called all my boys and said, this is the time we have to retaliate, and you have to answer brutality with brutality ... We were fighting those who attacked us ... We fought and killed them. So if we heard one murder has taken place, we committed ten more ... the ratio should be one to ten, that was the order to my boys." —Gopal Patha, BBC "50 years of India's independence".

"... I saw four trucks standing, all with dead bodies piled at least three feet high; like molasses in a sack, they were stacked on the trucks, blood and brain oozing out... that sight had a tremendous effect on me ... One murder would fetch ten rupees, and a wounding would bring five .." —Jugal Chandra Ghosh, BBC "50 years of India's independence".

The region most affected by the violence was the densely populated sector of the city bounded by Park Circus on the south, CIT Road on the east, Vivekananda Road on the north and Strand Road on the west. Official estimate put the casualties at 4,000 dead and 100,000 injured. Other sources put the death toll at 7,000–10,000. Some authors have claimed that most of the victims were Hindus. However, others indicate appreciably more Muslims were killed than Hindus.

Skirmishes between the communities continued for almost a week. Finally, on 21 August, 5 battalions British troops, supported by 4 battalions Indians and Gurkhas, were deployed in the city. Lord Wavell alleged that more British troops ought to have been called in earlier, and there is no indication that more British troops were not available. The rioting reduced on 22 August.

Characteristics of the Riot

In earlier riots in Calcutta, shops dealing with immediate consumer goods or items whose price had just risen were mostly looted. However, in the riot of 1946 any shop was an object of attack, the only discriminatory feature being Muslims exclusively pillaging Hindu shops and vice versa. Collective violence on either side also displayed features of organisation. The looted booty was carried to waiting lorries for transportation to a central place, shops were marked carefully with signs so that the crowd left untouched the establishments of their co-religionists. Houses of a particular community were attacked simultaneously. Both League and Congress volunteers used Red Cross badges to evade police detection. Perhaps at the height of antagonism the Hindu and Muslim crowd were impregnated with cross-fertilisation of ideas on collective conduct wherein one was copying the acts of others.

The Muslim League mobilised all its frontal organisations to make the Direct Action Day a success. Special coupons for gallons of petrol (gasoline) were issued in the names of League ministers to be used by their party functionaries, the petrol was used to incinerate Hindu businesses. One month's food ration for 10,000 people was drawn in advance to feed the League activists. Once the riots began the Chief Minister, Huseyn Shaheed Suhrawardy, accompanied by his political aids, spent considerable time in the Police Control Room while Muslims executed the riots. This made it extremely difficult for the Commissioner of Police, who was primarily responsible for handling the situation, to give clear and balanced decisions on all the numerous calls for help that were pouring in. It is not of course the function of a Minister to direct detailed operations, but the position was one of considerable delicacy as the Commissioner of Police could not insist on the extrusion from the Control Room of the Minister responsible for law and order.

At the same time, however, Suhrawardy put forth a great deal of effort to bring reluctant British officials around to calling the army in from Sealdah Rest Camp. Unfortunately, British officials did not send the army out until 1.45am on the 17th.

On the other hand, Marwari merchants purchased arms and ammunitions from American soldiers, which were later used during the riot. Acid bombs were manufactured and stored in Hindu-owned factories before the outbreak. Calcutta's Hindu blacksmiths were mobilised to prepare spearheads and other weapons. Violence in Calcutta, between 1945 and 1946, passed by stages from Indian versus European to Hindu versus Muslim. Indian Christians and Europeans were generally free from molestation as the tempo of Hindu-Muslim violence quickened. The decline of anti-European feelings as communal Hindu-Muslim tensions increased during this period is evident from the casualty numbers. During the riots of November 1945, casualty of Europeans and Christians were 46; in the riots of the 10 February–14 February 1946, 35; from February 15 to the August 15, only 3; during the Calcutta riots from August 15, 1946 to September 17, 1946, none.

Aftermath

During the riots, thousands began fleeing Calcutta. For several days the Howrah Bridge over the Hooghly River was crowded with evacuees headed for the Howrah station to escape the mayhem in Calcutta. Many of them would not escape the violence that spread out into the region outside Calcutta. Lord Wavell claimed during his meeting on August 27, 1946 that Gandhi had told him, "If India wants bloodbath she shall have it ... if a bloodbath was necessary, it would come about in spite of non-violence".

There was criticism of Suhrawardy, Chief Minister in charge of the Home Portfolio in Calcutta, for being partisan and of Sir Frederick John Burrows, the British Governor of Bengal, for not having taken control of the situation. The Chief Minister spent a great deal of time in the Control Room in the Police Headquarters at Lalbazar, often attended by some of his supporters. Short of a direct order from the Governor, there was no way of preventing the Chief Minister from visiting the Control Room whenever he liked; and Governor Burrows was not prepared to give such an order, as it would clearly have indicated complete lack of faith in him.

There are several views on the exact cause of the direct action day riots. According to intelligentsia, riots were instigated by members of the Muslim League and its affiliate Volunteer Corps' in the city in order to enforce the declaration by the Muslim League that Muslims throughout the subcontinent were to 'suspend all business' to support their demand for an independent Pakistan. However, supporters of the Muslim League believed that the Congress Party was behind the violence in an effort to weaken the fragile Muslim League government in Bengal. Members of the Indian National Congress, including Mohandas Gandhi and Jawaharlal Nehru responded negatively to the riots and expressed shock. The riots would lead to further rioting and pogroms between Hindus and Sikhs and Muslims. These events sowed the seeds for the eventual Partition of India.

Further Rioting in India

The Direct Action Day riots sparked off several riots between Muslims and Hindus/Sikhs in Noakhali, Bihar, Punjab, and the North Western Frontier Province in that year.

Noakhali–Tippera Riot

An important incident following Direct Action Day was the Noakhali and Tippera district massacres in October 1946. The Noakhali–Tippera riot was a direct sequel to the Great Calcutta

Riot and therefore, believed to be a repercussion of the latter. However, studies have indicated that violence was different in nature from Calcutta.

Rioting in the districts began in the Ramganj police station area in the northern Noakhali District on October 10, 1946. The violence unleashed was described as *"the organized fury of the Muslim mob"*. It soon engulfed the neighbouring police stations of Raipur, Lakshmipur, Begumganj and Sandip in Noakhali, and Faridganj, Hajiganj, Chandpur, Lakshman and Chudagram in Tippera. The devastation caused by widespread violence was quite extensive. Initial statistics regarding casualties remained doubtful. While the "Hindu" press placed the figures in thousands, the "League" press went on to the other extreme and even denied incidents of death. However, the official estimate was a conservative 200.

The immediate occasion for the outbreak of the disturbances was the looting of a *Bazaar* (market) in Ramganj police station following the holding of a mass meeting and provocative speech by Gholam Sarwar Hussein. This included attacks on the house of Surendra Nath Bose and Rajendra Lal Roy Choudhury, the erstwhile president of the Nokhali Bar and a prominent Hindu Mahasabha leader.

Rest of India

Some of the worst riots happened in Bihar and Garhmukteshwar in United Provinces. The Bihar riot began on 25 October 1946, which was being observed as Noakhali day. Severe violence broke out in Chapra and Saran district, between 25 and 28 of October. Very soon Patna, Munger and Bhagalpur became the sites of serious violence. By November 3, the official estimate put the figure of death at 445.

5

Hindu Nationalism

Hindu nationalism has been collectively referred to the expressions of social and political thought, based on the native spiritual and cultural traditions of India. Some scholars have argued that the term 'Hindu nationalism' which refers to the concept of 'Hindu Rashtra' is a simplistic translation and is better described by the term 'Hindu polity'.

The native thought streams became highly relevant in the Indian history when they helped form a distinctive identity to the Indian polity and provided a basis for questioning colonialism. They inspired the freedom movements against the British rule based on armed struggle, coercive politics and nonviolent protests. They also influenced social reform movements and economic thinking in India.

In India, the term 'nationalism' doesn't have the negative connotations which it has in Western intellectual circles of post-Marxist orientation. On the contrary, the term is hallowed by its association with the freedom movement against British colonialism and the establishment of democracy.

History

The term Hinduism derives from a Persian word that refers to the Sindhu (or Indus) river in northwest India; "Hindu" was first used in the 14th century by Arabs, Persians, and Afghans to describe the peoples of the region. The usage of the word 'Hindu' to describe the native polity of India have been found in the historical accounts of medieval India. These usages show that the word Hindu, until the early nineteenth century was emphasized by nativity rather than by religion. Prominent among the South Indian rulers of the fourteenth century were the Sangama rulers of Vijayanagara empire who were hailed as 'Hinduraya suratana', the best among the Hindu rulers. The Sangama rulers were in constant conflict with the Sultanate of Bijapur, and this usage of the word 'Hindu' in the title, was obviously to distinguish them as native rulers as against the Sultans who were "perceived to be foreign in origin". It has been noted by Historians that "Hindus" did not conceive themselves as a religious unity in any sense except in opposition to foreign rule. For example, the early seventeenth-century Telgu work, 'Rayavachakamu', condemns the Muslim rulers for being foreign and barbarian and only rarely for specifically religious traits.

The other references include the glorification of the Chauhana heroes of Jalor as 'Hindu' by Padmanabha in his epic poem, Kanhadade-prabandha, which he composed in AD 1455. The Rajput ruler, Maha Rana Pratap became renowned with the title of 'Hindu-kula-kamala-divakara' for his relentless fight against the Moghuls. 'Hindavi Swarajya' (self rule of the natives) was how the rule of Shivaji, the most notable of the rulers of the seventeenth century was described. The usage of 'Hindavi' (translated as 'of Hindus' in Marathi) in 'Hindavi Swarajya' is considered to mean Indian Independence rather than the rule by a religious sect or a community.

Hindu Renaissance in the Late 19th century

Many Hindu reform movements originated in the late nineteenth century. These movements led to the fresh interpretations of the ancient scriptures of Upanishads and Vedanta and also emphasized on social reform. The marked feature of these movements was that they countered the notion of western superiority and white supremacy propounded by the colonizers as a justification for British colonialism in India. This led to the upsurge of patriotic ideas that formed the cultural and an ideological basis for the freedom struggle in India.

Brahmo Samaj

The Brahmo Samaj was one of the earliest Hindu renaissance movements in India under the British rule. It was started by a Bengali scholar, Ram Mohan Roy in 1828. Ram Mohan Roy endeavored to create from the ancient Upanishadic texts, a vision of rationalist 'modern' India. Religiously he criticized idolatry and believed in a monotheistic religion devoid of any idolatry and religious customs. His major emphasis was social reform. He fought against caste discrimination and advocated equal rights for women. Although the Brahmos found favourable response from the British Government and the Westernized Indians, they were largely isolated from the larger Hindu society due to their intellectual Vedantic and Unitarian views. But their efforts to systematize Hindu spirituality based on rational and logical interpretation of the ancient Indian texts would be carried forward by other movements in Bengal and across India.

Arya Samaj

Arya Samaj is considered one of the overarching Hindu renaissance movements of the late nineteenth century. Swami Dayananda, the founder of Arya Samaj, rejected idolatry, caste restriction and untouchability, child marriage and advocated equal status and opportunities for women. He opposed "Brahmanism" (which he believed had led to the corruption of the knowledge of Vedas) as much as he opposed Christianity and Islam.. Although Arya Samaj was a social movement, many revolutionaries and political leaders of the Indian Independence movement like Ramprasad Bismil, Shyamji Krishnavarma, Bhai Paramanand and Lala Lajpat Rai were to be inspired by it.

Swami Vivekananda

Another 19th century Hindu reformer was Swami Vivekananda. Vivekananda as a student was educated in contemporary Western thought. He joined Brahmo Samaj briefly before meeting Ramakrishna, who was a priest in the temple of the mother goddess Kali in Calcutta and who was to become his Guru. Vivekananda's major achievement was to ground Hindu spirituality in a systematic interpretation of Vedanta. This project started with Ram Mohan Roy of Brahmo Samaj and which had produced rational Hinduism was now combined with disciplines such as yoga and the concept of social service to attain perfection from the ascetic traditions in what Vivekananda called the "practical Vedanta". The practical side essentially included participation in social reform.

He made Hindu spirituality, intellectually available to the Westernized audience. His famous speech at the Parliament of World religions at Chicago on September 11, 1893, followed huge reception of his thought in the West and made him a celebrity in the West and subsequently in India too.

A major element of Vivekananda's message was nationalist. He saw his effort very much in terms of a revitalization of the Hindu nation, which carried Hindu spirituality and which could counter Western materialism. The notions of White supremacy and Western superiority, strongly believed by the colonizers, were to be questioned based on Hindu spirituality. This kind of spiritual Hinduism was later carried forward by Mahatma Gandhi and Sarvepalli Radhakrishnan. It also became a main inspiration for the current brand of Hindu nationalism today. Historians have observed that this helped the nascent Independence movement with a distinct national identity and kept it from being the simple derivative function of European nationalisms.

Sri Aurobindo

Sri Aurobindo was a nationalist and one of the first to embrace the idea of complete political independence for India. He was inspired by the writings of Swami Vivekananda and the novels of Bankim Chandra.. He "based his claim for freedom for India on the inherent right to freedom, not on any charge of misgovernment or oppression". He believed that the primary requisite for national progress, national reform, is the free habit of free and healthy national thought and action and that it was impossible in a state of servitude. He was part of the revolutionary group Anushilan Samiti and was involved in armed struggle against the British In his brief political career spanning only four years, he led a delegation from Bengal to the Indian National Congress session of 1907 and contributed to the revolutionary newspaper Bande Mataram. In 1910, he withdrew from political life and spent his remaining life doing spiritual exercises and writing. But his works kept inspiring revolutionaries and struggles for freedom, including the famous Chittagong Uprising. Both Swami Vivekananda and Sri Aurobindo are credited with having found the basis for a vision of freedom and glory for India in the spiritual richness and heritage of Hinduism.

Independence Movement

The influence of the Hindu renaissance movements was such that by the turn of the century, there was a confluence of ideas of the Hindu cultural nationalism with the ideas of Indian nationalism. Both could be spoken synonymous even by tendencies that were seemingly opposed to sectarian communalism and Hindu majoritism.The Hindu renaissance movements held considerable influence over the revolutionary movements against the British rule and formed the philosophical basis for the struggles and political movements that originated in the first decade of the twentieth century.

Revolutionary Movements

Anushilan Samiti and Jugantar

Anushilan Samiti was one of the prominent revolutionary movements in India in the early part of twentieth century. It was started as a cultural society in 1902, by Aurobindo and the followers of Bankim Chandra to propagate the teachings of the Bhagavad-Gita. But soon the Samiti had its goal to overthrow the British rule in India. Various branches of the Samiti sprung across India in the guise of suburban fitness clubs but secretly imparted arms training to its members with the implicit aim of using them against the British administration On April 30, 1908 at Muzaffarpur, two revolutionaries, Khudiram Bose and Prafulla Chaki threw bombs at a British convoy aimed at British officer Kingsford. Both were arrested trying to flee. Aurobindo was also arrested on 2 May, 1908 and sent to Alipore jail. The report sent from Andrew Fraser, the then Lt Governor of Bengal to Lord Minto in England declared that although Sri Aurobindo came to Calcutta in 1906 as a Professor at the National College, "he has ever since been the principal advisor of the revolutionary party. It is of utmost importance to arrest his potential for mischief, for he is the prime mover and can easily set tools, one to replace another." But charges against Aurobindo were never proved and he was acquitted. Many members of the group faced charges and were transported and imprisoned for life. Others went into hiding.

In 1910, when, Aurobindo withdrew from political life and decided to live a life of renounciate, the Anushilan Samiti declined.

One of the revolutionaries, Jatindra Das Mukherjee, who managed to escape the trial started a group which would be called Jugantar. Jugantar continued with its armed struggle with the British, but the arrests of its key members and subsequent trials weakened its influence. Many of its members were imprisoned for life in the notorious Andaman Cellular jail.

India House

A revolutionary movement was started by Shyamji Krishnavarma, a Sanskritist and an Arya Samajist, in London, under the name of India House in 1905. The brain behind this movement was said to be V D Savarkar. Krishnaverma also published a monthly "Indian Sociologist", where the idea of an armed struggle against the British was openly espoused.. The movement had become well known for its activities in the Indian expatriates in London. When Gandhi visited London in 1909, he shared a platform with the revolutionaries where both the parties politely agreed to disagree, on the question of violent struggle against British and whether Ramayana justified such violence. Gandhi, while admiring the "patriotism" of the young revolutionaries, had dissented vociferously from their violent blueprints for social change. In turn the revolutionaries disliked his adherence to constitutionalism and his close contacts with moderate leaders of Indian National Congress. Moreover they considered his method of "passive resistance" effeminate and humiliating. The India House had soon to face a closure following the assassination of Sir Curzon-Wyllie by the revolutionary Madan Lal Dhingra, who was close to India House. Savarkar also faced charges and was transported. Shyamji Krishnaverma fled to Paris. India House gave formative support to ideas that were later formulated by Savarkar in his book named 'Hindutva'. Hindutva was to gain relevance in the run up to the Indian Independence and would also form the core to the political party named Hindu Mahasabha started by Savarkar.

Indian National Congress

"Lal-Bal-Pal"

"Lal-Bal-Pal" is the phrase that is used to refer to the three nationalist leaders Lala Lajpat Rai, Bal Gangadhar Tilak and Bipin

Chandra Pal who held the sway over the Indian Nationalist movement and the freedom struggle in the early parts of twentieth century.

Lala Lajpat Rai belonged to the northern province of Punjab. He was influenced greatly by the Arya Samaj and was part of the Hindu reform movement. He joined the Indian National Congress in 1888 and became a prominent figure in the Indian Independence Movement.. He started numerous educational institutions. The National College at Lahore started by him became the centre for revolutionary ideas and was the college where revolutionaries like Bhagat Singh studied. While leading a procession against the Simon Commission, he was fatally injured in the lathi charge by the British police. His death led the revolutionaries like Chandrashekar Azad and Bhagat Singh to kill the British officer J.P. Saunders, who they believed was responsible for the death of Lala Lajpat Rai.

Bal Gangadhar Tilak was a nationalist leader from the Central Indian province of Maharashtra. He has been widely acclaimed the "Father of Indian unrest" who used the press and Hindu occasions like Ganesh Chaturthi and symbols like the Cow to create unrest against the British administration in India. Tilak joined the Indian National Congress in 1890. Under the influence of such leaders, the political discourse of the Congress moved from polite accusation that imperial rule was "un-British" to the forth right claim of Tilak that "Swaraj is my birthright and I will have it".

Bipin Chandra Pal of Bengal was another prominent figure of the Indian nationalist movement, who is considered a modern Hindu reformer, who stood for Hindu cultural nationalism and was opposed to sectarian communalism and Hindu majoritism. He joined the Indian National Congress in 1886 and was also one of the key members of revolutionary India House.

Gandhi and Ramarajya

Though Gandhi never called himself a "Hindu nationalist", he believed in and propagated concepts like Dharma and "Rama Rajya" (Rule of Lord Rama) as part of his social and political philosophy. Gandhiji said "By political independence I do not mean an imitation to the British House of commons, or the soviet rule of Russia or the Fascist rule of Italy or the Nazi rule of Germany. They have systems suited to their genius. We must have ours suited to ours. What that can be is more than I can tell. I have described it as Ramarajya i.e., sovereignty of the people based on pure moral authority.. He emphasized that "Rama Rajya" to him meant peace and justice. "Whether Rama of my imagination ever lived or not on this earth, the ancient ideal of Ramarajya is undoubtedly one of true democracy in which the meanest citizen could be sure of swift justice without an elaborate and costly procedure.". He also emphasized that it meant respect for all religions " My Hinduism teaches me to respect all religions. In this lies the secret of Ramarajya."

Madan Mohan Malviya, an educationist and a politician with the Indian National Congress was also a vociferous proponent of the philosophy of Bhagavad-Gita. He was the president of the Indian National Congress in the year 1909 and 1918. He was seen as a 'moderate' in the Congress and was also considered very close to Gandhi. He popularized the Sanskrit phrase "Satyameva Jayate" (Truth alone wins), which today is the national emblem of the Republic of India. He founded the Benaras Hindu University in 1919 and became its first Vice-Chancellor.

Subhas Bose

Apart from Gandhi, revolutionary leader Netaji Subhas Chandra Bose referred to Vedanta and the Bhagavad-Gita as sources of inspiration for the struggle against the British.

Swami Vivekananda's teachings on universalism, his nationalist thoughts and his emphasis on social service and reform had all inspired Subhas Chandra Bose from his very young days. The fresh interpretation of the India's ancient scriptures appealed immensely to Subhas. Hindu spirituality formed the essential part of his political and social thought through his adult life, although there was no sense of bigotry or orthodoxy in it. Subhas who called himself a socialist, believed that socialism in India owed its origins to Swami Vivekananda. As historian Leonard Gordan explains "Inner religious explorations continued to be a part of his adult life. This set him apart from the slowly growing number of atheistic socialists and communists who dotted the Indian landscape." "Hinduism was an essential part of his Indianess".

His strategy against the British also included the use of Hindu symbols and festivals. In 1925, while in Mandalay jail, he went on a hunger strike when Durga puja was not supported by prison authorities.

Another leader of prime importance in the ascent of Hindu nationalism was Dr K. B. Hedgewar of Nagpur. Hedgewar as a medical student in Calcutta had been part of the revolutionary activities of the Anushilan Samiti and Jugantar. He was charged with sedition in 1921 by the British Administration and served a year in prison. He was briefly a member of Indian National Congress. In 1925, he left the Congress to form the Rashtriya Swayamsevak Sangh, which would become the focal point of Hindu movements in Independent India. After the formation of the RSS too, Hedgewar was to take part in the Indian National Congress led movements against the British rule. He joined the Jungle Satyagraha agitation in 1931 and served a second term in prison. The Rashtriya Swayamsevak Sangh started by him became one of the most prominent Hindu organization with its influence ranging in the social and political spheres of India.

Partition of India

The Partition of India outraged many majority Hindu nationalist politicians and social groups. Savarkar and members of the Hindu Mahasabha were extremely critical of Gandhi's leadership. They accused him of appeasing the Muslims to preserve a unity that in their opinion, did not exist; Savarkar endorsed the concept of the Two-nation theory while disagreeing with it in practice. Some Hindu nationalists also blamed Gandhi for conceding Pakistan to the Muslim League via appeasement. And they were further inflamed when Gandhi conducted a fast-unto-death for the Indian government to give Rs. 55 crores which were due to the Pakistan government, but were being held back due to the Indo-Pakistani War of 1947.

After the assassination of Mahatma Gandhi by Nathuram Godse, the Sangh Parivar was plunged into distress when the RSS was accused of involvement in his murder. Along with the conspirators and the assassin, Vinayak Damodar Savarkar was also arrested. The Court acquitted Savarkar, and the RSS was found be to completely unlinked with the conspirators. The Hindu

Mahasabha, of which Godse was a member, lost membership and popularity. The effects of public outrage had a permanent effect on the Hindu Mahasabha, which is now a defunct Hindutva party.

Evolution of Ideological Terminology

The word 'Hindu', throughout the history, had been used as an inclusive description which lacked a definition and was used to refer to the native traditions and people of India. It was only in late eighteenth century that the word 'Hindu' came to be used extensively with religious connotation, while still being used as a synecdoche describing the indigenuous traditions.

Hindutva and Hindu Rashtra

Savarkar

Savarkar was one of the first in the twentieth century to attempt a definitive description of the term 'Hindu' in terms of what he called *Hindutva* meaning Hinduness. The coinage of the term 'Hindutva' was an attempt by Savarkar who was an atheist and a rationalist, to delink it from any religious connotations that had become attached to it. He defined the word Hindu as "He who considers India as both his Fatherland and Holyland". He thus defined Hindutva ("Hindu-ness") or Hindu as different from Hinduism. This definition kept the Abrahamic religions (Christianity and Islam) outside its ambit and considered only native religious denominations as Hindu..

This distinction was emphasized on the basis of territorial loyalty rather than on the religious practices. In this book that was written in the backdrop of the Khilafat Movement and the subsequent Moplah riots, Savarkar wrote "Their (Muslims' and Christians') holy land is far off in Arabia or Palestine. Their mythology and Godmen, ideas and heroes are not the children of this soil. Consequently their names and their outlook smack of foreign origin. Their love is divided".

Savarkar, also defined the concept of Hindu Rashtra (translated as "Hindu polity"). The concept of Hindu Polity called for the protection of Hindu people and their culture and emphasized that political and economic systems should be based on native thought rather than on the concepts borrowed from the West.

Golwalkar

M S Golwalkar, the second head of the Rashtriya Swayamsevak Sangh, was to further this non-religious, territorial loyalty based definition of 'Hindu' in his book 'Bunch of thoughts'. 'Hindutva' and 'Hindu Rashtra' would form the basis of Golwalkar's ideology and that of the Rashtriya Swayamsevak Sangh. While emphasizing on religious pluralism, Golwalkar believed that Semitic monotheism and exclusivism were incompatible with and against the native Hindu culture. He wrote "Those creeds (Islam and Christianity) have but one prophet, one scripture and one God, other than whom there is no path of salvation for the human soul. It requires no great intelligence to see the absurdity of such a proposition". He added "As far as the national tradition of this land is concerned, it never considers that with a change in the method of worship, an individual ceases to be the son of the soil and should be treated as an alien. Here, in this land, there can be no objection to God being called by any name whatever. Ingrained in this soil is love and respect for all faiths and religious beliefs. He cannot be a son of this soil at all who is intolerant of other faiths."

He further would echo the views of Savarkar on territorial loyalty, but with a degree of inclusiveness, when he wrote "So, all that is expected of our Muslim and Christen co-citizens is the shedding of the notions of their being 'religious minorities' as also their foreign mental complexion and merging themselves in the common national stream of this soil."

Contemporary Descriptions

Later thinkers of the RSS, like H V Sheshadri and K S Rao, were to emphasize on the non theocratic nature of the word "Hindu Rashtra", which they believed was often inadequately translated, ill interpreted and wrongly stereotyped as a theocratic state. In a book by H.V. Sheshadri, the senior leader of the RSS writes "As Hindu Rashtra is not a religious concept, it is also not a political concept. It is generally misinterpreted as a theocratic state or a religious Hindu state. Nation (Rashtra) and State (Rajya) are entirely different and should never be mixed up. State is purely a political concept.... The State changes as the political authority shifts from person to person or party to party. But the people in the Nation remain the same.. They would maintain that the concept of Hindu Rashtra is in complete agreement with the principles of secularism and democracy.

The concept of 'Hindutva' is continued to be espoused by the organizations like the Rashtriya Swayamsevak Sangh and political parties like the Bharatiya Janata Party. But the definition, does not have the same rigidity with respect to the concept of 'holy land' laid down by Savarkar, and stresses on inclusivism and patriotism. BJP leader and the then leader of opposition, Atal Behari Vajpayee, in 1998, articulated the concept of 'holy land' in Hindutva as follows "Mecca can continue to be holy for the Muslims but India should be holier than the holy for them. You can go to a mosque and offer namaz, you can keep the roza. We have no problem. But if you have to choose between Mecca or Islam and India you must choose India. All the Muslims should have this feeling: we will live and die only for this country.".

In 1995, in a landmark judgment the Supreme Court of India observed that "Ordinarily, Hindutva is understood as a way of life or a state of mind and is not to be equated with or understood as religious Hindu fundamentalism. A Hindu may embrace a non-Hindu religion without ceasing to be a Hindu and since the Hindu is disposed to think synthetically and to regard other forms of worship, strange gods and divergent doctrines as inadequate rather than wrong or objectionable, he tends to believe that the highest divine powers complement each other for the well-being of the world and mankind."

The Rise of Hindu Nationalism

"Nationalism" and "Communalism" are synonymous in an Indian context and are negative concepts. They are identified with the misuse of religion in politics. Worldwide, the first such misuse of religion in politics took place in late 19th century in America when the Conservative Protestants in the face of rationalism and scientific values came up with reassertion of 'fundamentals' of Christianity. Essentially, this was an attempt to re-impose the pre-modern values of birth based hierarchy of gender and class. Later, in Europe, the Nazi and fascist onslaughts used race for similar reasons. In recent times, we have seen the rise of Islamic or communalism in several countries of the middle-east, typified by

Ayatullah Kohemini in the Iran of eighties and nineties. Communalism in India made its major appearance, in the pre-Independence era, in 1886, with the formation of two communal streams – the Muslim League (based on Islam) and the Hindu Mahasabha and the Rashtriya Swayamsevak Sangh (based on Hinduism). Over the years, these two streams have constantly tried to fan the communal passions of their followers, be it in the Shah Banoo case or the perennial dispute with regard to the Babri Masjid in Ayodhya. With the emergence of the Hindu right-wing party, the Bharatiya Janata Party (BJP) as a major political force in the country, the proponents of Hindu communalism, better known through its ideology "Hindutva", seem to have gained the upper hand.

Hindutva

The fundamental goal of the "Hindutva" ideology is the establishment of a Hindu-Nation state exemplified in the fascist doctrine of "one nation, one culture, one language, one religion". It is a very narrow type of "nationalism" which seeks legitimacy through demonizing other religions and faiths, very specially Islam and Christianity. Whilst it is not representative of the Hindu majority of the country, it makes every attempt to appear to champion the concerns of mainstream Hinduism.

These posturings have created a great deal of disharmony in various parts of the country particularly in the last fifteen years when in 1990 one of the main exponents of the "Hindu Rashtra" namely, Mr. L. K. Advani, (a former Deputy Prime Minister of the country and currently the President of the BJP) went across the country on a "Rath Yatra". This created a great deal of animosity, blood-shed and deepened the divide between the Hindus and Muslims of the country.

In the wake of the demolition of the Babri Masjid on 6th December 1992, India became divided even more, on communal lines. This was followed by several other instances of communal violence which include the bashing up of Christians in Gujarat (Northwest India) in 1998 – 99 and the Gujarat Genocide of 2002 (when more than 2000 Muslims were killed in Gujarat); among the other communal incidents were the horrendous murder of the Australian Missionary Graham Staines and his two sons (in January

1999 in Manoharpur, Orissa) and the attack on the Sisters of Mother Teresa in Kerala in October 2004.

Comparison between Hindu Rashtra and Secular Democratic India

It is important at this juncture to emphasis that the Constitution of India is a secular one in which all citizens are equal and which guarantees freedom of thought, expression and belief to every single Indian.

India is therefore not a theocratic state and any "nationalism" based on religion or on fundamentalism is bound to create chaos and confusion and ultimately division.

The Hindutva ideology, based on the theory of the nation-state, talks essentially about the "Hindu Rashtra" (nation). This is in total opposition to the Constitution of India which speaks about a sovereign, socialist, secular, democratic republic.

Those of us who have been trying to put a stop to this are convinced that religion should not be used in politics and vice-versa. In fact, religion, if true, has to be used only for the promotion of communal peace, harmony, justice, love and compassion. Any religion worth its salt will not do otherwise.

Hoping that this brief presentation into "The rise of Hindu nationalism in India would have given you some insight into the reality we face back home, I invite you in joining me in praying a favourite prayer of mine which was composed years ago by the poet laureate of India. He thus laid the first brick on which the edifice of Pakistan was raised.

Akhil Bharatiya Hindu Mahasabha

Akhil Bharat Hindu Mahasabha, a Hindu nationalist organization, was founded in 1915 to counter the Muslim League and the Indian National Congress. The president of Hindu Mahasabha was V.D. Savarkar. K.B. Hedgewar served as vice president of the organisation and later left the Mahasabha to form Rashtriya Swayamsevak Sangh. Dr Narayan Bhaskar Khare was the president of Mahasabha during 1949-1951.

Soon after India's Independence, and the subsequent assassination of Gandhi, a good number of Hindu Mahasabhaites joined Bharatiya Jana Sangh under the leadership of S.P. Mukherjee, who had left Hindu Mahasabha and joined hands with the RSS to float a political party under the control and supervision of RSS. Mukherjee had left Mahasabha after his proposal to allow Muslims to gain membership was turned down by the followers of V.D. Savarkar. The relationship between Savarkar's Mahasabha and RSS was strained mainly because the then chief of RSS, M.S. Golwalkar, felt overshadowed by the influence of Savarkar over the Hindu populace. Officially Mahasabha is still a distinct political entity but its election symbol has been withheld as it has not been getting enough votes. So now the party fights elections on different symbols in different constituencies.

Bishan Chandra Seth of Shahjahanpur elected from twice from Etah was one of the longest serving parliamentarians from Hindu Mahasabha. Other long serving parliamentarian from Sabha was Mahant Avaindnath.

The New leadership is dedicated towards the cause of HINDUS as defined by the Honble Supreme Court of India.

Vinayak Damodar Savarkar

Vinayak Damodar Savarkar (May 28, 1883 – February 26, 1966) was an Indian revolutionary and politician, who is credited with developing the Hindu nationalist political ideology *Hindutva.* He is considered to be the central icon of modern Hindu nationalist political parties. The commemorative blue plaque on India House fixed by the Historic Building and Monuments Commission for England reads "Vinayak Damodar Savarkar 1883-1966 Indian patriot and philosopher lived here".

Savarkar's revolutionary activities began when studying in India and England, where he was associated with the India House and founded student societies including Abhinav Bharat Society and the Free India Society, as well as publications espousing the cause of complete Indian independence by revolutionary means. Savarkar would publish *The Indian War of Independence* about the Indian rebellion of 1857 that would be banned by British authorities. He was arrested in 1910 for his connections with the revolutionary group India House. Following a failed attempt to escape while being transported from Marseilles, Savarkar was sentenced to 50-years imprisonment and moved to the Cellular Jail in the Andaman and Nicobar Islands. While in jail, Savarkar would pen the work describing *Hindutva,* openly espousing Hindu nationalism. He would be released in 1921 under restrictions after signing a plea for clemency in which he renounced revolutionary activities. Travelling widely, Savarkar became a forceful orator and writer, advocating Hindu political and social unity. Serving as the president of the Hindu Mahasabha, Savarkar endorsed the ideal of India as a *Hindu Rashtra* and opposed the *Quit India* struggle in 1942. He became a fierce critic of the Indian National Congress and its acceptance of India's partition, and was one of those accused in the assassination of Indian leader Mahatma Gandhi, though he was acquitted by the Court. He spent the last years of his life writing and expounding on *Hindutva.* Savarkar welcomed the establishment of the Jewish State in Palestine

The airport at Port Blair, Andaman and Nicobar's capital has been named Veer Savarkar International Airport.

Early Life

Vinayak was born in the family of Damodar and Radhabai Savarkar in the village of Bhagur, near the city of Nasik, Maharashtra. He had three other siblings namely Ganesh, Narayan, and a sister named Mainabai. Vinayak was born in a Marathi Chitpawan Brahmin family. The family had a good social standing due to their *jagirdars* (*landlords*) lineage. Vinayak's mother died when he was nine years old during an outbreak of cholera. The siblings also lost their father seven years later when he died of plague in 1899.

After death of parents the eldest sibling Ganesh, known as Babarao, took responsibility of the family. Babarao played a supportive and influential role in Vinayak's teenage life. During this period, Vinayak organised a youth group called *Mitra Mela* (*Band of Friends*) and encouraged revolutionary and nationalist views of passion using this group. In 1901, Vinayak Savarkar married Yamunabai, daughter of Ramchandra Triambak Chiplunkar, who supported his university education. Subsequently in 1902, he enrolled in Fergusson College, in Pune (then Poona). As a young man, he was inspired by the new generation of radical political leaders namely Bal Gangadhar Tilak, Bipin Chandra Pal and Lala Lajpat Rai along with the political struggle against the partition of Bengal and the rising Swadeshi campaign. He was involved in various nationalist activities at various levels. In 1905, during Dussehra festivities Vinayak organised setting up of a bonfire of foreign goods and clothes. Along with his fellow students and friends he formed a political outfit called *Abhinav Bharat*. Vinayak was soon expelled from college due to his activities but was still permitted to take his Bachelor of Arts degree examinations. After completing his degree, nationalist activist Shyam Krishnavarma helped Vinayak to go to England to study law, on a scholarship.. It was during this period that Garam Dal, (literally translated as *Hot Faction*) was formed under the leadership of Tilak, due to the split of Indian National Congress. The members of Garam Dal, did not acknowledge the moderate Indian National Congress leadership agenda which advocated dialogue and reconciliation with the British Raj. Tilak advocated the philosophy of Swaraj and was soon imprisoned for his support of revolutionary activities. Although generally espousing atheism, Vinayak began studying Indian history, Hindu scripture and observing religious traditions.

Activities at India House

After joining Gray's Inn law college in London Vinayak took accommodation at India House. Organised by expatriate social and political activist Pandit Shyamji, India House was a thriving centre for student political activities. Savarkar soon founded the Free India Society to help organise fellow Indian students with the goal of fighting for independence through a revolution.

Savarkar envisioned a guerrilla war for independence along the lines of the famous armed uprising of 1857. Studying the history of the revolt, from English as well as Indian sources, Savarkar wrote the book, *The History of the War of Indian Independence*. He analysed the circumstances of 1857 uprising and assailed British rule in India as unjust and oppressive. It was via this book that Savarkar became one of the first writers to allude the uprising as India's "First War for Independence." The book was banned from publication throughout the British Empire. Madame Bhikaji Cama, and expatriate Indian revolutionary obtained its publication in the Netherlands, France and Germany. Widely smuggled and circulated, the book attained great popularity and influenced rising young Indians and future revolutionaries, including Subhash Chandra Bose and Bhagat Singh. While Savarkar was studying revolutionary methods and he came into contact with a veteran of the Russian Revolution of 1905, who imparted him the knowledge of bomb-making. Savarkar had printed and circulated a manual amongst his friends, on bomb-making and other methods of guerrilla warfare. In 1909, Madan Lal Dhingra, a keen follower and friend of Savarkar, assassinated British MP Sir Curzon Wylie in a public meeting. Dhingra's action provoked controversy across Britain and India, evoking enthusiastic admiration as well as condemnation. Savarkar published an article in which he all but endorsed the murder and worked to organise support, both political and for Dhingra's legal defence. At a meeting of Indians called for a condemnation of Dhingra's deed, Savarkar protested the intention of condemnation and was drawn into a hot debate and angry scuffle with other attendants. A secretive and restricted trial and a sentence awarding the death penalty to Dhingra provoked an outcry and protest across the Indian student and political community. Strongly protesting the verdict, Savarkar struggled with British authorities in laying claim to Dhingra's remains following his execution. Savarkar hailed Dhingra as a hero and martyr, and began encouraging revolution with greater intensity.

Arrest, Imprisonment, Life in and Release from Cellular Jail

In India, Ganesh Savarkar had organised an armed revolt against the Morley-Minto reforms of 1909. The British police implicated Savarkar in the investigation for allegedly plotting the crime. Hoping to evade arrest, Savarkar moved to Madame Cama's home in Paris. He was nevertheless arrested by police on March 13, 1910. In the final days of freedom, Savarkar wrote letters to a close friend planning his escape. Knowing that he would most likely be shipped to India, Savarkar asked his friend to keep track of which ship and route he would be taken through. When the ship *S.S. Morea* reached the port of Marseilles on July 8, 1910, Savarkar escaped from his cell through a porthole and dived into the water, swimming a long distance to the shore in the hope that his friend would be there to receive him in a car. But his friend was late in arriving, and the alarm having been raised, Savarkar was re-arrested. Arriving in Mumbai (then Bombay), he was taken to the Yeravda Central Jail. Following a trial, Savarkar was sentenced to 50 years imprisonment and transported on July 4, 1911 to the infamous Cellular Jail in the Andaman and Nicobar Islands.

His fellow captives included many political prisoners, who were forced to perform hard labour for many years. Reunited with his brother Ganesh, the Savarkars nevertheless struggled in the harsh environment. Forced to arise at 5 a.m., tasks including cutting trees and chopping wood, and working at the oil mill under regimental strictness, with talking amidst prisoners strictly prohibited during mealtime. Prisoners were subject to frequent mistreatment and torture. Contact with the outside world and home was restricted to the writing and mailing of one letter a year. In these years, Savarkar withdrew within himself and performed his routine tasks mechanically. Obtaining permission to start a rudimentary jail library, Savarkar would also teach some fellow convicts to read and write.

Savarkar appealed for clemency in 1911 and again during Sir Reginald Craddock's visit in 1913, citing poor health in the oppressive conditions. In 1920, even as the Indian National Congress and leaders such as Mahatma Gandhi, Vithalbhai Patel and Bal Gangadhar Tilak demanded his unconditional release, Savarkar signed a statement endorsing the trial, verdict and British law, and renouncing violence, a bargain for freedom at the expense of ideals. "I hereby acknowledge that I had a fair trial and just sentence. I heartily abhor methods of violence resorted to in days gone by and I feel myself duty bound to uphold law and constitution to the best of my powers and I am willing to make the [1919 Montague-Chelmsford Reforms] a success in so far as I may be allowed to do so in future"

Joglekar considers this appeal for clemency a tactical ploy, to be like Shivaji's letter to Aurangzeb, during his arrest at Agra, Lenin's travel by sealed train through Germany as a part of a deal with Germany and Stalin's pact with Hitler. On May 2, 1921, the Savarkar brothers were moved to a jail in Ratnagiri, and later to the Yeravda Central Jail. He was finally released on January 6, 1924 under stringent restrictions – he was not to leave Ratnagiri District and was to refrain from political activities for the next five years. However, police restrictions on his activities would not be dropped until provincial autonomy was granted in 1937.

Hindutva

During his incarceration, Savarkar's views began turning increasingly towards Hindu cultural and political nationalism, and the next phase of his life remained dedicated to this cause. In the brief period he spent at the Ratnagiri jail, Savarkar wrote his ideological treatise – *Hindutva: Who is a Hindu?*. Smuggled out of the prison, it was published by Savarkar's supporters under his alias "Maharatta." In this work, Savarkar promotes a radical new vision of Hindu social and political consciousness. Savarkar began describing a "Hindu" as a patriotic inhabitant of Bharatavarsha, venturing beyond a religious identity. While emphasising the need for patriotic and social unity of all Hindu communities, he described Hinduism, Jainism, Sikhism and Buddhism as one and same. He outlined his vision of a "Hindu Rashtra" (*Hindu Nation*) as "Akhand Bharat" (*United India*), purportedly stretching across the entire Indian subcontinent:

"the Aryans who settled in India at the dawn of history already formed a nation, now embodied in the Hindus.... Hindus are bound together not only by the tie of the love they bear to a common fatherland and by the common blood that courses through their veins and keeps our hearts throbbing and our affection warm but also by the tie of the common homage we pay to our great civilisation, our Hindu culture."

Scholars, historians and Indian politicians have been divided in their interpretation of Savarkar's ideas. A self-described atheist, Savarkar regards being Hindu as a cultural and political identity. While often stressing social and community unity between Hindus, Sikhs, Buddhists and Jains, Savarkar's notions of loyalty to the fatherland are seen as an implicit criticism of Muslims and Christians, who regard Mecca, Medina and Jerusalem as their holiest places. Savarkar openly assailed what he saw as Muslim political separatism, arguing that the loyalty of many Muslims was conflicted. After his release, Savarkar founded the Ratnagiri Hindu Sabha on January 23, 1924, aiming to work for the social and cultural preservation of Hindu heritage and civilisation. Becoming a frequent and forceful orator, Sarvakar agitated for the use of Hindi as a common national language and against caste discrimination and untouchability. Focusing his energies on writing, Savarkar authored the *Hindu Padpadashashi* – a book documenting and extolling the Maratha empire - and *My Transportation for Life* – an account of his early revolutionary days, arrest, trial and incarcertaion. He also wrote and published a collection of poems, plays and novels.

Leader of the Hindu Mahasabha

Although disavowing revolution and politics, Savarkar grew disenchanted with the Congress's emphasis of non-violence and criticised Gandhi for suspending Non-cooperation Movement following the killing of 22 policemen in Chauri Chaura in 1922. He soon joined the Hindu Mahasabha, a political party founded in 1911 and avowed to Hindu political rights and empowerment. The party was disengaged from the Indian independence movement, allowing Savarkar to work without British interference. As his travel restrictions weakened, Savarkar began travelling extensively, delivering speeches exhorting Hindu political unity and criticising the Congress and Muslim politicians. Savarkar and the Mahasabha did not endorse the Salt Satyagraha launched by the Congress in 1930, and neither Savarkar nor any of his supporters participated in civil disobedience. Savarkar focused on expanding the party's membership, revamping its structure and delivering its message.

In the wake of the rising popularity of the Muslim League led by Muhammad Ali Jinnah, Savarkar and his party began gaining traction in the national political environment. Savarkar moved to Mumbai and was elected president of the Hindu Mahasabha in 1937, and would serve until 1943. The Congress swept the polls in 1937 but conflicts between the Congress and Jinnah would exacerbate Hindu-Muslim political divisions. Jinnah derided Congress rule as a "Hindu Raj," and hailed December 22, 1939 as a "Day of Deliverance" for Muslims when the Congress resigned en masse in protest of India's arbitrary inclusion into World War II. Savarkar's message of Hindu unity and empowerment gained increasing popularity amidst the worsening communal climate. However, Savarkar and the Mahasabha joined several political parties including the League and the Communist Party of India in endorsing the war effort. Savarkar publicly encouraged Hindus to enlist in the military, which his supporters described as an effort for Hindus to obtain military training and experience potentially useful in a future confrontation with the British. When the Congress launched the *Quit India* rebellion in 1942, Savarkar criticised the rebellion and asked Hindus to stay active in the war effort and not disobey the government. Under his leadership, the Mahasabha won several seats in the central and provincial legislatures, but its overall popularity and influence remained small.

Opposition to the Partition of India

The Muslim League adopted the Lahore Resolution in 1940, calling for a separate Muslim state based on the *Two-Nation Theory*, Bhimrao Ramji Ambedkar summaries Savarkar's position, in his *Pakistan or The Partition of India* as follows,

"Mr. Savarkar... insists that, although there are two nations in India, India shall not be divided into two parts, one for Muslims and the other for the Hindus; that the two nations shall dwell in one country and shall live under the mantle of one single constitution;... In the struggle for political power between the two nations the rule of the game which Mr. Savarkar prescribes is to be one man one vote, be the man Hindu or Muslim. In his scheme a Muslim is to have no advantage which a Hindu does not have. Minority is to be no justification for privilege and majority is to be no ground for penalty. The State will guarantee the Muslims any defined measure of political power in the form of Muslim religion and Muslim culture. But the State will not guarantee secured seats in the Legislature or in the Administration and, if such guarantee is insisted upon by the Muslims, such guaranteed quota is not to exceed their proportion to the general population."

Towards the end of the war, Savarkar and the Mahasabha became increasingly confrontational with the League and Muslim politicians. Hindu Mahasabha activists protested Gandhi's initiative to hold talks with Jinnah in 1944, which Savarkar denounced as "appeasement." He assailed the British proposals for transfer of power, attacking both the Congress and the British for making concessions to Muslim separatists. Soon after Independence, Dr Shyama Prasad Mookerjee resigned as Vice-President of the Hindu Mahasabha dissociating himself from its Akhand Hindustan plank, which implied undoing partition.

Support for Jewish State in the Palestine

Savarkar in a statement issued on 19 December 1947, expressed joy at the recognition of the claim of Jewish people to establish an independent Jewish state, and likened the event to the glorious day on which Moses led them out of Egyptian bondage. He considered that justice demanded restoration of entire Palestine to the Jews, their historical holyland and fatherland. He regetted India's vote at the United Nations Organisation against the creation of the Jewish state terming it a policy of appeasement of Muslims.

Works

Veer Savarkar wrote more than 10,000 pages in the Marathi language. His literary works in Marathi include "Kamala", "Mazi Janmathep" (My Life Sentence), and most famously "1857-The First War of Independence", about what the British referred to as the Sepoy Mutiny. Savarkar popularised the term 'First War of Independence'. Another noted book was "Kale Pani" (similar to Life Sentence, but on the island prison on the Andamans), which reflected the treatment of Indian freedom fighters by the British. In order to counter the then accepted view that India's history was a saga of continuous defeat, he wrote an inspirational historical work, "Saha Soneri Pane" (Six Golden Pages), recounting some of the Golden periods of Indian history. At the same time, religious divisions in India were beginning to fissure. He described what he saw as the atrocities of British and Muslims on Hindu residents in Kerala, in the book, "Mopalyanche Band" (Muslims' Strike) and also "Gandhi Gondhal" (Gandhi's Confusion), a political critique of Gandhi's politics. Savarkar, by now, had become a committed and persuasive critic of the Gandhian vision of India's future.

He is also the author of poems like "Sagara pran talmalala" (*O Great Sea, my heart aches for the motherland*), and "Jayostute" (written in praise of freedom), one of the most moving, inspiring and patriotic works in Marathi literature.

When in the Cellular jail, Savarkar was denied pen and paper. He composed and wrote his poems on the prison walls with thorns and pebbles, memorised thousands lines of his poetry for years till other prisoners returning home brought them to India. Savarkar is credited with several popular neologisms in Marathi and Hindi, like *Digdarshak* (leader or director, one who points in the right direction), *Shatkar* (a score of six runs in cricket), *Saptahik* (Weekly), *Sansad* (*Parliament*), "doordhwani" ("telephone"), "tanklekhan" ("typewriting") among others.

He chaired Marathi Sahitya Sammelan in 1938.

Books by Savarkar:

1. Saha Soneri Paane
2. 1857 che Svatantrya Samar
3. Hindupadpaatshahi
4. Hindutva
5. Jatyochhedak Nibandha
6. Moplyanche Banda
7. Maazi Janmathep
8. Kale Paani
9. Shatruchya Shibirat
10. Londonchi batamipatre
11. Andamanchya Andheritun
12. Vidnyan nishtha Nibandha
13. Joseph Mazeeni
14. Hindurashtra Darshan
15. Hindutvache Pnachapran
16. Kamala
17. Savarkaranchya Kavita
18. Sanyasta Khadg.

Gandhi Murder Case and Acquittal of Savarkar

Savarkar had become one of the fiercest critics of Gandhi, and attacked him and the Congress leadership for acquiescing to the partition of India. During the intense communal violence, Hindu Mahasabha activists were allegedly responsible for carrying out attacks on Muslim civilians. Savarkar blamed Gandhi for weakening Hindu society in face of Muslim separatism, and for agreeing to divide the Hindu homeland. The anger of some Hindu refugees from Pakistan provoked fears of assassination attempts on Gandhi's life. Gandhi's fast-unto-death in January 1948, demanding immediate communal peace and allegedly the payment of outstanding shares of the treasury to Pakistan in spite of the Indo-Pakistani War of 1947 increased the consternation and anger of many Hindu Mahasabha activists, including Savarkar. There is no evidence, however, that Gandhi's fast had anything to do with release of money to Pakistan.

Following the assassination of Gandhi on January 30, 1948, police arrested the assassin Nathuram Godse and rounded up his companions. Police investigation revealed that Godse and his chief conspirator Narayan Apte had been a close political confidantes of Savarkar in the Hindu Mahasabha. Despite having publicly denounced Gandhi's murder, Savarkar was arrested on suspicion of having inspired and planned Gandhi's murder, and but was acquitted for want of evidence.

Godse claimed full responsibility for planning and carrying out the attack, in absence of an independent corroboration of the prosecution witness Digambar Badge's evidence implicating Savarkar directly, the court exonerated him citing insufficient evidence.

Later Life

Despite his exoneration, Savarkar's role in the plot remains a source of intense controversy, but at the time the public held him answerable for instigating the murder. Public outrage over Gandhi's murder wrecked the fortunes of the Hindu Mahasabha, whose membership and activity dwindled into insignificance. Savarkar's home in Mumbai was stoned by angry mobs, and his political influence and activism sharply curtailed by widespread public anger. His activities remained confined to occasional speeches and publishing his writings.

He considered RSS and its associate organizations as too timid. But RSS had a stronger appeal to the votaries of Hindutva. RSS founder Keshav Baliram Hedgewar had the highest respect for Savarkar, and RSS continues to acknowledge Savarkar's efforts for the Hindu unity.

In 1966 Savarkar renounced medicines, food and water (Paryushana) leading to his death on February 26, 1966. He was mourned by large crowds that attended his cremation. He had written an article 'Atma-hatya or Deh-tyaag', arguing that suicide in most cases is taking one's life, but renouncing life after the body was no longer capable of functioning properly was a different matter. He left behind a son Vishwas and a daughter Prabha, who changed her surname to Chiplunkar after marriage. His first son,

Prabhakar, had died in infancy. His home, possessions and other personal relics have been preserved for public display.

K. B. Hedgewar

Keshava Baliram Hedgewar (April 1, 1889 – June 21, 1940) was the founder of the Rashtriya Swayamsevak Sangh (RSS). Hedgewar founded the RSS in Nagpur, Maharashtra in 1925, with the intention of promoting the concept of the *Hindu nation*. Hedgewar drew upon influences from social and spiritual Hindu reformers such as Swami Vivekananda, Vinayak Damodar Savarkar and Aurobindo to develop the core philosophy of the RSS.

He went to Kolkata to pursue a degree in medicine. After successful completion, Hedgewar was drawn into the influence of secret revolutionary organisations like the *Anushilan Samiti* and *Jugantar* in Bengal. He was also a member of the *Hindu Mahasabha* till 1929. Hedgewar was imprisoned for sedition by the British government in 1921 for a year and again in 1930 for nine months. After his spell in prison he instructed the RSS to remain aloof from political activities including the Salt Satyagraha (1930) and continue mainly as a social organisation.

Early Life and Career

Dr. Hedgewar was born in 1889 on the Marathi New Year. He hailed from a Deshastha Brahmin family which was originally from Kundakurti, a small village in Bodhan taluka near the border of Maharashtra and Andhra Pradesh states. Near this village, the rivers Godavari, Vanjara and Haridra meet to form a *Triveni* sangam.

Hedgewar was educated by his elder brother. After matriculating, he decided to go to Kolkata to study medicine. He was sent to Kolkata by Dr. B. S. Moonje in 1910 to pursue his medical studies and unofficially learn the techniques of fighting from the secret revolutionary organisations like the Anushilan Samiti and Jugantar in Bengal. He immediately joined Anushilan Samiti and had contacts with revolutionaries like Surya Sen. He came to believe that although the revolutionaries had immense determination, in a country of continental proportions it was impossible to instigate an armed insurrection. After completing his graduation, he returned to Nagpur, disillusioned with the armed movement. In his memoirs, the third chief of RSS, Balasahab

Deoras narrates an incident when Hedgewar saved him and others from following the path of Bhagat Singh and his comrades.

In Nagpur, Hedgewar became involved with social work and also with Tilak faction of the Congress Party, through which he developed a close association with Dr Moonje who later became his Mentor of Hindu Philosophy. In the 1920 session of Indian National Congress was held in Nagpur, Dr Hedgewar was appointed as the Deputy Chief of volunteers cader overseeing the whole function. This volunteer organisation was named as *Bharat Swayamsewak Mandal* which was headed by Dr. Laxman V. Paranjape (Dr. Hedgewar as his Deputy). All volunteers were told to wear Military type uniform (to be made at their own expense) which was later on adopted as RSS's official uniform from 1925 to 1940. This could be called as the real beginning of RSS because Dr L. V. Paranjpe had declared the intention of starting such an organisation in future. Dr B. S. Moonje and Dr. L. V. Paranjpe funded and actively supported Hedgewar to start RSS as the Top Senior Hindu Mahasabha Leaders of Nagpur region.

Background of RSS

Hedgewar slowly came to the conclusion that all the problems he felt the Hindu community in India faced-subjugation and oppression by 'foreigners' in the present and past, provincialism, and untouchability-were a result of an inherent flaw in the Hindu character rather than problems themselves. He felt a remedy was a cultural organisation that would unite Hindus on a common platform and instill among them discipline and national character. In this endeavour, he was blessed by Vinayak Damodar Savarkar, who was then under house imprisonment in Ratnagiri.

Inception of RSS

The Rashtriya Swayamsevak Sangh (RSS) first met in 1925 in a small ground in Nagpur with 5-6 persons on Vijaya Dashami. The basic element of RSS was to be the *Shakha* (branch) in every town/village, where *swayamsevaks* were to perform drills, exercise and chant slogans on an open ground everyday for an hour.

His initial folllowers included Appaji Joshi, Bhaiyyaji Dani,Babasaheb Apte, Gopal rao Yerkuntwar,Dada rao Parmarth, Balasaheb Deoras, Yadav Rao Joshi, Bhaurao Deoras, Moreshwar munje, K.D.Joshi, Raja Bhau Paturkar,Bapu rao Bhishikar, Abaji Hedgewar, Madhukar rao Bhagwat and Viththal rao Patki.

Narayan Bhaskar Khare

Dr. Narayan Bhaskar Khare (born 19 March 1884 Panvel-d 1970) was an Indian politician. He stayed with his uncle and studied highschool at Jabbulpore. He later joined Medical college Lahore and won Gold Medal. He was the forst M. D. of the Punjab University. He was member of Indian National Congress from 1916-1938. He was first elected as Member of Central Province Legislative Council during 1924-1930. He was Congress Member of Legislative Assembly M L A (Central) during 1935-1937. He was M L A of Central Provice from 1937-1943.

He served as prime minister in the first elected government of the Central Provinces and Berar in August 1937-July 1938. He resigned at the request of the Indian National Congress leadership.

He served on the Viceroy of India's Executive Council from 1943 to 1946. Afterward he was also Prime Minister of then Alwar State from 19th April 1947 to February, 1948. He also served as Member to Constituent Assembly of India during July 1947 to February, 1948. Later he joined Hindu Mahasabha on l5th August, 1949 and was its President from 1949—51.

After Indian Independence, he served in the 1st Lok Sabha, India's lower house of parliament, from 1952 to 1955. He was elected as Hindu Mahasabha candidate from Gwalior then Madhya Bharat. He later settled in Nagpur and died in 1970.

Biography: N.B. Khare

Dr.Khare's uniqueness rests on a character formed by a life of selfless service and determined action.

His energy and boldness make him the peer of great leaders. He is one of the creators of the Congress triumph in the Central Provinces.

He strove for a united Congress Party and he succeeded in his effort. He desires no pulling down of stone edifices. For, tumult is not his element. Being the solidest of men, he is a born enemy of disorder. Extremely practical, cautious, hopeful, quietly discerning, rough-tongued. Dr.Khare is remolding his province's ideal, which is leading to a strong and national development. Dr.Khare was born at Bhiwandi in 1884. His father Mr.Bhaskar Balla Khare was a lawyer with an unsteady income. Young Khare spent his youth in study and self-denial. He had poverty as a flower in his buttonhole.

Early in life he migrated to C.P and was brought up by his uncle at Jabbulpore. He was educated at Hitkarni High School and in 1902 graduated from the Government College. He secured the C.P government scholarship in Medicine and joined the Medical College, Lahore. In 1907 he took his degree in Medicine securing first rank. He won the Dr. Rahimkhan gold medal and another medal for Surgery.

The same year he joined the provincial Medical College. The airs of the European snobbish apostates was wormwood to his pride. He never pocketed an affront but hurled many at them. In 1913 he obtained the M.D degree. He was the first M.D of the Punjab University. In 1916 he resigned his post with view to set up private practice. The amount he realized by selling the furniture gave him a nice start. Very soon his fame reached spiral heights. As a physician he was renowned for his great skill and genuine sympathy.

Fearless independent is a true trait in the character of Dr.Khare. This streak in his nature which was prominent in his boyhood became more pronounced in his later life.

When he was an undergraduate in the Government College he was asked to write an essay on the "Blessings of British Rule To India". The future Premier of C.P wrote with great gusto.... He gave a vivid account of the curses of British Imperialism and how it was gnawing away our very vitals. The Principal, Mr. Browning read the essay. It was hard for hard meat for him to digest. He became the flaming pillar of wrath.

His essay breathed sedition. So he was asked to give an explanation. As a consequence Nationalist journals like Amrit Bazar Patrika and Kesari were not allowed to be subscribed by the library.

Imbued with Gandhian spirit he interested himself in politics. He became the trusted lieutenant of Narakesari Abhayankar. H played a notable part in imparting fresh vigour to the Congress movement in C.P. Form 1923-30 he was the prominent member of the C.P Legislative Council. In 1930 he participated in the Civil Disobedience movement. With inflexible purpose, untiring zeal and practical shrewdness he devoted himself to the Congress cause.

His deadly earnestness almost bordered on fanaticism. But it was saved from it by a gay sense of humour.

In 1930 he was imprisoned but was released before the expiry of the term on ground of health. After the sad demise of Abhayankar he was elected unopposed to the Central Assembly where he succeeded in placing the Arya Marriage Validation Bill on the Statute Book. More often than not he is a member of the A.I.C.C. he was elected the President of the joint parliamentary Board in C.P. he conducted the election campaign with unsurpassed vigour. As a mark of high esteem he was unanimously elected the leader of the Congress Party in the Assembly.

Lured by the smell of cold print he took up to journalism. He edited a Marathi Journal "Tarun Bharat" with marked ability.

He had to cease its publication when Civil Disobedience was started but its influence was not ceased to glow.

He is now the Prime Minister of the Central Provinces. He is the guide of its destiny at the most formative period of its history and posterity will honour him as a roving pioneer in the realms of constructive politics.

Identity Politics in India (Caste, Religion, Language and Ethnicity)

Identity Politics has become a prominent subject in the Indian politics in the past few years.

Rise of low castes, religious identities, linguistic groups and ethnic conflicts have contributed to the significance of identity politics in India. The discourse on Identity, many scholars feel, is distinctly a modern phenomenon. Craig Calhoun aptly describes the situation when he argues that it is in the modern times we encounter intensified efforts at consolidating individual and categorical identities and reinforce self-sameness. This is primarily a modern phenomenon because some scholars feel that emphasis on identity based on a central organising principle of ethnicity, religion, language, gender, sexual preferences, or caste positions, etc., are a sort of "compelling remedy for anonymity" in an otherwise impersonal modern world. It is thus said to be a "pattern of belonging, a search for comfort, an approach to community." However, the complex social changes and the imbrications of various forces, factors and events in this modern world have rendered such production and recognition of identities problematic. This is to say that any search for an *'authentic self* or *identity'* is not an innocent and unnuanced possibility; it involves negotiating other, often overlapping and contested, heterodox or multiple *'selves'*. Cascardi succinctly elucidates this by observing, "the modern subject is defined by its insertion into a series of separate value-spheres, each one of which tends to exclude or attempts to assert its priority over the rest", thereby rendering identity-schemes problematic. Nonetheless, the concerns with individual and collective identity that simultaneously seeks to emphasise differences and attempt to establish commonality with others similarly distinguished, have become a universal venture.

What is Identity Politics?

But the question is how do discourses on identity fit into the political landscape? What are the political underpinnings of these discourses on identity? What arc the organising principles of movements that characterise themselves as those based on identity concerns? Can we define movements of workers as an instance of identity politics? In short what is the politics of identity and what are its organising principles?

Identity Politics is said to "signify a wide range of political activity and theorising founded in the shared experiences of injustice of members of certain social groups". As a political activity it is thus considered to signify a body of political projects that attempts a "recovery from exclusion and denigration" of groups hitherto marginalised on the basis of differences based on their *'selfhood'* determining characteristics like ethnicity, gender, sexual preferences, caste positions, etc. Identity politics thus attempts to attain empowerment, representation and recognition of social groups by asserting the very same markers that distinguished and differentiated them from the others and utilise those markers as an assertion of selfhood and identity based on *difference* rather than *equality*. Contrastingly placed, it is to imply that adherents of identity politics essentialise certain markers that fix the identities of social groups around an ensemble of definitional absolutes. These markers may be those of language, culture, ethnicity, gender, sexual preferences, caste positions, religion, tribe, race, etc. institutionalised in jargons, metaphors, stereotypes, and academic literature and reinforced through practices of positive discrimination or affirmative action.

The proponents of identity politics thus, assign the primacy of some "essence" or a set of core features shared only by members of the collectivity and no others and accepts individual persons as singular, integral, altogether harmonious and unproblematic identities. These core markers are different from associational markers like those of the workers who are defined more by their common interests rather than by certain core essential naturally '*given*' identity attributes of the groups engaged in identity politics. Though many would argue that "worker" was an identity deserving legitimacy and as a group, its movements can be referred to as identity Politics, but probably the term "identity politics" as a body of political projects implied to in contemporary discourses refers to certain essential, local and particular categorical identities rather than any universalising ideals or agenda. The adherents of identity politics utilise the power of myths, cultural symbols and kinship relations to mould the feeling of shared community and subsequently politicise these aspects to claim recognition of their particular identities.

The strongest criticism against Identity Politics is that it often challenged by the very same markers upon which the sense of self or community is sought to be built. It is despite the fact that identity politics is engaged in numerous aspects of oppression and powerlessness, reclaiming and transforming negative scripts used by dominant groups into powerful instruments for building positive images of self and community. In other words the markers that supposedly defines the community are fixed to the extent that they harden and release a process of ingroup essentialism that often denies internal dialogicality within and without the group and itself becomes a new form of closure and oppression.

Identity Politics as a field of study can be said to have gained intellectual legitimacy since the second half of the twentieth century, i.e., between 1950s and 1960s in the United States when large scale political movements of the second wave-feminists, Black Civil Rights, Gay and Lesbian Liberation movements and movements of various Indigenous groups in the U.S. and other parts of the world were being justified and legitimated on the basis of claims about injustices done to their respective social groups. However, as scholars like Heyes point out that although "'Identity Politics' can draw on intellectual precursors from Mary Wollstonecraft to Frantz Fanon, writing that actually uses this specific phrase—Identity Politics—is limited almost exclusively to the last 15 years.

Identity Politics in India

In India we find that despite adoption of a liberal democratic polity after independence, communities and collective identities have remained powerful and continue to claim recognition. In fact, Beteille has shown that the Indian polity has consistently tried to negotiate the allegiance to a liberal [individual] spirit and the concerns and consciousness of community. According to Bikhu Parekh this process has recognised a wide array of autonomous and largely selfgoverning communities. It has sought to reconcile itself as an association of individuals and a community of communities, recognising both individuals and communities as bearer of rights. It was probably this claim for and granting of recognition of particular identities by the postindependence

state of India that led many scholars to believe that a material basis for the enunciation of identity claims has been provided by the post-independent state and its structures and institutions. In other words the state is seen as an "active contributor to identity politics through the creation and maintenance of state structures which define and then recognise people in terms of certain identities".

Thus, we find identity politics of various hues abound in India, the most spectacular however, are those based on language, religion, caste, ethnicity or tribal identity. But having said this it would be wrong on our part to assume that each of these identity markers operate autonomously, independent of the overlapping influence of the other makers. In other words a homogenous linguistic group may be divided by caste affiliations that may be sub-divided by religious orientations or all may be subsumed under a broader ethnic claim.

Caste

Caste-based discrimination and oppression have been a pernicious feature of Indian society and in the post-independence period its imbrications with politics have not only made it possible for hitherto oppressed caste-groups to be accorded political freedom and recognition but has also raised consciousness about its potential as a political capital. In fact Dipankar Gupta has poignantly exposed this contradiction when he elaborates the differences between Ambedkar and Mandal Commission's view of caste. While the former designed the policy of reservations or protective discrimination to remove untouchability as an institution from Indian social life and polity, the latter considered caste as an important political resource. Actually, the Mandal commission can be considered the intellectual inspiration in transforming castebased identity to an asset that may be used as a basis for securing political and economic gains.

Though it can also be said that the upper castes by virtue of their predominant position were already occupying positions of strengths in the political and economic system, and when the Mandal heightened the consciousness of the 'Dalits' by recognisisng their disadvantage of caste-identity as an advantage the confrontation ensues. The caste system, which is based on the notions of purity and pollution, hierarchy and difference, has despite social mobility, been oppressive towards the Shudras and the outcastes who suffered the stigma of ritual impurity and lived in abject poverty, illiteracy and denial of political power.

The origin of confrontational identity politics based on caste may be said to have its origin on the issue of providing the oppressed caste groups with state support in the form of protective discrimination. This groupidentity based on caste that has been reinforced by the emergence of political consciousness around caste identities is institutionalised by the caste-based political parties that profess to uphold and protect the interests of specific identities including the castes. Consequently, we have the upper caste dominated BJP, the lower caste dominated BSP (Bhaujan Samaj Party) or the SP (Samajwadi Party), including the fact that left parties (for example use of caste idioms for mobilising agricultural labourers in Andhra Pradesh elections in 1950) have tacitly followed the caste pattern to extract mileage in electoral politics. The Cumulative result of the politicisation can be summarised by arguing that caste-based identity politics has had a dual role in Indian society and polity. It relatively democratised the caste-based Indian society but simultaneously undermined the evolution of class-based organisations.

In all, caste has become an important determinant in Indian society and politics, the new lesson of organised politics and consciousness of caste affiliations learnt by the hitherto despised caste groups have transformed the contours of Indian politics where shifting caste-class alliances are being encountered.

Another form of identity politics is that effected through the construction of a community on the shared bond of religion. In India, Hinduism, Islam, Sikhism, Christianity, and Zoroastrianism are some of the major religions practised by the people. Numerically the Hindus are considered to be the majority, which inspires many Hindu loyalist groups like the RSS (Rashtriya Swayam Sevak Sangh) or the Siva Sena and political parties like the BJP (Bharatiya Janata Party) or the Hindu Mahasabha to claim that India is a Hindu State. These claims generate homogenising myths about India and its history. These claims are countered by other religious groups who foresee the possibility of losing autonomy of practise of their religious and cultural life under such homogenising claims. This initiates contestations that have often resulted in communal riots. The generally accepted myths that process the identity divide on religious lines centre on the 'appeasement theory', 'forcible religious conversions', general 'anti-Hindu' and thus 'anti-India' attitude of the minority religious groups, the 'hegemonic aspirations' of majority groups and 'denial of a socio-cultural space' to minority groups.

Historically, the Hindu revivalist movement of the 19th century is considered to be the period that saw the demarcation of two separate cultures on religious basis—the Hindus and the Muslims that deepened further because of the partition. This division which has become institutionalised in the form of a communal ideology has become a major challenge for India's secular social fabric and democratic polity. Though communalism for a major part of the last century signified Hindu-Muslim conflict, in recent years contestations between Hindus and Sikhs, Hindus and Christians have often crystallised into communal conflict. The rise of Hindu national assertiveness, politics of representational government, persistence of communal perceptions, and competition for the socioeconomic resources are considered some of the reasons for the generation of communal ideologies and their transformation into major riots. Identity schemes based on religion have become a major source of conflict not only in the international context but since the early 1990s it has also become a challenge for Indian democracy and secularism. The rise of majoritarian assertiveness is considered to have become institutionalised after the BJP, that along with its 'Hindu' constituents gave political cohesiveness to a consolidating Hindu consciousness, formed a coalition ministry in March 1998. However, like all identity schemes the forging of a religious community glosses over internal differences within a particular religion to generate the "we are all of the same kind" emotion. Thus differences of caste groups within a homogenous Hindu identity, linguistic and sectional differences within Islam are shelved to create a homogenous unified religious identity. In post-independence India the majoritarian assertion has generated its own antithesis in the form of minority religions assertiveness and a resulting confrontational politics that undermines the syncretistic dimensions of the civil society in India. The process through which this religious assertiveness is being increasingly institutionalised by a 'methodical rewriting of history' has the potential to reformulate India's national identity along communal trajectories.

Language

Identity claims based on the perception of a collectivity bound together by language may be said to have its origin in the pre-independence politics of the Congress that had promised reorganisation of states in the post-independent period on linguistic basis. But it was the "JVP" (Jawaharlal Nehru, Vallabhbai Patel and Pattabhi Sitaramayya) Committee's concession that if public sentiment was "insistent and overwhelming", the formation of Andhra from the Teluguspeaking region of the then Madras could be conceded which as Michael Brecher mentions was the "opening wedge for the bitter struggle over states reorganisation which was to dominate Indian Politics from 1953 to 1956". Ironically, the claim of separate states for linguistic collectivities did not end in 1956 and even today continues to confront the concerns of the

Indian leadership. But the problem has been that none of the created or claimed states are mono-ethnic in composition and some even have numerically and politically powerful minorities. This has resulted in a cascading set of claims that continue to threaten the territorial limits of existing states and disputes over boundaries between linguistic states have continued to stir conflicts, as for instance the simmering tensions between Maharastra and Karnataka over the district of Belgaum or even the claims of the Nagas to parts of Manipur. The linguistic divisions have been complicated by the lack of a uniform language policy for the entire country. Since in each state the dominant regional language is often used as the medium of instruction and social communication, the consequent affinity and allegiance that develops towards one's own language gets expressed even outside one's state of origin. For instance the formation of linguistic cultural and social groups outside one's state of origin helps to consolidate the unity and sense of community in a separate linguistic society. Thus language becomes an important premise on which group identities are organised and establishes the conditions for defining the 'in-group' and 'out-group'.

Though it is generally felt that linguistic states provide freedom and autonomy for collectivities within a heterogeneous society, critics argue that linguistic states have reinforced regionalism and has provided a platform for the articulation of a phenomenal number of identity claims in a country that has 1,652 'mother tongues' and only fourteen recognised languages around which states have been reorganised. They argue that the effective result of recognition for linguistic groups has disembodied the feelings of national unity and national spirit in a climate where 'Maharastra for Marathis, Gujrat for Gujratis, etc." has reinforced linguistic mistrust and defined the economic and political goods in linguistic terms.

Ethnicity

You will study in detail about the ethnicity in unit 26 of the book 2 of this course. There are two ways in which the concept of ethnic identity is used; one, it insiders the formation of identity on the basis of single attribute-language, religion, caste, region, etc.; two, it considers the formation of identity on the basis, of multiple attributes cumulatively. However, it is the second way formation of identity on the basis of more than one characteristics- culture, customs, region, religion or caste, which is considered as the most common way of formation of the ethnic identity. The one ethnic identity is formed in relation to the other ethnic identity. The relations between more than one ethnic identities can be both harmonious and conflictual. Whenever there is competetion among the ethnic identities on the real or imaginary basis, it expressed in the form of autonomy movements, demand for session or ethnic riots. You will study about the major examples of ethnicityd possibly leading to a growing crisis of governability

Rashtriya Swayamsevak Sangh

The Rashtriya Swayamsevak Sangh (RSS) also known as the Sangh, is a Hindu volunteer organization in India. It was founded in 1925 by Dr. K. B. Hedgewar, a doctor from Nagpur, as a cultural organisation in British India.

The volunteers of the RSS participated in various political and social movements including the freedom movement. The RSS volunteers are also known for their role in the relief and rehabilitation work during natural calamities and for running more than 100,000 service programs in education, health care, rural development, tribal emancipation, village self-sufficiency, and the rehabilitation of lepers and special needs children etc.

Some critics have referred to the RSS as a Hindu nationalist organization. Many have also accused it of supporting militancy, which the RSS has vehemently denied and protested, often going to the extent of suing the accusers in court.. Accusations have led to the RSS being banned thrice by the Government of India, prominently in 1948 when it was accused of being involved in the assassination of Mahatma Gandhi. But it has been acquitted of all charges..

History

RSS was founded in 1925 by Dr. Keshav Baliram Hedgewar, who was a doctor in the central Indian city of Nagpur. Hedgewar as a medical student in Kolkata had been a part of the revolutionary activities of the Anushilan Samiti and Jugantar striving to free India from British rule. He had been charged with sedition in 1921 by the British Administration and was imprisoned for a year. After returning to Nagpur, he was briefly a member of Indian National Congress before he left it in 1925, to form the Rashtriya Swayamsevak Sangh. After the formation of the RSS, Hedgewar kept the organization from having any direct affiliation with any of the political organisations then fighting British rule. But Hedgewar and teams of volunteers, took part in the Indian National Congress, led movements against the British rule. Hedgewar was arrested in the Jungle Satyagraha agitation in 1931 and served a second term in prison.

The RSS was established as a educational body whose objective was to train a group of Hindus, who on the basis of their character would work to unite the Hindu community so that India could become an independent country and a creative society. *Encyclopedia Britannica* opines that "Hedgewar was heavily influenced by the writings of the Hindu nationalist ideologue Vinayak Damodar Savarkar and adopted much of his rhetoric concerning the need for the creation of a 'Hindu nation'. Hedgewar formed the RSS as a disciplined cadre consisting mostly of upper-caste Brahmins who were dedicated to independence and the protection of Hindu political, cultural, and religious interests."

Activities During Partition

The Partition of India was a very traumatic event in the young nation's history with millions of Sikhs, Hindus and Muslims, attempting to escape the violence and carnage that followed..

RSS was involved in major attacks on minority groups in which 1,000 individuals were killed in the incident at Garmukteswar on November 1946. These types of major attacks and counterattacks by RSS, Sikh and Muslim organizations cemented the public perception regarding the Two-Nation theory.

Noted Gandhian and recipient of the highest civilian award in India, Bharat Ratna, Dr. Bhagwan Das commended the role of the "high-spirited and self-sacrificing boys" of the RSS in protecting the newly formed Republic of India, from a planned coup to topple the Jawaharlal Nehru Administration in Delhi

Gandhi's Assassination, the Ban and the Acquittal

Following Mahatma Gandhi's assassination in 1948 by former member of the RSS Nathuram Godse, many prominent leaders of the RSS were arrested and RSS as an organization was banned on February 4, 1948. Godse's connection with the RSS was investigated. Justice Kapur Commission setup to look into the conspiracy to murder Mahatma Gandhi noted the following

"...RSS as such were not responsible for the murder of Mahatma Gandhi, meaning thereby that one could not name the organization as such as being responsible for that most diabolical crime, the murder of the apostle of peace". "It has not been proved that they (the accused) were members of the RSS which shows that they (the accused) were believers in a more violent form of activities..." – Kapur Commission Report, Vol. 1.

"As a final result of the poison, the country had to suffer the sacrifice of the invaluable life of Gandhiji. Even an iota of the sympathy of the Government or of the people no more remained for the RSS. In fact, opposition grew. Opposition turned more severe when the RSS men expressed joy and distributed sweets after Gandhiji's death." – Sardar Patel-freedom fighter, first Home Minister and Deputy Prime Minister of India

Sardar Patel also pointed out that members of RSS have indulged in attacking "innocent and helpless men, women and children".

RSS Leaders were acquitted of the conspiracy charge by the Supreme Court of India and following an intervention by the Court, the Indian Government agreed to lift the ban with condition that the RSS adopt a formal constitution. The second Sarsanghachalak, Golwalkar drafted the constitution for the RSS which he sent to the government in March 1949. In July of the same year, after many negotiations over the constitution and its acceptance, the ban on RSS was lifted.

On January 15, 2000, a daily, *The Statesman,* carried a story about the RSS by A G Noorani, which depicted the RSS as the killer of Gandhi. Subsequently the Delhi unit of the RSS filed a criminal case of defamation against author of the article A G Noorani along with the cartoonist and the Managing Director of the publishing house. When two of the accused did not respond to the Court summons, non-bailable warrants were issued in their name by the Court. On February 25, 2002, Noorani wrote an unconditional apology to the court in which he regretted writing the defamatory article against the RSS. On March 3, 2002, 'The Statesman' also published an apology regretting the publication of the said article.

Liberation of Dadra and Nagar Haveli and Goa

After the Independence of India, many organizations including the RSS aspired to liberate Dadra and Nagar Haveli from Portuguese occupation. In early 1954, volunteers Raja Wakankar and Nana Kajrekar of the RSS visited the area round about Dadra and Nagar Haveli and Daman several times to study the topography and also to get acquainted with the local workers who were agitating for the liberation. In April 1954, the RSS formed a coalition with the National Movement Liberation Organization (NMLO), the and Azad Gomantak Dal (AGD) for the liberation of Dadra and Nagar Haveli. On the night of 21 July, United front of Goans, a group, working independently of the coalition, captured the Portuguese police station at Dadra and declared Dadra as free. Subsequently on 28 July, volunteer teams of the RSS and AGD captured the territories of Naroli and Phiparia and ultimately the capital of Silvassa. The Portuguese forces which escaped and moved towards Nagar Haveli, were assaulted at Khandvel and were forced to retreat till they surrendered to the Indian border police at Udava on 11 August 1954. A native administration was setup with Appasaheb Karmalkar of NMLO as the Administrator of Dadra and Nagar Haveli on 11 August 1954.

The liberation of Dadra and Nagar Haveli gave a boost to the freedom movement against the Portuguese in Goa. In 1955, RSS leaders demanded the end of Portuguese rule in Goa and its integration into India. When Prime Minister of India, Jawaharlal Nehru refused to obtain it by armed intervention, RSS leader Jagannath Rao Joshi led the satyagraha agitation straight into Goa itself. He was imprisoned with his followers by the Portuguese police. The peaceful protests continued but met with severe repressions. On 15 August 1955, the Portuguese police opened fire on the satyagrahis, killing thirty or so people.

Role During the 1962 Sino-Indian War

The RSS which had been keeping low profile after the lifting of the ban, earned recognition based on its volunteer work during the Sino-Indian War in 1962. RSS was invited by Prime Minister Jawaharlal Nehru to take part in the Indian Republic day parade of 1963. It along with several other civilian organizations took part in the parade. This event helped the RSS increase its popularity and its patriotic image.

Later in 1965 and 1971 Indo-Pak wars too, the RSS volunteers offered their services to maintain law and order of the country and were apparently the first to donate blood.

Movement for the Restoration of Democracy

In 1975, the Indian Government under the Prime Minister Mrs. Indira Gandhi, proclaimed emergency rule in India, thereby suspending the fundamental rights and curtailing the rights of the press. This extreme step was taken after the Supreme Court of India, cancelled her election to the Indian Parliament on charges of malpractices in the election. The democratic institutions were kept under suspended animation and prominent opposition leaders including Gandhian Jayaprakash Narayan, were arrested and thousands of people were detained without any charges being framed against them. RSS, which was seen close to opposition leaders, and with its large organizational base was seen to have potential of organizing protests against the Government, was also banned. Police clamped down on the organization and thousands of its workers were imprisoned.

The RSS defied the ban and thousands participated in Satyagraha (peaceful protests) against the ban and against the curtailment of fundamental rights. Later, when there was no letup, the volunteers of the RSS formed underground movements for the restoration of democracy. Literature that was censored in the media was clandestinely published and distributed on a large scale and funds were collected for the movement. Networks were established between leaders of different political parties in the jail and outside for the coordination of the movement.

'The Economist', London, described the movement as "the only non-left revolutionary force in the world". It said that the movement was "dominated by tens of thousands of RSS cadres, though more and more young recruits are coming". Talking about its objectives it said "its platform at the moment has only one plank: to bring democracy back to India". The Emergency was lifted in 1977 and as a consequence the ban on the RSS too was lifted.

Participation in Land Reforms

It has been noted that the RSS volunteers participated in the Bhoodan movement organized by Gandhian leader Vinobha Bhave. Vinobha Bhave had met the RSS leader M. S. Golwalkar in Meerut in November 1951. Golwalkar had been inspired by the movement that encouraged land reforms through voluntary means. He pledged the support of the RSS for this movement. Consequently, many RSS volunteers led by Nanaji Deshmukh participated in the movement.. But Golwalkar has also been critical of the Bhoodan movement, on other occasions for being reactionary and for working "merely with a view to counteracting Communism". He believed that the movement should inculcate a right and positive faith in the masses that can make them rise above the base appeal of Communism.

Organization

Although the RSS claims not to keep membership records, it is estimated that the organization has between 2.5–6 million members.

Sarsanghchalaks

The *Sarsanghchalak* is the head of the RSS organization. The individuals who have been Sarsanghchalaks are:

- Dr. Keshav Baliram Hedgewar (founder), also known as *Doctorji* (1925-1930 & 1931-1940)
- Dr. Laxman Vaman Paranjpe (1930–1931) (when Dr. Hedgewar was in jail during Forest Satyagraha)
- Shri Madhav Sadashiv Golwalkar, also known as, *Guruji* (1940–1973)
- Shri. Madhukar Dattatraya Deoras, also known as, *Balasaheb* (1973–1993)
- Prof. Rajendra Singh, also known as, *Rajjubhaiya* (1993–2000)
- Dr. Kuppahalli Sitaramayya Sudarshan (2000–2009)
- Dr. Mohan Madhukar Bhagwat (21 March 2009-till date).

The position is decided by nomination by predecessor. The current *Sarsanghachalak* of RSS is Dr. Mohan Madhukar Bhagwat.

Shakha

"*Shakha*" is Hindi for "branch". Most of the organizational work of the RSS is done through the coordination of *shakhas* or branches. These *shakhas* are run for 1 hour in public places. In 2004, more than 60,000 *shakhas* were run throughout India..

The *shakhas* conduct various activities for its volunteers which include physical fitness activities through yoga, exercises and games. It has other activities which emphasize on qualities like civic sense, social service, community living and patriotism. The volunteers are trained in first aid and in rescue and rehabilitation operations. The volunteers are also encouraged to get involved in the developmental activities of the village or locality.

IT Milan

For swayamsevaks who work in IT (Information Technology) related sectors another form of Shakha is set, called as "IT Milan". These are weekly meetings unlike the regular *Shakhas* which run daily. There are as many as 3,000 techies in Bangalore who meet regularly this way. This 60–90 minutes weekly gathering includes a Prayer, Surya Namaskara, Yoga, games, song and sermon. IT Milans are user friendly; the prayer is available as a printout, usually everyone is addressed in English, and there are enough people to aid newcomers on the Surya Namaskara and seven *yoga asanas*. These exercises have been designed for IT professionals who suffer from chronic lower backache due to long hours at computers. It also helps that their employers respect their RSS links. Games are played during the Milan to relieve tension in the minds of IT *Swayamsevaks* and foster team spirit. An IT Milan also serves as a forum for discussion on various issues of national and international importance like the Copenhagen Summit and West Bengal government's decision to grant religion based reservation to Muslims.

Mission

The mission of Rashtriya Swayamsevak Sangh has been described as the revitalization of Indian value system based on universalism and peace and prosperity to all. Vasudhaiva Kutumbakam, the worldview that the whole world is one family, propounded by the ancient thinkers of India, is considered as the ultimate mission of the organization. But the immediate focus, the leaders believe, is on the Hindu renaissance, which would build an egalitarian society and a strong India that could propound this philosophy.

Hence, the focus is on social reform, economic upliftment of the downtrodden and the protection of cultural diversity of the natives in India. The organization says, it aspires to unite all Hindus and build a strong India, which could contribute to the welfare of the world.

In the words of RSS ideologue and the second head of the RSS, M S Golwalkar, "in order to be able to contribute our unique knowledge to mankind, in order to be able to live and strive for the unity and welfare of the world, we stand before the world as a self-confident, resurgent and mighty nation".

In *Vichardhara* (English: *"Bunch of Thoughts"*), M S Golwalkar, affirms the RSS mission of integration as:

"Realising the national character of Hindu People, the RSS has been making determined efforts to inculcate in them burning devotion for Bharat and its national ethos; kindle in them the spirit of dedication and sterling qualities and character; rouse social consciousness, mutual good-will, love and cooperation among them all; to make them realise that casts, creeds and languages are secondary and that service to the nation is the supreme end and to mold their behaviour accordingly; instill in them a sense of true humility and discipline and train their bodies to be strong and robust so as to shoulder any social responsibility; and thus to create all-round Anushasana in all walks of life and build together all our people into a unified harmonious national whole, extending from Himalayas to Kanyakumari." – M S Golwalkar, *Bunch of Thoughts*

Golwalkar also explains that RSS does not intend to compete in electioneering politics or share power. He asserts that there is no place in RSS for any hatred or opposition towards any particular caste, creed or party.

Christopher Jaffrelot opines that RSS's objective has been the establishment of a Hindu nation in India and that its two-fold objective was to propagate the Hindutva ideology and infuse physical strength to the Hindu community.

Sangh Parivar

Organizations which are inspired by the Rashtriya Swayamsevak Sangh's ideology refer themselves as the members of the *Sangh Parivar*. In most of the cases, *pracharaks* (full-time volunteers of the RSS) were deputed to start and manage these organizations. The organizations within the Sangh include the Vishwa Hindu Parishad, Rashtriya Sevika Samiti, Akhil Bharatiya Vidyarthi Parishad, Vanavasi Kalyan Ashram, Bharatiya Mazdoor Sangh, Vidya Bharati, Sewa Bharati and many others spread in all parts of society. Numerous other Hindutva organizations take inspiration from the RSS's philosophy.

RSS has never directly contested elections, but supports parties that are ideologically similar. Although RSS generally endorses the Bharatiya Janata Party (BJP), yet at times had refused to do so due to difference of opinion with the party. Also, RSS is open to support any political party that subscribes to its views..

Of late, the volunteers of the RSS have also held prominent political and administrative positions in India including the Prime Minister of India, the Vice President of India, the Home Minister and Ministers in the Central Government, Governors and Chief Ministers of various states and the members of elected bodies at the state and the national level and also the Indian ambassador to the US

Social Reform

The RSS has advocated the training of Dalits and other backward classes as temple high priests (a position traditionally reserved for Caste Brahmins and denied to lower castes). They argue that the social divisiveness of the Caste system is responsible for the lack of adherence to Hindu values and traditions and reaching out to the lower castes in this manner will be a remedy to the problem. The RSS has also condemned 'upper' caste Hindus for preventing Dalits from worshipping at temples, saying that "even God will desert the temple in which Dalits cannot enter"

Christophe Jaffrelot finds that "there is insuficient data available to carry out a statistical analysis of social origins of the early RSS leaders" but goes on to conclude, based on some known profiles that most of the RSS founders and its leading organisers, with exceptions were Maharashtrian Brahmins from middle or lower class and argues that the pervasiveness of the Brahminical ethic in the organisation was probably the main reason why it failed to attract support from the low castes. He argues that the "RSS resorted to instrumentalist techniques of ethno-religious mobilisation – in which its Brahminism was diluted – to overcome this handicap." However Anderson and Damle 1987, find that members of all castes have been welcomed into the organisation and are treated as equals.

During M. K. Gandhi's visit to RSS Camp accompanied by Mahadev Desai and Mirabehn at Wardha in 1934, he was surprised by the discipline and the absence of untouchability in RSS and commented "When i visited the RSS Camp. I was very much surprised by your discipline and absence of untouchablity ". He personally inquired to Swayamsevaks and found that they were living and eating together in the camp without bothering to know their castes.

Dr Bhimrao Ambedkar while visiting the RSS camp at Pune in 1939 observed that Swayamsevaks were moving in absolute equality and brotherhood without even caring to know the cast of others. In his address to the Swayamsevaks, he said that " This is the first time that I am visiting the camp of Sangh volunters. I am happy to find absolute equality between Savarniyas (Upper cast) and Harijans (Lower cast) without any one being aware of such difference existing." When he asked Dr Hedgewar whether there were any untouchables in the camp, he replied that there are neither "touchables" nor "untouchables" but only Hindus.

Relief and Rehabilitation

Natural Calamities

RSS has participated in many relief activities during natural calamities. For instance, in the 2001 Gujarat earthquake, Indian newsmagazine Outlook's reporter Saba Naqvi Bhaumik reported that:

"Literally within minutes RSS volunteers were at the scenes of distress. Across Gujarat, the (RSS) cadres were the saviors. Even as the state machinery went comatose in the first two days after the quake, the cadre-based machinery of the Sangh fanned out throughout the state. Approximately 35,000 RSS members in uniform were pressed into service." – Saba Naqvi Bhaumik, Outlook, Feb 12, 2001

"This is an old tradition in the RSS. To be the first at any disaster strike: floods, cyclone, drought and now quake. In Kutch, too, the RSS was the first to reach the affected areas. At Anjar, a town in ruins, the RSS was present much before the Army took the lead in finding survivors and fishing out the dead." – K. Srinivas, District collector of Ahmedabad

India-Today, reported in its Feb. 12, 2001 issue that,

"It is conceded by even their worst detractors that the RSS has been in the forefront of the non-official rescue and relief (operations). This has led to an upsurge of goodwill for the Sangh"– India Today

The RSS assisted in relief efforts quite extensively during the 2001 Gujarat earthquake. They helped rebuild villages. They "earned kudos" from many varied agencies and sources for their actions.

This is a long and continuous tradition with the RSS. The RSS was instrumental in relief efforts after the 1971 Orissa Cyclone and the 1977 Andhra Pradesh Cyclone.

An RSS-affiliated NGO, Seva Bharati, has adopted 57 children (38 Muslims and 19 Hindus) from militancy affected areas of Jammu and Kashmir to provide them education at least up to Higher Secondary level. They have also taken care of many victims of the Kargil War of 1999.

Seva Bharati conducted relief operations in the aftermath of the 2004 Indian Ocean earthquake. Activities included building shelters for the victims, providing food, clothes and medical necessities..

The RSS assisted relief efforts during the 2004 Sumatra-Andaman earthquake and the subsequent tsunami..

In 2006, RSS participated in relief efforts to provide basic necessities such as food, milk and potable water to the people of Surat, Gujarat who were affected by massive floods in the region.

The RSS volunteers carried out massive relief and rehabilitation work after the floods ravaged North Karnataka and some districts of the state of Andhra Pradesh.

Protection of Sikhs During the 1984 Anti-Sikh Riots

Sikh intelectual and author of A History of the Sikhs Khushwant Singh, credits members of the RSS with helping and protecting Sikhs who were being targeted by members of the Congress(I) political party during the 1984 Anti-Sikh Riots. Singh who otherwise has been critical of the RSS and believes that it is a " communal organization and dangerous to the country's secular fabric" has said:

"RSS has played an honourable role in maintaining Hindu-Sikh unity before and after the murder of Indira Gandhi in Delhi and in other places"

"It was the Congress (I) leaders who instigated mobs in 1984 and got more than 3000 people killed. I must give due credit to RSS and the BJP for showing courage and protecting helpless Sikhs during those difficult days" – Khushwant Singh

Discrimination against RSS Volunteers

Many cases have been reported in post-independence India where RSS volunteers have been discriminated against by the government due to their allegiance to the RSS and its ideology. In a court case of a teacher who was dismissed from service due to his past links with the RSS, the Supreme Court labelled the government's action as "McCarthyism" and a "violation of fundamental rights".

A municipal school teacher, Ramshanker Raghuvanshi, was dismissed by the Congress government of Madhya Pradesh in 1974, which stated that he had taken "part in the RSS" activities and hence was "not a fit person to be entertained in Government service". The Supreme Court dismissed the arguments of the government and said that the government had not adhered to the provisions of the Indian Constitution. The Supreme Court bench consisting of Justice Syed Murtuza Fazalali and Justice O. Chinnappa Reddy observed that "India is not a police state" and pleaded that the "promise of fundamental rights enshrined in the Indian Constitution not become a forgotten chapter of history". Delivering the landmark judgment, the Court observed that "seeking a police report on person's political faith", in the first place, "amounted to the violation of fundamental rights". The Supreme Court ruled in favour of the municipal teacher and ordered his reinstatement. Similar observations were made by the High courts of different provinces of India in different cases of political persecution of RSS volunteers. One case involved Ranganathacharya Agnihotri, who was selected for the post of Munsiff but was not absorbed into service as he had been a volunteer of the RSS in his past. When Agnihotri approached the High Court of Mysore, he was reinstated. The Court observed:

"Prima facie the RSS is a non-political cultural organization without any hatred or ill will towards non-Hindus and that many eminent and respected persons in the country have not hesitated to preside over the functions or appreciate the work of its volunteers. In a country like ours which has accepted the democratic way of life (as ensured by the Constitution), it would not be within reason to accept the proposition that mere membership of such peaceful or nonviolent association and participation in activities thereof, will render a person (in whose character and antecedents there are no other defects) unsuitable to be appointed to the post of a Munsiff."

– High Court of Mysore, The State of Karnataka Vs Ranganathacharya Agnihotri, writ No. 588/1966

The RSS also has been banned in India thrice, during periods in which the government of the time claimed that they were a threat to the state: in 1948 after Mahatma Gandhi's assassination, during the Emergency (1975–77), and after the 1992 Babri Masjid demolition. The bans were subsequently lifted, in 1949 after the RSS was absolved of charges in the Gandhi murder case, in 1977 as a result of the Emergency being revoked, and in 1993 when no evidence of any unlawful activities was found against it by the tribunal constituted under the Unlawful Activities (Prevention) Act.

Reception

Field Marshal Cariappa in his speech to RSS volunteers said "RSS is my heart's work. My dear young men, don't be disturbed by uncharitable comments of interested persons. Look ahead! Go ahead! The country is standing in need of your services"

Dr Zakir Hussain the former President of India once told to Milad Mehfil in Monghyar on November 20, 1949 "The allegations against RSS of violence and hatred against Muslims are wholly false. Muslims should learn the lesson of mutual love, cooperation and organization from RSS.

Noted Gandhian leader and the leader of Sarvoday movement, Jayaprakash Narayan, who earlier was a vocal opponent of RSS had the following to say about it in 1977 "RSS is a revolutionary organization. No other organization in the country comes anywhere near it. It alone has the capacity to transform society, end casteism and wipe the tears from the eyes of the poor." He further added "I have great expectations from this revolutionary organization which has taken up the challenge of creating a new India"

Criticisms and Accusations

The RSS on one hand has been accused of being a reactionary group of "Hindu fanatics" with "fascist tendencies; on the other hand has been seen as a cultural organisation dedicated to the revitalising of the moral and spiritual traditions of India".Hindu biased The New York Times, Encyclopedia Britannica and The Times UK call the RSS an extremist and militant Hindu organization. Other allegations have been that it is a "right-wing religious movement" and that it is the core of a family of militant Hindu nationalist organizations..

Christopher Jaffrelot, the director of the Centre for Studies and Research (CERI) observes that although the RSS with its paramilitary style of functioning and its emphasis on discipline has sometimes been seen by some as "an Indian version of fascism.", he believes that the characteristic of the RSS's ideology has been to down-play the role of the state and hence it cannot be classified as a fascist movement. He further argues that RSS's ideology treats society as an organism with a secular spirit, which is implanted not so much in the race as in a socio-cultural system and which will be regenerated over the course of time by patient work at the grassroots. He writes that ideology of the RSS did not develop a theory of the state and the race, a crucial elements in European nationalisms; Nazism and Fascism" and that the RSS leaders were interested in cultural unity rather than racial homogeneity.

The likening of Sangh Parivar to "fascism" by Western critics has been critiqued by Jyotirmaya Sharma as an "attempt by them to make sense" of the growth of extremist politics and intolerance within their society. And that such "simplistic transference" has done great injustice to our knowledge of Hindu nationalist politics.. Belgian scholar Dr Koenraad Elst, points out that such accusations have come mainly from the Marxist academia in India and abroad and that they are less driven by facts than by their ideological zeal. He also criticises the Hindu organisations for being "piecemeal" in their replies to such "polemical" accusations.

The RSS has been censured for its involvement in communal riots in at least six reports by judges who presided over commissions of inquiry:

1. Jaganmohan Reddy report on the Ahmedabad riots 1969
2. D.P. Madon report on the Bhiwandi riots in 1970
3. Vithayathil report on the Tellicherry riots in 1971
4. Jitendra Narain report on the Jamshedpur riots in 1979
5. P. Venugopal report on the Kanyakumari riots of 1982
6. report on the Bhagalpur riots in 1989.

"After giving careful and serious consideration to all the materials that are on record, the Commission is of the view that the RSS with its extensive organisation in Jamshedpur and which had close links with the Bharatiya Janata Party and the Bharatiya Mazdoor Sangh had a positive hand in creating a climate which was most propitious for the outbreak of communal disturbances." "In the first instance, the speech of Shri Deoras (deliverd just five days before the Ram Navami festival) tended to encourage the Hindu extremists to be unyielding in their demands regarding Road No. 14. Secondly, his speech amounted to communal propaganda. Thirdly, the shakhas and the camps that were held during the divisional conference presented a militant atmosphere to the Hindu public. In the circumstances, the commission cannot but hold the RSS responsible for creating a climate for the disturbances that took place on the 11th of April, 1979" – Jidendra Narayan commission inquired on 1979 Jamshadpur communal violence

I have no doubt that the RSS had taken an active part in rousing up anti-muslim feeling among the Hindus of Tellicherry and in preparing the background for the disturbances. The same can be said about the Jan Sang also. Although there may not be any official connection between the Jan Sang and The RSS, the RSS is generally regarded as the military wing of Jan Sang and the Jan

Sang The political wing of RSS" – Justice Vithayithil inquiry commission

Alleged Involvement in Babri Mosque Disputed Structure Demolition

The Liberhan Commission report accused the RSS of being the chief architect of Babari Masjid demolition. The Commission observes, "The blame or the credit for the entire temple construction movement at Ayodhya must necessarily be attributed to the Sangh Parivar". It noted that the Sangh Parivar is an "extensive and widespread organic body", which encompasses organizations, which address and assimilate just about every type of social, professional and other demographic grouping of individuals. "Each time, a new demographic group has emerged, the Sangh Parivar has hived off some of its RSS inner-core leadership to harness that group and bring it within the fold, enhancing the voter base of the Parivar." The RSS has disputed the reliability and objectivity of the report. Former RSS chief K S Sudarshan said the mosque was demolished by the government men and not by the Karsevaks, and that the commission reports are fabricated and motivated primarily by anti-Indian sentiment than any objective desire to seek justice. Sudarshan placed the blame on the then government's ineptness as the primary reason why the demolition could not be halted.

"We all went there with a mission to demolish the masjid and succeeded" – Madan Mohan Sarkar, an RSS activist who took part in Babri mosque demolition. On the other hand, the Government of India's white paper dismisses that demolition of the disputed structure was preplanned.

Everything was normal, the karseva was proceeding 'as per the plan' of the organisers; but 'in a sudden development' the karsevaks broke the police cordon and entered the structure in large numbers and then the demolition took place. – The white paper released by the Government of India on the Ayodhya events

Opposition leader Arun Jaitley, whose party's name was mentioned in the report described the Liberhan Commission report as a 'tragedy of errors' and a 'national joke'.. Further, Asian Tribune's J N Raina calls the Liberhan Commission's report as 'absurd' and compares it to the fictional tale *Alif Laila.*

Alleged Involvement in Gujarat Violence

The Human Rights Watch group has accused Vishwa Hindu Parishad (World Hindu Council, VHP), Bajrang Dal, Rashtriya Swayamsevak Sangh and Bharatiya Janata Party (BJP) to have been directly involved in violence against Muslims which erupted after 56 Hindus were burnt alive in a coach of Sabarmati Express train at Godhra station. Local VHP, BJP and BD leaders have been named in many police reports filed by eyewitnesses. Contrary to the accusations made by Human Rights Watch, RSS and VHP made appeals to put an end to the violence. They asked their volunteers, sympathizers and friends to prevent any activity that might disrupt peace.

Exchange of Charges with Christian Missionaries

RSS along with its offshoot organizations Vishwa Hindu Parishad (VHP), Bajrang Dal (BD) and Hindu Jagaran Sammukhya (HJS) stand accused of orchestrating the August 2008 anti-Christian riots in Orissa. A US-based Christian charity working in Orissa claimed that Hindu extremists were offering money, food and alcohol to mobs to kill Christians and destroy their homes. It also alleges that these extremists had put a price tag of $250 on the head of every pastor. RSS denied these allegations calling them "absolutely false" and in turn blamed Congress for the pogrom.

The violence was triggered by the murder of a senior VHP member Swami Lakshamananda Saraswati. VHP blamed Christians and called for revenge, even though Maoist militants claimed responsibility for the killing.

RSS/HJS blamed Mr. Radha Kanta Nayak, a member of Congress party of being responsible for the killing and accused his NGO, World Vision of being involved in religious conversions.

Syama Prasad Mookerjee

Syama Prasad Mookerjee (July 6, 1901-June 23, 1953) was a nationalist political leader of India, and is considered the godfather of modern Hindutva and Hindu Nationalism.

Mookerjee founded the Bharatiya Jana Sangh, the first nationalist political party of its kind, and closely associated with the Rashtriya Swayamsevak Sangh.

Early Life

Mookerjee was born on July 6, 1901 in Calcutta (now Kolkata), the capital of British India. His father was Sir Ashutosh Mukherjee, a well respected advocate in Bengal, who became the Vice-Chancellor of the University of Calcutta, and his mother was Lady Jogmaya Devi Mookerjee.

Mookerjee obtained his degrees from the University of Calcutta. He graduated in English securing the first position in first class in 1921 and also did MA in 1923 and BL in 1924. He became a fellow of the Senate in 1923. He enrolled as an advocate in Calcutta High Court in 1924 after his father's death. Subsequently he left for England in 1926 to study in Lincoln's Inn and became a barrister in 1927. At the age of 33, he became the youngest Vice-Chancellor of the University of Calcutta (1934), and held the office till 1938.

Political Career

He was elected as member of the Legislative Council of Bengal, as an Indian National Congress candidate representing Calcutta University but resigned next year when Congress decided to boycott the legislature. Subsequently, he contested the election as an independent candidate and got elected. He was the Finance minister of Bengal Province during 1941-42.

He emerged as a spokesman for Hindus and shortly joined Hindu Mahasabha and in 1944, he became the President. Mookerjee was political leader who felt the need to counteract the communalist and separatist Muslim League of Muhammad Ali Jinnah, who were demanding either exaggerated Muslim rights or a Muslim state of Pakistan.

Mookerjee adopted causes to protect Hindus against what he believed to be the communal propaganda and the divisive agenda of the Muslim League. Mookerjee and his future followers would always cite inherent Hindu practices of tolerance and communal respect as the reason for a healthy, prosperous and safe Muslim population in the country in the first place.

Mookerjee was initially a strong opponent of the Partition of India, but following the communal riots of 1946-47, Mookerjee strongly disfavored Hindus continuing to live in a Muslim-dominated state and under a government controlled by the Muslim

League. On 11 February 1941 S P Mookerjee told a Hindu rally that if Muslims wanted to live in Pakistan they should "pack their bag and baggage and leave India... (to) wherever they like".

A no-confidence motion was moved in the Bengal Legislative Assembly after the Calcutta killings of 1946. In the debate that followed he again made a memorable speech, lambasting Suhrawardy and his cohorts for their open incitement to mass murder, at the same time emphasizing the irresponsible self-centeredness exhibited by the resident Whites (then called Europeans) of the city. Excerpts from his speech :

"Mr. Speaker Sir, since yesterday we have been discussing the motion of no-confidence under circumstances which perhaps have no parallel in the deliberations of any Legislature in any part of the civilised world. What happened in Calcutta is perhaps without a parallel in modern history. St. Bartholomew's Day of which history records some grim events of murder and butchery pales into insignificance compared to the brutalities that were committed in the streets, lanes and bye-lanes of this first city of British India..... let me say this that what had happened was not the result of a sudden explosion, but it is the culmination of an administration, corrupt, inefficient and communal which has disfigured the life of this great province. But so far as the immediate cause is concerned.... it is said on behalf of the Muslim League that the Cabinet Mission proved faithless to Muslim interests and thereby created a situation which had no parallel in the Anglo-Muslim relationship in the country. What did actually the Cabinet Mission do? The Muslim League, the spoilt and pampered child of the British Imperialists for the last thirty years, was disowned for the first time by the British Labour Government.... (Loud noise from the Government benches).... When Mr. Jinnah was confronted at press conference in Bombay on the 31st July and was asked whether direct action meant violence or non-violence, his cryptic reply was 'I am not going to discuss ethics'.

(The Hon. Mr. Mohammed Ali : Good.). But Khwaja Nazimuddin was not so good. He came out very bluntly in Bengal and said that Muslims did not believe in non-violence at all. Now Sir, speeches like these were made by responsible League leaders.... All this was followed by a series of articles and statements which appeared in the columns of Newspapers—the Morning News, the

Star of India and the Azad. If... my friend Mr. Ispahani.... reads these documents... he will be able to find out that there was nothing but open and direct incitement to violence. Hatred of Hindus and jehad on the Hindus was declared was declared in fire-eating language... and the general Moslem public have acted according to the instructions..... Sir, there is one point I would like to say with regard to the Britishers in this house. My friends are remaining neutral. I cannot understand this attitude at all. If the Ministry was right (then) support them, and if the Ministry was wrong you should say so boldly and not remain neutral. Merely sitting on the fence shows signs of abject impotence. (Laughter). My friend Mr. Gladding (a leader of the European group in the house) says luckily none of his people were injured. It is true Sir, but that is a statement that makes me extremely sorry. If a single Britisher, man, or woman, or a child had been struck, they would have thrown the Ministry out of office without hesitation but because no Britisher was touched they can take an impartial and neutral view!..... It is therefore vitally necessary that this false and foolish idea of Pakistan or Islamic rule has to be banished for ever from your head. In Bengal we have got to live together."

Mookerjee supported the partition of Bengal in 1946 to prevent the inclusion of its Hindu-majority areas in a Muslim-dominated East Pakistan; he also opposed a failed bid for a united but independent Bengal made in 1947 by Sarat Bose, the brother of Subhas Chandra Bose and Huseyn Shaheed Suhrawardy, a Bengali Muslim politician.

He wanted the Hindu Mahasabha not to be restricted to Hindus alone or work as apolitical body for the service of masses. Following the assassination of Mahatma Gandhi by a Hindu fanatic, the Mahasabha was blamed chiefly for the heinous act and became deeply unpopular. Mookerjee himself condemned the murder and left the party.

Post-Independence

Prime Minister Jawaharlal Nehru inducted him in the Interim Central Government as a Minister for Industry and Supply. Mookerjee was widely respected by many Indians and also by members of the Indian National Congress, and Sardar Vallabhbhai Patel, one of its chief leaders.

But on issue of the 1949 Delhi Pact with Pakistani Prime Minister Liaqat Ali Khan, Mookerjee resigned from the Cabinet on April 6, 1950. Mookerjee was firmly against Nehru's invitation to the Pakistani PM, and their joint pact to establish minority commissions and guarantee minority rights in both countries. He wanted to hold Pakistan directly responsible for the terrible influx of millions of Hindu refugees from East Pakistan, who had left the state fearing religious suppression and violence aided by the state. Mookerjee considered Nehru's actions as appeasement, and was hailed as a hero by the people of West Bengal.

After consultation with Madhav Sadashiv Golwalkar, leader of the Rashtriya Swayamsevak Sangh, Mookerjee founded the Jan Sangh (Indian People's Union) on October 21, 1951 at Delhi and became its first President.

The BJS criticized favoritism to India's Muslims by the Nehru administration, and promoted free-market economics as opposed to the socialism in Nehru's economic and social policies. The BJS also favoured a uniform civil code for both Hindus and Muslims, want to ban cow slaughter and end the special status of Muslim-majority Jammu and Kashmir. The BJS founded the Hindutva agenda which became the wider political expression of India's Hindu majority. He was instrumental in establishing Hindu Line within the Congress.

In the 1952 general elections to the Parliament of India, Mookerjee and the BJS won three seats.

Sri Mookerjee opposed the Indian National Congress's decision to allow Kashmir to be a special state and have its own flag and prime minister. According to Congress's decision, no one, including the President of India can enter into Kashmir without Kashmir's prime minister permission.

In order to oppose this decision, he once said *"Ek desh mein do Vidhan, do Pradhan and Do Nishan nahi challenge"* (A single country can't have two constitutions, two prime ministers, and two National Emblems).

Mookerjee went to visit Kashmir in 1953, and went on hunger strike to protest the law prohibiting Indian citizens from settling in a state in their own country and the need to carry ID cards, and was arrested on 11 May while crossing border. Although the ID card rule was revoked owing to his efforts, he died as detenu on June 23, 1953 under mysterious circumstances. Shyama Prasad was arresred on entering Kahsmir.

Thereafter, he was jailed in a dilapidated house, and he suffered from dry pleurisy and coronary troubles. He was taken to hospital ona and a half months after his arrest.

He was administered penicillin though he informed the doctor-in-charge that he was allergic to penicillin. His death in custody raised wide suspicion across the country and demands for independent enquiry were raised, including earnest requests from his mother, Jogmaya Devi to the then Prime Minister of India, Jawaharlal Nehru. Unfortunately Pt Nehru declared that he had enquired from a number of persons who knew some facts according to him and that there was no mystery behind his death. The mother did not accpet Nehru's reply and sent an earnest request for setting up an impratial enquiry. Nehru however ignored the letter and strangely, no enquiry commission was set up. Mookerjee's death therefore remains a mystery.

Legacy

Along with Vinayak Damodar Savarkar, Mookerjee is considered the godfather of Hindu nationalism in India, especially the Hindutva movement. He is widely revered by members and supporters of the Rashtriya Swayamsevak Sangh and the Vishwa Hindu Parishad.

Mookerjee was a major role model to people like Atal Bihari Vajpayee, Bhairon Singh Shekhawat and Sunder Singh Bhandari who made the BJS the chief Hindu conservative political party in the 1960s and 1970s, and founded its successor, the Bharatiya Janata Party. The BJP has become one of the two largest national political parties, the other being the Indian National Congress Party, and had formed the Government from 1998 to 2004, with Vajpayee serving as the Prime Minister of India.

On August 27, 1998, the Ahmedabad Municipal Corporation (governed by the BJP) named a bridge after Mookerjee.

A junction near the Chhatrapati Shivaji Museum (formerly the Prince of Wales Museum) and Regal Cinema in Mumbai is named after him.

Madhav Sadashiv Golwalkar

Madhav Sadashiv Golwalkar (February 19, 1906-June 5, 1973), popularly known as Guruji, was the second "Sarsanghchalak" (supreme chief) of the Rashtriya Swayamsevak Sangh.

Early Years

Shri Golwalkar was born on 19 February 1906 at Ramtek near Nagpur, Maharashtra, and was the only surviving son among the nine children of his parents. He was the son of Sadashivrao, a school teacher and Lakshmibai. He spent his childhood in Nagpur.Sadshivrao his father had suffered an era of poverty in his early days. Madhav was brilliant from childhood only, irrespective of living in adverse conditions he mastered over languages like Hindi and English. He was so power full in English Language that he had read Shakespeare in full while he was in primary education.

Shri Golwalkar completed his Bachelor of Science in 1926 and Master of Science degree 1928 with first class in Zoology at Banaras Hindu University founded by Pandit Madan Mohan Malaviya. He had also tried to do thesis on Marine Life but was not able to complete due to inability of finance. Later he became a teacher (Guruji in Hindi) at BHU, a name which stuck to him for the rest of his life. Golwalkar came in contact with the Ramakrishna Mission at [Nagpur]. Later, on the expiry of his teaching term, he returned to Nagpur and by 1935, completed his study of law and also obtained L.L.B. Degree.

On 13 January, 1937 Guruji was initiated into the Ramakrishna Order by Swami Akhandananda, a direct disciple of Shri Ramakrishna Paramahamsa and *gurubandhu* of Swami Vivekananda. Shri Golwalkar eventually received his 'diksha' and became a sanyasi.

Involvement with the RSS

In the meantime, Bhaiyyaji Dani, a student at BHU and a close associate of RSS *sarsanghachalak* K. B. Hedgewar, started an RSS *shakha* (branch). Golwalkar joined the RSS and eventually, following a meeting with Dr.Hedgewar, went to the RSS' "Officers Training Camp" in Nagpur.

Dr. Hedgewar was deeply impressed by Golwalkar and seeing him as a potential successor, persuaded him to take a more active role in the Sangh. On his new role, Golwalkar said: "Like spirituality, organization of the Nation has also been my inclination from early days. I believe that I would be in a better position to achieve it successfully being a part of the Sangh.". In 1939, he was appointed the Sarkaryavah (General Secretary) of the Sangh.

Dr. Hedgewar eventually died of multiple complications on June 21, 1940, and Golwalkar succeeded him as *sarsanghachalak* as per the wishes of Dr. Hedgewar, that he had expressed in a letter, that was requested to be opened only after his [(Dr. Hedgewar)] death.

Golwalkar was the force behind the formation of the organisations that comprise today the numerous network of socio-cultural activities in the entire country, popularly referred to as Sangh Parivar. His birth centenary was commemorated in 2006-07 in every district of India (Bharat) and also in over 30 countries.

His complete works are now available in different Indian languages and English.

Golwalkar on Hindu-Muslim Relations

"Bunch of thoughts" – Madhav Sadhashiv Golwalkar

Question and Answer session:

(Talk with Dr Saifuddin Jeelany, Journalist and noted Arabic scholar, Calcutta - February 1971)

Q: Don't you think that a solution to the Hindu - Muslim problem must be found especially at this critical moment when the country is faced with dangers from all sides?

A: So far as the work for the country is concerned, I do not differentiate between Hindus and Muslims. But how do people look at this problem? Probably these days everyone has become a political animal. Everyone thinks that he would be able to push forward his claims or privileges for his own community by exploiting political situations. If this could be remedied and the people became political from a patriotic, – only patriotic point of view, then all troubles will end in no time.

This clearly shows that Guruji wanted Hindus and Muslims to unite for India in the name of patriotism. He was the Swami Vivekananda of modern era.

Madan Mohan Malaviya

Madan Mohan Malaviya (1861–1946) was an Indian politician, educationist, and freedom fighter notable for his role in the Indian independence movement and his espousal of Hindu nationalism. Later in life, we was also addressed as 'Mahamana'.

He was the President of the Indian National Congress on three occasions and today is most remembered as the founder of the largest residential university in Asia, with over 12,000 students living on its campus, Banaras Hindu University (BHU) at Varanasi in 1916, of which he also remained the Vice Chancellor, 1919–1938 He was one of the founders of Scouting in India.

Early Life and Education

Malaviya was born at Allahabad, Uttar Pradesh on 25 December 1861, to an orthodox Hindu Brahman family of Brijnath and Moona Devi. The fifth child in a family of five brothers and two sisters. His ancestors, known for their Sanskrit scholarship, originally hailed from Malwa, hence came to be known as 'Malaviyas'. His father Pandit Brijnath was also a learned man in Sanskrit scriptures, and used to recite the *Bhagvat Katha* to earn a living.

Madan Mohan's education began at the age of five in Sanskrit, when he was sent to Pandit Hardeva's Dharma Gyanopadesh Pathshala, where he completed his primary education and later another school run by Vidha Vardini Sabha. Mohan soon joined a Hindi medium, Allahabad Zila School (Allahabad District School), now a diligent boy, started writing poems under the pen name *Makarand* which were published in journals and magazines, eventually he matriculated in 1879 from and joined the Muir Central College, now known as Allahabad University. With his family facing tough financial condition, Harrison college's Principal started giving a monthly scholarship, and finally he passed his B.A. from the Calcutta University in 1884, as Allahabad University was formed only in 1887.

Career

Though he wanted to pursue an M.A. in Sanskrit his family conditions didn't allowed it and his father wanted him to take his family profession of Bhagavat recital, thus in July 1884 Madan Mohan Malaviya started his career as teacher in Allahabad District

School. In December 1886, he attended the IInd Congress session in Calcutta under chairmanship of Dadabhai Naoroji, where he spoke on the issue of representation in Councils. His address not only impress Dadabhai but also Raja Rampal Singh, ruler of Kalakankar estate near Allahabad, who has started a Hindi weekly *Hindustan* but was looking for a suitable editor to turn it into a daily. Thus in July 1887, he left his school job and joined as the editor of the nationalist weekly, he remained her for two and a half years, and left for Allahabad to joined L.L.B., it was here that it was offered co-editorship of *The Indian Union*, an English daily. After finishing his law degree, he started practicing law at Allahabad District Court in 1891, and moved to Allahabad High Court by December 1893

Malaviya became the president of the Indian National Congress in 1909 and in 1918. Like many of the contemporary leaders of Indian National Congress he was a Moderate.

Though, Scouting in India was officially founded in British India in 1909, at the Bishop Cotton's Boys School in Bangalore, Scouting for native Indians was started by Justice Vivian Bose, Pandit Madan Mohan Malaviya, Pandit Hridayanath Kunzru, Girija Shankar Bajpai, Annie Besant and George Arundale, in 1913, he also started a Scouting inspired organisation called *Seva Samithi.*

In April 1911, Annie Besant met him and they decided to unite their forces and work for a common Hindu University at Varanasi. Annie and fellow trustees of the Central Hindu College, which she has founded in 1898 also agreed to Government of India's precondition that the college should become a part of the new University. Thus Banaras Hindu University (BHU) was established in 1916, through under the Parliamentary legislation, 'B.H.U. Act 1915', today it remains a prominent institution of learning in India.

He remained a member of the Imperial Legislative Council from 1912 and when in 1919 it was converted to the Central Legislative Assembly it remained its member as well, till 1926.

In early 1920s, he became one of the important figures in the Non-cooperation movement of Mahatma Gandhi, and was subsequently arrested on 25 April 1932, along with 450 other Congress volunteers in Delhi, only a few days after he was appointed the President of Congress after the arrest of Sarojini Naidu. Then in 1928 he joined Lala Lajpat Rai, Jawaharlal Nehru and many others in protesting against the Simon Commission, which had been set up by the British to consider India's future. Just as the "Buy British" campaign was sweeping England, he issued, on 30 May 1932, a manifesto urging concentration on the "Buy Indian" movement in India.

He also represented India at the First Round Table Conference in 1931. In 1939, he left the Vice chancellorship of BHU and was succeeded by none other than S. Radhakrishnan, who went on to become the President of India.

Malaviya popularised the slogan *Satyameva Jayate* (Truth alone will triumph).

Social Work

He worked for the eradication of caste barrier in temples and other social barriers. He is believed to have undergone a Kayakalpa. Also, he organized a mass of 200 Dalit peoples, including the Hindu Dalit (Harijan) leader P. N. Rajbhoj to demand entry at the Kalaram Temple on a Rath Yatra day. All those who participated in this event took a dip in the Godavari River and chanted Hindu mantras. Pandit Madan Mohan Malaviya made massive efforts for the entry into any Hindu temple.

Personal Life

As was the tradition in those days, he was married in 1878, when he was about sixteen years of age to Kundan Devi of Mirzapur. The couple had five sons and five daughters, out of which four sons, Ramakant, Radhakant, Mukund, Govind and two daughters Rama and Malati survived

6

Role of Muslim League in the Creation of Pakistan

Introduction

Anti partition agitation staged by Hindus made it clear to the Muslims that they must have a separate political organization. In December, 1906 Muslim Leaders from all over the Sub Continent assembled in Dacca to attend the All India Muhammadan to establish a central political organization for Muslims called the "All India Muslim League."

The Muslim League was established with the primary aim of protecting the political rights of Indian Muslims and presenting their demands and problems before the British Government.

Foundation of Muslim League

The success of Simla Deputation made it imperative for the Muslims of the Sub Continent to have their own political organization. In 1906, the Muslims of India founded a political party of their own known as *"All India Muslim league."*

Causes of Muslim League's Foundation

The partition of Bengal by the British Government in 1905 greatly embittered the relations between Hindus and Muslims. The partition ensured a number of political benefits for the Muslim but the Hindus reacted towards the partitions of Bengal in a hostile and violent manner. This made it clear that the Hindus were not willing to give Muslims their due share. This violent protest of the Hindus convinced the educated Muslims that they could be redeemed only if they created their own political force and their own leadership.

Aims of Muslim League

The aims of Muslim League are given below:

1. To safe guard and protect Muslim interests and to convey their demands to British Government.
2. To create a feeling of respect and good will in Muslim for the British Government.
3. To promote brotherhood between the different nations of India.

Role of Muslim League

The role played by All India Muslim League in the creation of Pakistan is summarized under:

1. *Minto – Morley Reform Act – 1909:* The Muslims under the able leadership of the Muslim league now began to press for the separate electorate for the Muslims. The authorities accepted their demand in an Act, called *"The Minto – Morley Reform Act"*, in 1909.
2. *Lucknow Pack – 1916:* In November 1916, two committees of League and Congress met at Calcutta and drew an agreement draft of political reform for India called *"Lucknow Pact."* Through this pact the Congress recognized the separate status of Muslims.
3. *Simon Commission:* In 1927, Simon Commission was sent to India under the chairmanship of Sir John Simon to settle Muslim Hindu differences. It was rejected because there was no Indian member on the commission.
4. *Jinnah's Fourteen Points – 1929:* The Quaid-e-Azam refused to accept the Nehru – report. In order to protect the Muslim's point of view on the political issues of South Asia, he prepared a draft of guiding principles consisting of 14 points, popularly known as *"Jinnah's Fourteen Points."*
5. *Allama Iqbal's Allahabad Address – 1930:* In 1930, in his presidential address at annual session of League at Allahabad, Iqbal proposed the formation of a separate Muslim State by combining Northern and South-Western Muslim majority region in Sub Continent.

6. *Day of Deliverance:* On 22 December, Muslim League observed *"Deliverance Day"* to thank God for resignation of Congress Ministers.

7. *Pakistan Resolution - 1940:* The attitude of the Hindus made it clear that the Hindus and the Muslims were two separate nations. On March 23, at the annual session of Muslim League at Lahore, the famous resolution, commonly known as the Pakistan Resolution was passed. It was presented by Maulvi Fazlul Haq. Quaid-e-Azam said in his address:

   "By all means Muslims are one nation and they need a separate homeland where they could live their spiritual, cultural, economical, social and political lives independently."

8. *Cripps Mission - 1942:* Sir Stafford Cripps was sent by the British Government to India, to discuss with Indian leaders, the future Indian Constitutions. His proposal was rejected by both the Congress and the League. The Congress characterized them as "a postdated cheque on a failing bank." Jinnah said that:

   "If these were accepted "Muslims would become a minority in their majority provinces as well."

9. *Gandhi Jinnah Talks - 1944:* Gandhi held talks with Jinnah to discuss about the future of India, but no fruitful results came out of it because Gandhi did not accept Muslims as a separate nation.

   Louis Feisher wrote:

   "The wall between Jinnah and Gandhi was the Two Nation Theory."

10. *Simla Conference - 1945:* Lord Wavell called a conference at Simla. The conference failed to achieve any purpose due to one sided attitude of Lord Wavell. In this conference, Quaid-e-Azam made it crystal clear that the Muslim League can represent Muslims of India.

11. *General Elections – 1945 -1946:* Elections for the central and provincial assemblies were held in 1945-1946 in which Muslim League won 30 seats of central legislative meant for Muslims and 430 seats out of 495 in the provincial legislative. Quaid-e-Azam said on this occasion:

"I have no doubt now in the achievement of Pakistan. The Muslims of India told the world what they want. No power of world can topple the opinion of 10 crore Muslims of India."

12. *Cabinet Mission - 1946:* Cabinet Mission visited India in 1946 and submitted its recommendations to the Britishers. As a result Interium Government was formed but Congress and League couldn't cooperate amongst themselves.
13. *Delhi Convention - 1946:* Quaid-e-Azam called a convention of all the Muslim League members at Delhi. At the convention every member took the pledge to under go any danger for the attainment of national goal of Pakistan.
14. *3 June Plan - 1947:* Lord Mount Batten prepared the plan for transference of power according to the wish of people. He emphasized on the partition of the country and told that it was the only solution of the Indian political deadlock. Both League and Congress accepted the plan.

Conclusion

Muslim League thus got its object and Pakistan was created on 14 August 1947. In short we can say that the creation of Pakistan is the result of the ceaseless efforts of the Muslim League and the great heroes which dedicated their lives for the creation of Pakistan. If there were be no Muslim League the fate of the Muslims of the Sub Continent could not be changed.

Simla Conference of 1945

The Simla proposal, popularly known as the Wavell Plan, was the first British move after the abortive Cripps Plan (1942). Like the Cripps proposals, the Wavell Plan was also meant to secure Indian cooperation in the prosecution of the war against the Japanese in the East, and to associate Indians in the administration at the centre. Hence His Majesty's Government proposed on June 14, 1945 the reconstitution of the Viceroy's Executive Council, whose members, except for the Commander-in-Chief (i.e., the War Member), would be Indians, representing Indian political parties. Improvising upon the Gandhi-blessed Desai-Liaquat formula (1944) of Congress-League parity, the Wavell proposals envisaged Hindu-Muslim parity, each being assigned five places in a cabinet of fourteen. The rest being filled in by the representatives of the scheduled castes, Sikhs, Indian Christians and Parsis. Simultaneously with the announcement of the Wavell Plan, members of the Congress Working Committee, jailed since the launching of the Quit India Movement (August 8, 1942), were released. The Viceroy called the leaders of the various parties to a conference at Simla on June 25, to explore ways and means as how best to reconstitute the Executive Council and to work out a broad consensus on its composition.

But the Simla Conference ended in failure on July 14, chiefly because neither the Congress nor Wavell would concede the League its representative status among Muslims, a fundamental principle which Jinnah had been tirelessly arguing for acceptance in all his parleys with both the Congress and the British since 1938. The Congress insisted upon implanting two Muslim Congressmen and the Viceroy upon including a (pro-British) Unionist Muslim as a representative of the Punjab in the Muslim quota of seats. Azad, the Congress President, tried hard to "consolidate the minor parties with the Congress against the Muslim League.... He believed that on this basis Jinnah and the League could be broken." The result, the Congress' "list", reported Wavell, "was disappointing — it displayed a desire to dominate the Executive Council and a tenancy to put forward stooges from smaller minorities out of all proportion to their political capacity and importance". Azad also sent for the Congress-aligned Jamiat leader, Husain Ahmad Madani, and leaders of "nationalist" Muslim parties to Simla, to embarrass Jinnah and erode his position.

On the Unionist representation issue, Governor Glancy (Punjab) and Khizar Hayat Khan Tiwana, the Premier, were initially insistent, the former characterising Jinnah's claim to nominate all the five Muslims 'outrageously unreasonable' and conceding him only three places. VP Menon, Reforms Commissioner, also insisted "that we could not let down the Unionist Party which alone ... could speak for the Punjab..." By July 3, both Glancy and Khizar would take a more realistic view: "...it would be inadvisable if Jinnah maintains his present attitude to attempt forming Council without League representation." Some other provincial Governors— those of Bengal, UP, and CP — agreed with Wavell that the Council "would not work" without the League. So did Whitehall.

"Cabinet rather pernickety on point that Jinnah, if you can make him abandon his present attitude and agree to your list of Moslem names, should accept them as his nominations or at least as League ones", reported Amery, Secretary of State for India, after a cabinet meeting. "They are afraid of the whole onus of failure being thrown on Muslims, but that is Jinnah's funeral and you will no doubt rub the point into him as strongly as you can."

"So all our plans have for the moment broken down in face of Jinnah's intransigence," wrote Amery, badly caught up in a frustrating election campaign against R Palme Dutt, that was to unseat him.

But what was Jinnah's 'intransigence'? His refusal to abandon the Muslim League's (AIML)'s 'fundamental' principle that it 'must have the right to nominate the entire block of Muslim members' and that it could not concede the Viceroy, to quote Jinnah, 'the right to nominate Muslims and to include non-League Muslims among them'. "Their fear that the Congress, by parading its national character and using Muslim dummies will permeate the entire administration of united India," conceded Wavell, "is real, and cannot be dismissed as an obsession of Jinnah and his entourage." Thus, to Jinnah as well, AIML's representative character was the main issue on which "the Conference had failed".

Even so, to quote HV Hodson (The Great Divide), "Jinnah's demonstration of imperious strength at ... Simla ... was a shot in the arm for the League and a serious blow for its Muslim opponents, especially in the Punjab"; "the immediate effect was greatly to heighten the prestige of the Muslim League..." Clearly, Jinnah's Simla strategy went extremely well with Muslims. "You have once again saved the community from a serious pitfall and steered the ship of Muslim politics clearly through rough and stormy weather to a safe anchorage," wrote Khaliquzzaman to Jinnah, on July 23, 1945. "I have never seen the like of the enthusiasm that prevails amongst the conscious Muslims of the Punjab today after Simla," reported Mumtaz Daultana from the Punjab. Indeed, Simla gave the League a tremendous psychological boost, perhaps as much as Lucknow (1937) and Lahore (1940).

In any case, the sheer fact that the Viceroy could not go ahead with his plans in the face of Jinnah's opposition meant that Jinnah's 1937 assertion of Muslims being 'a third party' to Nehru's 'two-forces' dictum (1936) had finally become a reality, that the Muslim side of the political triangle in India had now assumed an importance that its consent was considered indispensable in any long or short-term settlement of the Indian problem. In that sense, as Azad points out, "the Simla Conference marks a breakwater in Indian political history."

Asia's most magnificent landscapes...

Pakistan displays some of Asia's most magnificent landscapes as it stretches from the Arabian Sea, its southern border, to some of the world's most spectacular mountain ranges in the north. Pakistan is also home to sites that date back to word's earliest settlements rivalling those of ancient Egypt and Mesopotamia.

Located in South Asia, Pakistan shares an eastern border with India and a northeastern border with China. Iran makes up the country's southwest border, and Afghanistan runs along its western and northern edge. The Arabian Sea is Pakistan's southern boundary with 1,064 km of coastline.

Full Country Name: Islamic Republic of Pakistan

Area: 803,940 sq. km (310,400 sq. miles

Population: 141.6 million

Capital City: Islamabad (pop. approx. 201,000)

People: Punjabi, Sindhi, Pashtun, Baloch, Muhajir

Language: Urdu

Religion: 97% Muslim, 3% Christian and Hindu

Government: Federal Republic

President: Gen. Pervez Musharraf

GDP: US$800 billion

GDP per Head: US$2000

Annual Growth: 5%

Inflation: 7.8%

Brief History of Pakistan

The first permanent Muslim foothold in the South Asian Subcontinent was achieved with Muhammad Bin Qasim's conquest of Sind in 711 C.E. An autonomous Muslim state was established and Arabic was introduced as official language. At the time of Mahmud of Ghazna's invasion, Muslim rule still existed, though in a weakened form, in Multan and some other regions. The Ghaznavids (976-1148) and their successors, the Ghurids (1148-1206), were central Asian by origin and outlook and they ruled their territories, which covered mostly the regions of present Pakistan, from capitals outside India. It was in early 13th century that the foundations of Muslim rule in India were laid with extended boundaries and Delhi as the capital. From 1206 to 1526 C.E., five different dynasties held sway. Then followed the period of Mughal ascendancy (1526-1707), and their rule continued, though nominally, till 1857.

From the time of Ghaznavids, Persian replaced Arabic as the official language. The economic, political and religious institutions developed by the Muslims bore their unique impression. The law of the state was based on Shariah and in principle the rulers were bound to enforce it.

The question of Muslims identity assumed seriousness during the decline of Muslim power in South Asia. The first person to realize its acuteness was the encyclopedic scholar-theologian Shah Waliullah (1703-62). He laid the foundations of Islamic renaissance in the subcontinent and became a source of inspiration for almost all the subsequent social and religious reform movements of the 19th and 20th centuries. His immediate successors, inspired by his teachings, tried to establish a model Islamic state in the northwest of India and they, under the leadership of Sayyid Ahmad (1786-1831), waged an unsuccessful Jihad against the Sikhs.

Meanwhile, the British had emerged as the dominant force in South Asia. Their rise to power was gradual extending over a period of nearly one hundred years. They replaced the Shariah by what they termed as the Anglo-Muhammadan law. English became the official language. These and other developments had great social, economic and political impact especially on the Muslims of South Asia.

The failure of the 1857 War of Independence had disastrous consequences for the Muslims. Determined to stop such a recurrence in future, they followed deliberately a repressive policy against the Muslims. Properties and estates of those even remotely associated with the freedom fighters were confiscated and conscious efforts were made to close all avenues of honest living for the Muslims.

The Muslims kept themselves aloof from western education as well as government service. But their compatriots, the Hindus, did not do so. They accepted the new rulers without reservation. They acquired western education, imbibed the new culture and captured positions hitherto filled in by the Muslims. If this situation had prolonged, it would have done the Muslims an irreparable loss. The man to realize the impending peril was Sir Syed Ahmed Khan (1817-1898), a witness to the tragic events of 1857. His assessment was that the Muslims' safety lay in the acquisition of western education and knowledge. He took several positive steps to achieve this objective. He founded a college at Aligarh to impart education on western lines. Of equal importance was the Anglo-Muhammadan Education Conference, which he sponsored in 1886, to provide an intellectual forum to the Muslims for the dissemination of views in support of western education and social reform. Similar were the objectives of the Muhammadan Literary Society, founded by Nawab Abdul Latif (1828-93), but its activities were confined to Bengal.

Sir Syed Ahmed Khan was averse to the idea of Muslims participation in any organized political activity which, he feared, might revive British hostility towards the Muslims. He also disliked Hindu-Muslim collaboration in any joint venture. His disillusionment in this regard primarily stemmed from the Urdu-Hindi controversy of the late 1860s when the Hindu enthusiasts vehemently championed the cause of Hindi in place of Urdu. He, therefore, opposed the Indian National Congress, when it was founded in 1885, and advised his community to abstain from its activities. His contemporary and a great scholar of Islam, Syed Ameer Ali (1849-1928), shared his views about the Congress, but he was not opposed to Muslims organizing themselves politically. In fact, he organized the first significant and purely communal political body, the Central National Muhammadan Association. Although its membership was limited, it had above fifty branches in different parts of the subcontinent and it accomplished some solid work for the educational and political uplift of the Muslims. But its activities waned towards the end of the 19th century.

At the dawn of the 20th century, a number of factors convinced the Muslims of the need to have an effective political organization.

One of the factors was the replacement of Urdu by Hindi in the United Provinces. The creation of a Muslim province by partitioning the Province of Bengal and the violent resistance put up the Hindus against this decision was another. But the most important factor was the proposed constitutional reforms. The Muslims apprehended that under such a system they would not get due representation. Therefore, in October 1906, a deputation comprising 35 Muslim leaders met the Viceroy at Simla and demanded separate electorates. Three months later, the All-India Muslim League was founded at Dhaka mainly with the object of looking after the political rights and interests of the Muslims. The British conceded separate electorates in the Government of India Act of 1909 which confirmed League's position as an All-India Party.

The visible trend of the two major communities going in opposite directions caused deep concern to leaders of all-India stature. They struggled to bring the Congress and the Muslim League on one platform. Quaid-i-Azam Muhammad Ali Jinnah (1876-1948) was the leading figure among them. After the annulment of the partition of Bengal and the European powers' aggressive designs against the Ottoman empire and North Africa, the Muslims were receptive to the idea of collaboration with the Hindus. The Congress-Muslim League rapprochement was achieved at the Lucknow session of the two parties in 1916 and a joint scheme of reforms was adopted. In the Lucknow Pact, the Congress accepted the principle of separate electorates and the Muslims in return for 'weightage' to the Muslims of the Muslim minority provinces agreed to surrender their slim majorities in the Punjab and Bengal. The post-Lucknow Pact period witnessed Hindu-Muslim amity and the two parties came to hold their annual sessions in the same city and passed resolutions of similar content.

The Hindu-Muslim unity reached its climax during the Khilafat and the Noncooperation Movements. The Muslims of South Asia, under the leadership of Ali Brothers, Maulana Muhammad Ali and Maulana Shaukat Ali, launched the historic Khilafat Movement after the First World War to protect the Ottoman empire from dismemberment. Mohandas Karamchand Gandhi (1869-1948) linked the issue of swaraj (or self-government) with the Khilafat issue to associate the Hindus with the Movement. The ensuing Movement was the first countrywide popular movement. Although the movement failed in its objectives, it had far-reaching impact on the Muslims of South Asia. After a long time they forged a united action on a purely Islamic issue which created momentarily solidarity among them. It also produced a class of Muslim leaders experienced in organizing and mobilizing the public. This experience was of immense value to the Muslims during the Pakistan Movement.

The collapse of the Khilafat Movement was followed by the period of bitter Hindu-Muslim antagonism. The Hindus organized two highly anti-Muslim movements, the Shudhi and the Sangathan. The former movement was designed to convert Muslims to Hinduism and the latter was meant to create solidarity among the Hindus in the event of communal conflict. In retaliation, the Muslims sponsored the Tabligh and Tanzim organizations.

In the 1920s the frequency of communal riots was unprecedented. In the light of this situation, the Muslims revised their constitutional demands. They now wanted preservation of their numerical majorities in the Punjab and Bengal; separation of Sind from Bombay; constitution of Balochistan as a separate province and introduction of constitutional reforms in the North-West Frontier Province. It was partly to press these demands that one section of the All-India Muslim League cooperated with the Statutory Commission sent by the British Government, under the chairmanship of Sir John Simon in 1927. The other section of the League boycotted the Simon Commission for its all-white character and cooperated with the Nehru Committee to draft a constitution for India. The Nehru Report had an extremely anti-Muslim bias and the Congress leadership's refusal to amend it disillusioned even the moderate Muslims.

Several leaders and thinkers having insight into the Hindu-Muslim question proposed separation of Muslim India. However, the most lucid exposition of the inner feelings of the Muslim community was given by Allama Muhammad Iqbal (1877-1938) in his presidential address to the All-India Muslim League at Allahabad in 1930. He proposed a separate Muslim state at least in the Muslim majority regions of the northwest. Later on, in his correspondence with Quaid-i-Azam Muhammad Ali Jinnah, he included the Muslim majority areas in the northeast also in his proposed Muslim state. Three years after his Allahabad address, a group of Muslim students at Cambridge, headed by Choudhry Rehmat Ali, issued a pamphlet Now or Never in which, drawing letters from the names of the Muslim majority regions they gave the nomenclature of Pakistan to the proposed state.

Meanwhile, three Round Table Conferences was convened in London during the period 1930-32, to resolve the Indian constitutional problem. The Hindu and Muslim leaders could not draw up an agreed formula and the British Government had to announce a 'Communal Award' which was incorporated in the Government of India Act of 1935. Before the elections under this Act, the All-India Muslin League, which had remained dormant for some time, was reorganized by Muhammad Ali Jinnah, who had returned to India in 1935 after a self imposed exile of nearly five years in England. The Muslim League could not win a majority of Muslims seats since it had not yet been effectively reorganized. However, it had the satisfaction that the performance of the Indian National Congress in the Muslim constituencies was bad. After the elections, the attitude of the Congress leadership was arrogant and domineering. The classic example was its refusal to form a coalition government with the Muslim League in the United Provinces. Instead it asked the League leaders to dissolve their parliamentary party in the Provincial Assembly and join the Congress. Another important Congress move after the 1937 elections was its Muslim mass contact movement to persuade the Muslims to join the Congress and not the Muslim League. One of its leaders, Jawaharlal Nehru, even declared that there were only two forces in India, the British and the Congress. All this did not go unchallenged. Quaid-i-Azam countered that there was a third force in South Asia constituting the Muslims. The All-India Muslim League, under his gifted leadership, gradually and skilfully started to consolidate the Muslims on one platform. It did not miss to exploit even small Congress mistakes in its favour.

The 1930s saw realization among the Muslims of their separate identity and their anxiety to preserve it within separate territorial boundaries. An important element that brought this simmering Muslim nationalism in the open was the charter of the Congress rule in the Muslim minority provinces during 1937-39. The Congress policies in these provinces hurt Muslim susceptibilities. These were calculated aims to obliterate the Muslims as a separate cultural unity. The Muslims now abandoned to think in terms of seeking safeguards and began to consider seriously the demand for a separate Muslim state. During 1937-1939, several Muslim leaders and thinkers inspired by Allama Iqbal's ideas, presented elaborate schemes of partitioning the subcontinent on communal lines. The All-India Muslim League on March 23, 1940, in a resolution at its Lahore session, demanded separate homeland for the Muslims in the Muslim majority regions of the subcontinent. The resolution was commonly referred to as the Pakistan Resolution.

The British Government recognized the genuineness of the Pakistan demand indirectly in the proposals for the transfer of power which, Sir Stafford Cripps brought to India in 1942. Both the Congress and the All-India Muslim League rejected these proposals for different reasons. The principle of secession of Muslim India as a separate dominion was, however, conceded in these proposals. After the failure, a prominent Congress leader, C. Rajagopalacharya, suggested a formula for a separate Muslim state in the Working Committee of the Indian National Congress, which was rejected at the time but later on, in 1944, formed the basis of the Gandhi-Jinnah talks.

The Pakistan demand was popularized during the Second World War. Every section of the Muslim community - women, students, Ulema and businessmen - was organized under the banner of the All-India Muslim League. Branches of the party were opened in the remote corners on the subcontinent. Literature in the form of pamphlets, books, magazines and newspapers was produced to explain the Pakistan demand and distributed largely.

The support gained by the All-India Muslim League and its demand for Pakistan was tested after the failure of the Simla Conference 1945. Elections were called to determine the respective strength of the political parties. The Muslim League swept all the thirty seats in the central legislature and in the provincial elections also its victory was outstanding. After the elections, on April 8-9, 1946, the All-India Muslim League called a convention of the newly elected League members in the central and provincial legislatures at Delhi. This convention which constituted virtually a representative assembly of the Muslims of South Asia, on a motion by the Chief Minister of Bengal, Hussein Shaheed Suhrawardy, reiterated the Pakistan demand in clearer terms.

In early 1946, the British Government sent a Cabinet Mission to the subcontinent to resolve the constitutional deadlock. The

Mission conducted negotiations with various political parties but failed to evolve an agreed formula. Finally, Cabinet Mission announced its own plan which, among other provisions, envisaged three federal groupings, two of them comprising the Muslim majority provinces, linked at the Centre in a loose federation with three subjects. The Muslim League accepted the Plan, as a strategic move, expecting to achieve its objective in a not-too-distant future. The Congress also agreed to the Plan but soon realizing its implications to the Congress, its leaders began to interpret in a way not visualized by the authors of the Plan. This provided the All-India Muslim League an excuse to withdraw its acceptance of the Plan and the party observed August 16 as a 'Direct Action Day' to show Muslim solidarity in support of the Pakistan demand.

In October 1946, an Interim Government was formed. The Muslim League sent its representatives under the leadership of its General Secretary, Mr. Liaquat Ali Khan, with the aim to fight for the party objective from within the Interim Government. After a short time the situation inside the Interim Government and outside convinced the Congress leadership to accept Pakistan as the only solution of the communal problem. The British Government, after a last attempt to save the Cabinet Mission Plan in December 1946, also moved toward a plan for the partition of India. The last British Viceroy, Lord Louis Mountbatten, came with a clear mandate to draft a plan for the transfer of power. After holding talks with political leaders and parties, he prepared a Partition Plan for the transfer of power which, after its approval by the British Government, was announced on June 3, 1947. Both the Congress and the Muslim League accepted the plan. Two largest Muslim Majority provinces, Bengal and Punjab was partitioned. The assemblies of west Punjab, East Bengal, and Sind; and in Balochistan, the Quetta Municipality and the Shahi Jirga voted for Pakistan. Referenda were held in the North-West Frontier Province and the District of Sylhet in Assam which resulted in an overwhelming vote for Pakistan. On August 14, 1947, the new state of Pakistan came into existence.

Rin Mutiny and Muslim League

Sarkar's disapproval of the Congress and the Muslim League's discouragement to the rebels in the Royal Indian Navy (RIN) mutiny is candidly expressed. Gandhi said on February 23, 1946:

"A combination between Hindus and Muslims and others for the purpose of violent action is unholy." In his view, it was "a bad and unbecoming example for India". Aruna Asaf Ali disagreed. She said in a rejoinder it would be far easier "to unite Hindus and the Muslims at the barricade than on the constitutional front". Sarkar agrees with this romanticised, thoughtless recipe and wishes we had "radical mass actions forcing an unqualified imperial retreat". Under whose leadership, pray? His view that even in 1946 the British tried to "cling" to power is palpably wrong as Ambedkar realistically noted. The consequence of "mass actions" would have been violence and anarchy.

The effort at documentation is enormous. The documents are grouped under five broad heads – anti-British protests and movements; political organisations; labour and peasants; communalism; economy and society. The section on communalism explains the BJP regime's ire: while not ignoring the Muslim League, the editor exposes the Rashtriya Swayamsewak Sangh (RSS) thoroughly. The volume provides invaluable source material for the events of 1946.

The latest volume of *The Jinnah Papers* includes material from *The Transfer of Power* volumes besides other documents from the archives, which are published in this volume for the first time. There are some very interesting documents. One correspondent, a Delhi lawyer, S.M. Rahman, wrote to Jinnah a year before Partition, on April 5, 1946, a long and angry letter. Parts of it were wild. But in some others he wrote sense.

"...Have you not seen all the Christian people in Europe having the same civilisation, religious faith and social customs, conflicting among themselves and cutting off each other's head? How can you bring the theory of Islamic culture and religion in social unity as an excuse for Muslim separation from political unity? Do you think Muslims of NWFP [North-West Frontier Province] shall tolerate [the] culture of Punjabis or Sindhis or Bengalis or Assamese? Do you know that a Bengali Muslim shall think a Bengali Hindu nearer to his culture and habits than a Punjabi or Sindhi Muslim? Do you know Pakistan shall have as many nationalities and cultures as you claim about India? Every district of the Punjab has its own culture, customs and even the language that is spoken. Have you ever been to Kangra in the north and D.I. [Dera Ismail] Khan in the west and Ferozepore in the south and Karnal in the east of Punjab? What have you to say about their nationalities and cultures? How can it be possible that Hindus who have lived [for] millions of years in Pakistan-defined area, can ever start thinking that the name of their motherland (place of birth not only of theirs but that of their hundreds of forefathers), is Pakistan when they know well it [is] Bharat or Hindustan or India and they know it long before you got the new invention of Pakistan saying that there are two nations and countries [sic] in India.

"Do you know that Hindus have started now taking very seriously the danger of your political stunt and that underground preparations are going on for a civil war to finish the Muslims? Do you know that so long as there is one Sikh in the Punjab, he will not allow it to be ruled by your majesty? He will take the full toll of yourself and your comrades in arms before you can reach the seat of your fascist govt. in the so-called Pakistan.

"Cannot you think, how foolish it is to assume that the two zones of Pakistan – Eastern and Western – can ever have any connection with each other unless there is a corridor? You might be thinking, let you have the Pakistan conceded, and then you will again put [sic] Islam in danger and demand a corridor. You must know that once Pakistan is conceded, the Hindus are not going to sit calm and digest your Pakistan easily. With the creation of Pakistan there shall be permanent ending of Hindu-Muslim political inter-relationship. Hindus shall be far bitter in their feelings against the Muslims. Their resolve shall be to build military strength far more than that of Pakistan. Their natural development in science and industry shall be a net asset to them in achieving their success. The result will be that when your majesty raises the issue of a corridor, which you will and must, a clash will occur. The result is evident and that is the death of Muslim community." There were not a few thinking Muslims who opposed the partition of India. Another correspondent from Calcutta (now Kolkata) pointed out that the two wings of Pakistan could not form one state and that Bengal would have to be partitioned into two parts. The Premier of Bengal, H.S. Suhrawardy, introduced the Jharkhand leader Jaipal Singh to Jinnah as "a supporter of the Muslim League".

A brutally frank letter of July 12, 1946, from Syed Ali Bux to Jinnah, after the latter's disastrous meeting with the Nizam of

Hyderabad, records Jinnah's clumsy and arrogant behaviour, for which the Nizam duly ticked him off. It also reveals Jinnah's reliance on people in the State who were not worthy of trust. Jinnah indiscreetly discussed matters with two such persons *before* meeting the Nizam. The letter was written while Jinnah was still in Hyderabad. It was a sincere attempt to bring about a compromise. It foreshadowed Jinnah's suicidal policy towards the princely states generally. There are some interesting nuggets; for instance, Ambedkar's request to Jinnah to persuade Ramkrishna Dalmia to donate at least Rs.3 lakh for the college he proposed to set up in Mumbai. The letter was written because Dalmia told Ambedkar that he would have to consult Jinnah in that matter.

The seeds of Jinnah's disastrous policy towards Kashmir were sowed in 1946. On May 23, 1946, Agha Shaukat Ali wrote to Jinnah from Srinagar mentioning Sheikh Abdullah's overtures to the Muslim Conference. The Congress was not pleased with his slogan "Quit Kashmir", which alienated the Maharaja. The Muslim Conference was in a pathetic state. Jinnah simply had no policy worth the name. Pandit Prem Nath Bajaj also sought Jinnah's advice. Ironically, the League press in Lahore supported Sheikh Abdullah while Jinnah did not. In 1947 he expected the Maharaja to accede to Pakistan. Jinnah insisted that the decision on accession belonged to the ruler and not to the people as Nehru rightly asserted.

A long letter by Jinnah's staunch follower Shaukat Hayat Khan, dated July 11, 1947, should serve as an eye opener to Pakistanis. It was written after a trip to Kashmir only a month before Independence and bears quotation *in extenso*: "I went underground to meet Ghulam Mohiuddin, their [the National Conference's] underground leader. He has achieved considerable amount of popularity.... He is not at all averse to Pakistan but says he is handicapped by our silence. If, he says, a little sympathy was shown to them they would see that Pakistan issue is not decided upon adversely. *They feel that the interests of thirty lakhs of your subjects were being sacrificed at the altar of Hyderabad and Bhopal.* Though they understood that your moves have greater strategy in view on account of various repressions, they were impatient of delay and may be reluctant to make greater sacrifices required of them. It was suggested that even a little bit of sympathy from us, in the form of a statement for release of Abbas, Shaukat of the

Muslim Conference, and Sheikh Abdullah of the National Conference, in addition to a recommendation for the grant of basic civil rights to the people would give an excuse for them to support Pakistan openly. They discounted the news of Abdullah's assurance to the Maharaja and said that he was in favour of a referendum. My impression was that this party is still most powerful and had the support of the intelligentsia. They had advantage of having a good many honest workers. I did not think that they were in the pay of the Congress....

"*The People:* They are hounded, hunted and hungry. Officials are playing havoc into *[sic]* them. Each day they are being oppressed by illegal arrests and their food is being taken away under a system of most cruel taxation; and worst of all their women-folk every day are being molested with impunity. They are very bitter and look upon you as their saviour and are confident that you will rescue them.

"They are curiously torn between two loyalties, one to Pakistan and the other to Abdullah. They are indeed bewildered. *They pray for Pakistan and for the release of Abdullah in almost the same breath.* If Abdullah fights against Pakistan it would be a very hard test for these poor people and God knows what the result is going to be. My impression, however, is that we will probably win" (emphasis added throughout).

That was not to be. Jinnah rejected Mountbatten's offer, at Lahore on November 1, 1947, of a plebiscite in all the three disputed states – Kashmir, Junagadh and Hyderabad. He wanted Hyderabad excluded, a perverse idea India could not possibly accept. In truth, Jinnah wanted Kashmir and ignored Sheikh Abdullah while Nehru wanted Abdullah but ignored the people of Kashmir. We are paying for their mistakes still.

The documents on Jinnah's parleys with the Cabinet Mission show that on April 16, 1946, he was offered two alternatives – the Pakistan of today and a Centre confined to defence, foreign affairs and communications. He preferred the latter. Jinnah was asked to give his own plan, which he did on May 12. It was for an all-India confederation – not partition. He accepted the Mission's Plan of May 16, 1946, which envisaged a federal India based on groups of provinces. It was wrecked by the Congress at the instance of Gandhi who demurred at the proposals from the very outset.

Jinnah said in Nehru's presence on May 11 that "if the Congress would agree to Groups of Provinces as desired by the Muslim League, he would seriously consider a Union".

Peter Clarke's biography of a member of the Mission, Stafford Cripps, narrated the story of the destruction of the last chance for preserving India's unity ("Cripps and India's Partition"; *Frontline*; August 2 and 16, 2002). He has now written a history of the last days of the British Empire as seen from London. The chapters on Palestine and India are particularly useful. Both were partitioned, but with a difference.

"One difference was that it was demanded by a religious minority in India with the price to pay of receiving a 'motheaten' Pakistan; whereas partition was demanded by a religious minority in Palestine with the evident ambition of leaving the motheaten fragments to the Arab majority."

At the end of a careful survey, Clarke concludes: "The work of the Cabinet delegation in 1946, which has usually been derided, surely offered the Indian parties independence on the basis of a historic compromise which they would have to make themselves. It was, by definition, hardly the best solution in the eyes of either side; but each side needed to reconcile itself to a second-best solution if hasty partition and predictable bloodshed were to be avoided. Unfortunately, this is not how Gandhi, still the most powerful man in India, looked at the world. His failure to rise to the political challenge in 1946 emerges as the most significant missed opportunity in the whole story... In the final months, Gandhi's response was heroic on a personal moral level, but that need not blind us to the degree of his own responsibility for engendering this situation."

A tell-tale document in Sarkar's collection exposes the Congress' game. It was a letter by Vallabhbhai Patel in reply to Ambedkar's memorandum of demands, which he wrote as a basis for a pact with the Congress. Patel cited difficulties. One of them, incredibly, was the grouping provisions of the Mission's Plan, which he had helped to sabotage. Read this: "For instance, the provincial Constitution will be *settled by the sections* and the Congress will not be in a majority in Sections B (NWFP, Balochistan, Punjab and Sindh) and C (Bengal and Assam)." This was to fob off Ambedkar. For, to the League and the authors of the Plan, the Congress insisted that the provincial Constitution would be drafted *by the province alone*; not by the Section or Group. In December 1946, Gandhi said the Assamese would not be men but mannequins if they joined Section C (with Bengal).

Not Nehru alone by his famous outburst in July 1946 but the entire Congress rejected the Plan under Gandhi's determined leadership.

Kashmir and Partition of India

Historical Perspective

India under the British was divided into two distinct entities, British Provinces and Princely States. Princely States under the Government of India Act 1935 were defined as including any territory, whether described as a state, an estate, a jagir or otherwise. They were under the suzeranity of His Majesty and not a part of the British India. The code of conduct governing the relations of the princely states with the British Government was, therefore, different from that which governed the relations between provinces and the British Government. In the case of the provinces, the authority of the British Government was direct. It was exercised through the British Parliament, the Secretary of State for India, Governor General in Council or Provincial Governors. In the case of the princely states, the authority was indirectly exercised by various treaties, engagements and sanads, supplemented by usage and sufferances. In 1945, Churchill's coalition government was voted out and Clement Attlee's Labour Party came to power in London. British Prime Minister Clement Attlee announced in the House of Commons, in February 1946, that a Parliamentary delegation would visit India with a view to meeting the national leaders and discuss various problems connected with self government in India. The Cabinet Mission, consisting of Lord Pethic Lawrence, Sir Stafford Cripps, and Mr. L. V. Alexander, all members of the British Government, arrived in India on 23rd March, 1946, and held conferences with four representatives, two each of the Congress and the Muslim League. But the conference failed to devise and agreed formula and the Mission announced their own proposals in the State Paper of May 16,1946.

Their plan rejected the Muslim League's demand for Pakistan and proposed a federal union of India including British India and

Indian Princely States. It provided for the establishment of a Constitutional Assembly to frame the future Constitution of India, which was to be based on the principle that the centre would control only three subjects, viz, Foreign Affairs, Defence and Communications, all other subjects were to be administered by autonomous provinces and states.

It was proclaimed by the Secretary of State for India that paramountcy was to lapse after India had achieved independence and that the future relationship of the states with the rest of India was to be decided by the parties themselves through consultations and negotiations. In the meantime, 200 delegates of All India State People's Conference from all over India, met to discuss the Cabinet Mission Plan, on 8-11 June, 1946. During his speech in the meeting Pandit Jawahar Lal Nehru insisted on democratisation of the states to bring them at par with the rest of India. He said," Rulers alone can't decide the fate of nearly 100 million people."

The Cabinet Mission Plan was accepted by the princes, but they wanted to make some proposals during interim period. All these proposals were not at all concerned with people of the states. The situation however changed when the Muslim League, after joining the Interim Government, refused to join the Constitutional Assembly and continued to insist on its demand for Pakistan. It was felt all over the country and in England that events in India were leading towards a dangerous impasse. In order to face the situation more effectively, the British Government appointed Lord Viscount Mountbatten in place of Lord Wavell as Governor-General of India.

Lord Mountbatten, plunged himself in the negotiations with the leaders of different political parties and announced that long before June 1948, the Dominions of India and Pakistan would be established and that the question of Indian states would be dealt with in the light of the Cabinet Mission's memorandum of May 12,1946 .To approve the British plan, a conference between Mountbatten and several Indian leaders was held on June 2, 1947. It was approved on June 3,1947. The plan stated; "while paramountcy will lapse, according to His Majesty's Governments declaration of May 12, and May 16,1946, His Majesty's Government will not enter into military or any other agreement with the Indian states." Most of the states were under the impression that the lapse of paramountcy meant independent status for the states and they could either join the Constitution Assembly or remain independent. Seeing the attitude of the rulers in taking decision, Pandit Nehru said on June 15,1947, in the All India Congress Committee: Owe will not recognise the independence of the states in India and any recognition of such independence by any foreign power will be considered as unfriendly act ". Mr. Jinnah contested the views of Pandit Nehru. On June 17,1947, he said," Constitutionally and legally the Indian states will be independent sovereign states on the termination of paramountcy and they will be free to decide for themselves and adopt any course they like; it is open to them to join the Hindustan Constitutional Assembly or decide to remain independent. In case they opt for independence they would enter into such agreements or relationships with Hindustan or Pakistan as they may choose."

Throughout the negotiations on the Cabinet Mission proposals as well as the subsequent schemes of partition and transfer of power, the question of states and State People's right was kept in the foreground by the Congress and assurances were extracted from the British Government that on the lapse of paramountcy the princes would not become sovereign rulers .... "Sovereignty must reside in the people and not in any individual. The State people's claim to represent for themselves is justified and will see to it that they are heard. And certainly their rulers cannot speak for them," said Nehru on June 8,1947 before the delegates of State People's conference.

Whereas the Congress supported the cause of the people of the states to determine their relations with the Dominions, Muslim League's attitude towards them was antipathetic. The League's policy of not estranging the princes had become apparent when Mr. Jinnah made the following observations as far back as 1940:

> *The only important states which matter are not in the Eastern but in the North-Western one. They are Kashmir, Bahawalpur, Patiala etc. If these states willingly agree to come into the federation of the Muslim Homeland, we shall be glad to come to a reasonable and honourable settlement with them. We, however, have no desire to force them or coerce them in any way.*

With the passing of Indian Independence Act 1947, all the states were released from their obligations to the Crown. They became free to align their future with either of two Dominoins.

All the negotations that had already been held on Cabinet Mission proposal of 1946 and the transfer of power and Independence Act of 1947, made it evident that if Indian states became separate independent entities, it would create a serious vacuum between the Central Government and the States; this would effect not only political relations but also economic and other relations between the two. Taking into consideration these problems, Heartley Showcross, the under secretary of States for India in a speech emphatically maintained that the British Government would not recognise any state as a separate international entity, and Prime Minister Atlee speaking on Independence Bill, hoped that no irrevocable decision to stay out prematurely will be taken. State Department was set up on 27 June, 1947, to deal with matters concerning states. It was divided into two sections; one to be headed by a Congress leader and the other by a Muslim League leader. Sardar Patel and Abdur Rab Nishtar headed these sections. Sardar Patel issued agenda for the conference of rulers of princely states to be held on 25 July, 1947. It included (i) Acession of the states on defence, external affairs, and communications, (ii) Standstill Agreement. It was enthusiastically welcomed by states. The same was repeated by Lord Mountbatten in his capacity as Crown Representative, when the special session of Chamber Princes was held on 25 July, 1947. He assured the princes that their accession on these three subjects would involve no financial liability and that in other matters there would be no encroachment on their sovereignty. Finally he appealed to them to join any one of the two dominions before 15 August, 1947.

In order to expedite work, the Negotiating Committee of Chamber of Princes prepared the draft of Instrument of Accession and Standstill Agreement which were approved by the General Conference of the Chamber of Princes on August 1, 1947. Some of the rulers were inclined to execute Standstill Agreements but wait as the Instrument of Accession was concerned. It was, however, made clear to such rulers in the conference that the Government of India had decided to execute Standstill agreement with only those who had already signed the Instrument of Accession. Therefore the only bases which constituted the basis of relationship between the Indian states and the successor government in British India were the Instrument of Accession and the Standstill Agreement.

Thus before 15th August, 1947, all the states except Hyderabad, Junagarh and Kashmir had acceded either to India or Pakistan. In Hyderabad the public opinion was divided; while the majority who were Hindus favoured accession with Indian Union, a strong minority under the leadership of Kasim Rizvi wanted to remain independent as the Muslim state of Hyderabad, and was aggressively hostile to Indian Union. The Government of Hyderabad failed to check the frequent raids of Muslim razakars and the militant communists of Telegana into the territory of Indian Union. These hostile designs were overcome by police action, before the Nizam consented to accede to the Indian Union.

Junagarh had a Muslim ruling family and 85% Hindu majority population. It had stated it would go along with the policy of other 279 Kathiawar states, many encircling it, all of which acceded to India. It was not contiguous at any point with Pakistan, and its railways, posts and telegraph were an integral part of the Indian communication system. There was a coup de tat on August 10, 1947, by a group of Sindhi Muslims (pro-Pakistan) under the leadership of Bhutto, took over the government and the Nawab became a virtual prisioner in his palace. On September 15, 1947, he eventually acceded to Pakistan. On November 9, 1947, India occupied the state at the invitation of the Prime Minister. On February 24, 1948, a plebiscite was held resulting in an overwhelming vote for accession to India. Finally, in January 1949, Junagarh was merged with Saurashtra, a union of princely states of Kathiawar. Jammu and Kashmir was the only state whose Maharaja delayed the accession of the state to India.

Bengal

The Muslim League

In 1906, as Bengal was divided, Dutch Christians overtook beautiful Bali after the Puputan massacres in which they murdered the Hindu Balinese royal families.

Bengal was divided by Lord Curzon, an arrogant British viceroy, to control the rebellious province. (An important building in the University of Dhaka shamefully bears Curzon's name.) This division was an outrage for the people of Bangla but the landlords gave their support to the British. The British were eventually forced to undo the division in 1911 under popular pressure.

The same year, one of the worst things of Indian history happened. This was the formation of the All-India Muslim League. The party was formed in Dhaka (presently capital of Bangladesh) in 1906. It was founded by the rich Muslim landlords. It was indeed a dark day in Bangla when the movement for independence was betrayed.

The Muslim League declared allegiance to the British and sought to draw Muslims away from the independence movement. In their first resolution on December 30, 1906 in Dhaka, the very first thing they declared was, "To promote, among the Musalmans of India, feelings of loyalty to the British Government, and to remove any misconception that may arise as to the intention of Government with regard to any of its measures." This was moved by Nawab Salimullah, whose name is also borne by a student hall in the University of Dhaka. (SHAME).

In 1913, on their 6th session, at Lucknow on March 22-23rd, 1913, there was an ammendment to their constitution. The first objective of Muslim League was then: "According to the revised Constitution, the first object of the League is `to maintain and promote among the people of this country feelings of loyalty towards the British Crown'... It is the British Crown alone which is the permanent and ever-abiding symbol of Empire. It is not to this Government or to that we acknowledge allegiance: it is to the British Crown itself that we owe unswerving and abiding loyalty... It is the paramount duty of every loyal subject of the King Emperor to abstain from doing anything calculated to impair the permanence and stability of British rule in India."—Mian Muhammad Shafi (Leader of Punjab Muslim League and Chairman of session.). The betrayal continued. There were allegations that the Muslim League was a stooge for the British and were financed and supported by them. By their history the Muslim League validates and confirms the allegations.

Muslim League and many Hindu upper caste members fuelled the differences among Hindus and Muslims. Relations further worsened as Muslim League convinced many educated Muslims that there was a Hindu conspiracy against the Muslims. Since then many educated Muslims saw the Hindus encroaching on their rights and saw the Muslim League as championing the rights of Muslims. The Muslim League was in reality trying to create panic among Muslims.

However, Muslim League initially was not very popular. Their leaders had hoped that the Muslims, seeing the name of their party would flock to them out of religious faith. However, initially that did not happen. Their pro-British stance did not help their popularity. But gradually, however, their propaganda paid off. The Muslims started abandoning the national movement to join the sectarian Muslim League. However, not all were swayed by the propaganda and many remained in the Congress. But they were considered to be "Hindu minded".

Hindu Muslim Riots

Some rich Hindus are also to blame for the Hindu-Muslim rift. They treated the Muslims as inferiors. Many Hindu moneylenders were extremely tyrannical and also caused Muslims to distrust Hindus. Hindus also did not condone the killing of cows by Muslims, since it is sacred to them. The Muslims took that as an attack on their faith. Many realities and the myth of a conspiracy gradually drew a seizable portion of the Muslims away from the united independence movement. However, many Muslims stayed on in the fight. And among them of course, was Maulana A. K. Azad, one of the great Indian leaders.

The Hindu Muslim division further grew with the Muslim League's defeat in the 1937 elections. When Muhammad Ali Jinnah took over the Muslim League in 1930s, hatred seeped in gradually leading to terrible violence. Muslim league resorted to violence against the Congress and the young Congress members fought back. This was used then by the Muslim League as evidence that the Hindus were attacking the Muslims and further agitated their supporters.

In the light of these results (1937 elections), the leader of the Muslim League, Mohammed Ali Jinnah decided that "... the League should strengthen its attraction to Muslim voters by an appeal to Islamic anxieties". (Denis Judd: ibid.; p. 27).

As India slowly slipped out of British control, the British concentrated their efforts to divide India along religious lines. In 1939, Muhammad Ali Jinnah proclaimed the doom of united India. He called for a separate Muslim land. Muslim League cadres adopted terror tactics all over India. Hindu Muslim riots marred the decade of 1940 through out India.

This part is from an eyewitness: August 16, 1946 was an ominous day. It was declared as the Direct Action Day. Most had thought that it was going to be a day when Muhammad Ali Jinnah was going to give a national address at Gorer (Garh, Gaur, Gaud) Math, in Baliganj, Calcutta. However, many Hindus were fearful of anti-Hindu violence. At the very start of the day, there was much rumours of violence. Processions of Muslim League supporters chanting *Arabic* slogans were picketed by their opponents. This got out of hand as the sun climbed the sky. Non-Bengali Muslims (possibly Biharis) armed themselves and other Muslims with sticks (about 5 ft). Some were armed with hockey sticks and iron bars. Knives and other sharp objects were also wielded.

Thus began the '46 riots in Bengal with heavy casualties on both sides. It was apparent that the Muslim League, pawns of the British had succeeded in dividing the Indian people in the name of Islam. Their violent tactics worked to drive a wedge between the people of India.

The Partition

In February 1947, the new Labour Prime Minister, Clement Attlee, "...announced in the House of Commons that the British would withdraw from India not later than June 1948". (Denis Judd: ibid.; p. 49).

After the second world war, the British were severely weakened. India on the other hand had also become too rebellious to control. Besides India was no longer a golden egg laying goose for the British. It had become more of a liability. They were weary and finally decided to give up India. However, they played one last nasty trick of "divide and rule" before leaving. They divided India on religious grounds.

And in March 1947 Lord Mountbatten was sworn in as the last Viceroy of India, charged with bringing about "... a transfer of power". (Denis Judd: ibid.; p. 50). to "... 'responsible' hands". ('New Encyclopaedia Britannica', Volume 21; p. 109). (britneo)

They dealt with reformist moderate leaders like Gandhi and Nehru who were not wholly nationalist and had more faith in western systems and the British than on India and her glorious past. The British knew they would be easier to handle.

In May 1947 Mountbatten showed Nehru a 'secret' British plan, called significantly 'Plan Balkan', which "... devolved power to the provinces, including the princely states". (Denis Judd: ibid.; p. 52). Nehru denounced the plan as producing "... fragmentation and conflict and disorder". (Jawaharlal Nehru: Letter to Mountbatten, May 1947, in: Denis Judd: ibid.; p.52). (britneo)

As the riots accelerated out of control, Gandhi, and the other leaders of the nation called for an end to the violence. The Congress fought a half hearted battle to save the unity of the nation. The Muslim League armed its separatist cadres and the Congress watched reluctant to take action, as that would be against their pacifism. Muhammad Ali Jinnah under the tacit support of the British blackmailed the nation causing it to be divided in what I consider a heinous crime against the people. Jinnah was bent on becoming the Prime Minister. He said that he would give up the division of India, and end the violence if he were made the first Prime Minister. But that was not to be.

After much ado, finally Gandhi gave in, much to the disbelief of many of the freedom leaders, and accepted the formation of two separate states, the creation of Pakistan and India. A great tragedy. (Gandhi really had no real authority to make this call in my opinion. One man with a few others did not have that authority to decide to mutilate a nation).

Mass migration that followed was a nightmare, with tremendous suffering. Gandhi's passive resistance led to a passive ethnic cleansing. 600, 000 died and 14 million were displaced in this unfortunate event. It cemented the hatred between Hindus and Muslims. Whatever unity was there was destroyed... may be permanently.

People think of Gandhi brought great success to India. But in reality he was a failure, despite his great popularity. He caused the birth of a nation out of hatred. The division of India was a curse that caused great suffering to millions who were displaced by this ill decision of Gandhi and the treachery of Jinnah. The curse still haunts the people of the subcontinent, by causing many more wars and much more hatred. The only excuse Gandhi may have had was that he made an honest mistake and had no idea of the great tragedy of his decision. For Jinnah, the British puppet, there is perhaps no excuse.

In 1947, India had a bittersweet celebration... India was independent but had lost 27% of her territory which became Pakistan. (Many claim that the partition was by popular demand. There was an election but it was farcical and will be discussed here next.) Mahatma Gandhi (one of the greatest men despite the division of India) was killed on January 7th by Nathuram Godse, a 25 year old editor and publisher of a Hindu Mahasabha weekly in Poona for conceding the division of the country. Many believe that since most of the Muslim upper class were descendants of foreign occupiers of India just as the British were, they could live in India if they chose to be Indians but Gandhi had no right to give up 27 % of the country to them. It was seen as an act no less than treason by some.

Fate of Bangla

During the partition of India, Bangla was redivided (was first divided in 1906) into two with the western half given to India and the eastern half to Pakistan. East Bengal became the eastern province of Pakistan, called East Pakistan after 1956. The new state of Pakistan consisted of West Pakistan (now Pakistan) on the Arab Sea and East Pakistan (now Bangladesh) on the Bay of Bengal, separated in the middle by 1100 miles of the vast expanse of India. This was an unnatural division since the Bengalis of East Pakistan and the different ethnic peoples of West Pakistanis spoke different languages and followed different customs and had different history and culture. It also divided many Bengali families. The only thing that was common between the two peoples was their religion. Both nations were predominantly Islamic. Of course, the degree of fanaticism varied. In Bangla, many Muslims did not even go to the mosque (now they do).

Other States

To further aggravate the situation, a number of states were left with their fate undecided. The British did not decide whether they should join India or Pakistan. This was a big problem. One of these states was KASHMIR, the beautiful mountain state. The British left the decision to the King of Kashmir. The big problem with Kashmir was that it was a Muslim majority region under the rule of a Hindu king. Pakistan decided arbitrarily, since much of the division was done according to religious distribution, that Kashmir should belong to them. And no sooner had they decided, they sent in tribal warriors and soldiers into Kashmir. Unfortunately for them, the King of Kashmir decided to join India. He officially joined India and India rushed its fledgling troops to Kashmir but Pakistan had already taken much of Kashmir. That was the first war. It ended in the UN. India decided to hold a referendum to allow the people of Kashmir to decide their fate. The UN also said that Pakistan must withdraw its forces as a precondition for India to hold the referendum. Pakistan never withdrew and no referendum was held. That was just the beginning of the Kashmir problem!

The Partition of India

14 August, 1947, saw the birth of the new Islamic Republic of Pakistan. At midnight the next day India won its freedom from colonial rule, ending nearly 350 years of British presence in India. During the struggle for freedom, Gandhi had written an appeal "To Every Briton" to free their possessions in Asia and Africa, especially India (Philips and Wainwright, 567). The British left India divided in two. The two countries were founded on the basis of religion, with Pakistan as an Islamic state and India as a secular one.

Whether the partition of these countries was wise and whether it was done too soon is still under debate. Even the imposition of an official boundary has not stopped conflict between them. Boundary issues, left unresolved by the British, have caused two wars and continuing strife between India and Pakistan.

The partition of India and its freedom from colonial rule set a precedent for nations such as Israel, which demanded a separate homeland because of the irreconcilable differences between the Arabs and the Jews. The British left Israel in May 1948, handing the question of division over to the UN. Un-enforced UN Resolutions to map out boundaries between Israel and Palestine has led to several Arab-Israeli wars and the conflict still continues.

Reasons for Partition

By the end of the 19th century several nationalistic movements had started in India. Indian nationalism had grown largely since British policies of education and the advances made by the British in India in the fields of transportation and communication. However, their complete insensitivity to and distance from the peoples of India and their customs created such disillusionment with them in their subjects that the end of British rule became necessary and inevitable.

However, while the Indian National Congress was calling for Britain to Quit India, the Muslim League, in 1943, passed a resolution for them to Divide and Quit. There were several reasons for the birth of a separate Muslim homeland in the subcontinent, and all three parties-the British, the Congress and the Muslim League-were responsible.

The British had followed a divide-and-rule policy in India. Even in the census they categorised people according to religion and viewed and treated them as separate from each other. They had based their knowledge of the peoples of India on the basic religious texts and the intrinsic differences they found in them instead of on the way they coexisted in the present. The British were also still fearful of the potential threat from the Muslims, who were the former rulers of the subcontinent, ruling India for over 300 years under the Mughal Empire. In order to win them over to their side, the British helped establish the M.A.O. College at Aligarh and supported the All-India Muslim Conference, both of which were institutions from which leaders of the Muslim League and the ideology of Pakistan emerged. As soon as the League was formed, they were placed on a separate electorate. Thus the idea of the separateness of Muslims in India was built into the electoral process of India.

There was also an ideological divide between the Muslims and the Hindus of India. While there were strong feelings of nationalism in India, by the late 19th century there were also communal conflicts and movements in the country that were based on religious communities rather than class or regional ones.

Some people felt that the very nature of Islam called for a communal Muslim society. Added to this were the memories of power over the Indian subcontinent that the Muslims held on to, especially those in the old centres of Mughal rule. These memories might have made it exceptionally difficult for Muslims to accept the imposition of colonial power and culture. They refused to learn English and to associate with the British. This was a severe drawback for them as they found that the Hindus were now in better positions in government than they were and thus felt that the British favoured Hindus. The social reformer and educator, Sir Syed Ahmed Khan, who founded M.A.O. College, taught the Muslims that education and cooperation with the British was vital for their survival in the society. Tied to all the movements of Muslim revival was the opposition to assimilation and submergence in Hindu society. Sir Syed Ahmed Khan was also the first to conceive of a separate Muslim homeland.

Hindu revivalists also deepened the chasm between the two nations. They resented the Muslims for their former rule over India. Hindu revivalists rallied for a ban on the slaughter of cows, a cheap source of meat for the Muslims. They also wanted to change the official script form the Persian to the Hindu Devanagri script, effectively making Hindi rather than Urdu the main candidate for the national language.

Congress made several mistakes in their policies which further convinced the League that it was impossible to live in a undivided India after freedom from colonial rule because their interests would be completely suppressed. One such policy was the institution of the "Bande Matram," a national anthem which expressed anti-Muslim sentiments, in the schools of India where Muslim children were forced to sing it.

The Muslim League gained power also due to the Congress. The Congress banned any support for the British during the Second World War. However the Muslim League pledged its full support, which found favour form them from the British, who also needed the help of the largely Muslim army. The Civil Disobedience Movement and the consequent withdrawal of the Congress party from politics also helped the league gain power, as they formed strong ministries in the provinces that had large Muslim populations. At the same time, the League actively campaigned to gain more support from the Muslims in India, especially under the guidance of dynamic leaders like Jinnah.

There had been some hope of an undivided India, with a government consisting of three tiers along basically the same lines as the borders of India and Pakistan at the time of Partition. However, Congress' rejection of the interim government set up under this Cabinet Mission Plan in 1942 convinced the leaders of the Muslim League that compromise was impossible and partition was the only course to take.

Impact and Aftermath of Partition

"Leave India to God. If that is too much, then leave her to anarchy."—Gandhi, May 1942

The partition of India left both India and Pakistan devastated. The process of partition had claimed many lives in the riots. Many others were raped and looted. Women, especially, were used as instruments of power by the Hindus and the Muslims; "ghost trains" full of severed breasts of women would arrive in each of the newly-born countries from across the borders.

15 million refugees poured across the borders to regions completely foreign to them, for though they were Hindu or Muslim, their identity had been embedded in the regions where there ancestors were from. Not only was the country divided, but so were the provinces of Punjab and Bengal, divisions which caused catastrophic riots and claimed the lives of Hindus, Muslims and Sikhs alike.

Many years after the partition, the two nations are still trying to heal the wounds left behind by this incision to once-whole body of India. Many are still in search of an identity and a history left behind beyond an impenetrable boundary. The two countries started of with ruined economies and lands and without an established, experienced system of government. They lost many of their most dynamic leaders, such as Gandhi, Jinnah and Allama Iqbal, soon after the partition. Pakistan had to face the separation of Bangladesh in 1971. India and Pakistan have been to war twice since the partition and they are still deadlocked over the issue of possession of Kashmir. The same issues of boundaries and divisions, Hindu and Muslim majorities and differences, still persist in Kashmir.

Partition of Punjab

Scholarly works on the partition of India are legion, but those focusing on the partition of the Punjab are very few. Ian Talbot and Kirpal Singh indeed have pioneering works on the Punjab partition to their credit, but much more research needs to be done to shed light on the dynamics of that cataclysmal event. After all the greatest forced migration in history with its gory tales of massacres, looting, arson, rape, abduction of women and children and other acts of savagery were essentially facets of a Punjabi tragedy. Why and how this happened will be elaborated in my forthcoming book. On the 60th anniversary of the partition of the Punjab it is appropriate that a sketch of the main events is shared with the public. I shall in a series of articles trace the main events that culminated in the bloody division of that province.

Although ideas of partitioning Punjab had existed since at least the beginning of the twentieth century it was only in the wake of the March 23, 1940 Lahore Resolution adopted by the Muslim League that the Sikhs began to demand that the Punjab should also be partitioned on a religious basis.

Sikh religion, culture and history were inextricably linked to the Punjab—the founder of the Sikh faith, Baba Guru Nanak (1469-1539) and his spiritual successors were Punjabis, the only great kingdom ruled a Sikh, the Kingdom of Lahore under Maharaja Ranjit Singh (1799-1839), was essentially a Punjabi state, most of the holy shrines of the Sikhs and the vast majority of their community were based in the Punjab. Therefore the Sikhs demanding partition appears to be a contradiction in terms. But they did and the question is: why? Certainly the clues are not to be found in their demographic complexion.

Unlike the Muslims who were in majority in the northwestern and northeastern zones of the subcontinent, the Sikh were not in a majority anywhere in the Punjab, not even in the central districts where they were mainly located or in their holy city of Amritsar. According to the 1941 census their overall proportion of the total Punjab population was 13.2 per cent in the British-administered areas and it increased to 14. 9 per cent if the Sikh states were also included. The Muslims had an overwhelming majority of 57.1 per cent in the British areas, which decreased to 53.2 per cent if the Sikh states were included. The Hindu population was 29.1 per cent in British districts and it declined to 26.6 if the Sikh states were included. The Sikhs were not in a majority in any of the major Sikh states either.

The Sikh argument was that India should not be partitioned, but if it became inevitable then the Punjab should be divided and the borders between a predominantly Muslim Punjab in the West and a Hindu-Sikh majority East Punjab should be drawn on the Chenab, so that East Punjab would include their holy places as well as the majority of the community. The Sikh leadership feared persecution in a predominantly Muslim Pakistan, just as the Muslim leadership argued that permanent Hindu Raj based on caste prejudices will be established if India remained united.

On February 20, 1947 Prime Minister Clement Attlee announced that His Majesty's Government intended to transfer power to Indian hands, in a united or partitioned India, by June 1948. The Sikhs reacted angrily to that declaration because no mention of a Sikh right to a separate homeland was included in it.

In the meantime, the Muslim League had launched on January 24 1947 direct action in the Punjab against the coalition government headed by Sir Khizr Hayat Tiwana, which it alleged was not representative of the Muslims of Punjab. The main supporters of Punjab Unionist Party, the Muslim landlords, had decamped and were now members of the Punjab Muslim League. The Muslim League won 75 out of the 83 seats fixed for Muslims. Two Unionists crossed the floor and joined it but it was still short of a majority by 10 seats in a house of 175.

On the other hand, the Unionist Party led by Tiwana was routed in the election. It won only 18 seats. Tiwana managed to put together a coalition government, which included the Akalis and other Panthic Sikhs who won 23 seats and the Congress which did very well by winning 50 general seats. The coalition government also included some scheduled caste members of the Punjab Assembly.

Direct action or a civil disobedience movement as the Muslim League preferred to call it lasted from January 24 to February 26. Its mass character multiplied every day and the jails were filled with leaders and cadres who defied Section 144 and were arrested. Although it remained peaceful, each day the slogans the crowds shouted became more and more menacing and threatening, striking fear and terror in the hearts of the non-Muslims.

Slogans such as, 'Pakistan ka nara kiya? La illahah illillah (what is the slogan of Pakistan? It is, there is no God but Allah), 'Assey lein gey Pakistan jaisey liya tha Hindustan' (we will take Pakistan the way we took India) were raised all over the Punjab. Some slogans directly insulted the Punjab premier in a most abusive and shallow manner. Towards the end of the agitation the demonstrators began to harass Hindus and Sikhs and made them fly the Muslim League flag on their cars and shops. The government and the Muslim League, however, reached an agreement on February 26 according to which the agitation was called off and the Muslim League leaders and cadres were released. But those several weeks of mass agitation provoked a determined reaction from the Hindu and Sikh leaders in the Punjab who vowed not to let a Muslim League minority government come to power. On March 2 Khizr resigned. He had been badly shaken and demoralised by the abuse directed at him and by the fact that the landlords had abandoned him.

The Punjab Governor, Sir Evan Jenkins, invited the Muslim League leader Nawab Iftikhar Hussain Khan Mamdot to prove that he had a majority in the house. Although he claimed that he could muster a majority with the help of some scheduled castes members of the Punjab Assembly Mamdot failed to do so. That created a political impasse. Governor Jenkins therefore imposed governor rule on March 5 under Section 93 of the India Act of 1935. Punjab continued to remain under governor's rule until partition in mid-August 1947.

British Rule and Muslim League

The British ruled the Indian subcontinent for nearly 200 years-from 1756 to 1947. After the Indian Mutiny of 1857, the British government abolished the powers of the British East India Company, which had ruled the subcontinent on behalf of the British Crown, and took on direct powers of governance. Political reforms were initiated, allowing the formation of political parties. The Indian National Congress, representing the overwhelming majority of Hindus, was created in 1885. The Muslim League was formed in 1906 to represent and protect the position of the Muslim minority. When the British introduced constitutional reforms in 1909, the Muslims demanded and acquired separate electoral rolls. This guaranteed Muslims representation in the provincial as well as national legislatures until the dawn of independence in 1947. The idea of a separate Muslim state in south Asia was raised in 1930 by the poet and philosopher Sir Muhammad Iqbal.

He suggested that the northwestern provinces of British India and the native state of Jammu and Kashmir should be joined into such a state. The name "Pakistan", which came to be used to describe this grouping, is thought to have originated as a compound abbreviation made up of letters of the names of the provinces involved, as follows: Punjab, Afghania (North West Frontier Province), Kashmir, Indus-Sindh, and Balochistan. An alternative explanation says the name means "Land of the Pure". By the end of the 1930s, Muhammad Ali Jinnah, leader of the Muslim League and considered the founding father of Pakistan, had also decided that the only way to preserve Indian Muslims from Hindu domination was to establish a separate Muslim state.

Creation of Pakistan

In 1940 the Muslim League formally endorsed the partitioning of British India and the creation of Pakistan as a separate Muslim state. During pre-independence talks in 1946, therefore, the British government found that the stand of the Muslim League on separation and that of the Congress on the territorial unity of India were irreconcilable. The British then decided on partition and on August 15, 1947, transferred power dividedly to India and Pakistan. The latter, however, came into existence in two parts: West Pakistan, as Pakistan stands today, and East Pakistan, now known as Bangladesh. The two were separated by 1,600 km (1,000 mi) of Indian territory.

Problems of Partition

The division of the subcontinent caused tremendous dislocations of populations.

Some 6 million Hindus and Sikhs moved from Pakistan into India, and about 8 million Muslims migrated from India to Pakistan.

The demographic shift was accompanied by considerable inter-ethnic violence, including massacres, that reinforced bitterness between the two countries. This bitterness was further intensified by disputes over the accession of the former native states of India to either country. Nearly all of these 562 widely scattered polities had joined either India or Pakistan; the princes of Hyderabad, Junagadh, and Kashmir, however, had chosen to join neither country. On August 15, 1947, these three states became technically independent, but when the Muslim ruler of Junagadh, with its predominantly Hindu population, joined Pakistan a month later, India annexed his territory. Hyderabad's Muslim prince, ruling over a mostly Hindu population, tried to postpone any decision indefinitely, but in September 1948 India also settled that issue by pre-emptive annexation. The Hindu ruler of Jammu and Kashmir, whose subjects were 85 per cent Muslim, decided to join India. Pakistan, however, questioned his right to do so, and a war broke out between India and Pakistan. Although the UN subsequently resolved that a plebiscite be held under UN auspices to determine the future of Kashmir, India continued to occupy about two thirds of the state and refused to hold a plebiscite. This deadlock, which still persists, has intensified suspicion and antagonism between the two countries.

Pre-Republican Era

The first independent government of Pakistan was headed by Prime Minister Liaquat Ali Khan. Muhammad Ali Jinnah was Governor-General until his death in 1948. From 1947 to 1951 the country functioned under unstable conditions. The government endeavoured to create a new national capital to replace Karachi, organize the bureaucracy and the armed forces, resettle refugees, and contend with provincial politicians who often defied its authority. Failing to offer any programmed of economic and social reform, however, it did not capture the popular imagination.

In his foreign policy Liaquat established friendly relations with the United States, when he visited President Harry S. Truman in 1950. Liaquat's United States visit injected bitterness into Pakistan's elations with the Union of Soviet Socialist Republics (USSR) because Liaquat had previously accepted an invitation from Moscow that never materialized in a visit. The United States gave no substantial aid to Pakistan until three years later, but the USSR, Pakistan's close neighbor, had been alienated.

After Liaquat was assassinated in 1951, Khawaja Nazimuddin, an East Pakistani who had been Governor-General since Jinnah's death, became Prime Minister. Unable to prevent the erosion of the Muslim League's popularity in East Pakistan, however, he was forced to yield to another East Pakistani, Muhammad Ali Bogra, in 1953.

When the Muslim League was routed in East Pakistani elections in 1954, the Governor-General dissolved the constituent assembly as no longer representative. The new assembly that met in 1955 was no longer dominated by the Muslim League. Muhammad Ali Bogra was then replaced by Chaudhuri Muhammad Ali, a West

Pakistani. At the same time, Iskander Mirza became the Governor-General of the country. The new constituent assembly enacted a bill, which became effective in October 1955, integrating the four West Pakistani provinces into one political and administrative unit.

The assembly also produced a new constitution, which was adopted on March 2, 1956. It declared Pakistan an Islamic republic. Mirza was elected Provisional President.

Jinnah and Haroon

More than two decades before Muhammad Ali Jinnah was acclaimed as Quaid-i-Azam (the Great Leader), K.M. Munshi, a colleague at the Bombay Bar and in the Congress, lauded him as a man the like of whom he had never seen before. These two volumes of his papers only confirm what was known to all except the detractors. He established an ascendency in leadership by sheer dint of example in personal and political rectitude, discipline and commitment, tactical skills and organisational talent.

B.R. Ambedkar wrote: "It is doubtful if there is a politician in India to whom the adjective incorruptible can be more fittingly applied. Any one who knows what his relations with the British government have been, will admit that he has always been their critic, if indeed, he has not been their adversary. No one can buy him. For it must be said to his credit that he has never been a soldier of fortune" *(Pakistan and Partition of India;* 1946; page 323).

These volumes cover the Gandhi-Jinnah talks in 1944 based on "the C.R. formula" which Rajaji (C. Rajagopalacharya) drew up and Gandhi amended slightly during the talks; the Shimla Conference on the Wavell Plan in 1945, which came to nothing; the release of Congress leaders from prison at the end of the war and the general elections to the Central and Provincial Assemblies in 1946.

Liaquat Ali Khan ran the Central Office of the Muslim League in Delhi. But Jinnah kept vigil and control over the funds for which he kept accounts meticulously and insisted others did likewise. A respected leader like Nawab Mohammed Ismail Khan of Meerut sought additional funds for the Committee of Action of which he was chairman. He was No. 3 in the League hierarchy after general secretary Liaquat Ali Khan. While sending a cheque,

Jinnah asked him to send an account of the previous advances to the committee. On receiving the account, Jinnah commented: "I find this method of accounting is not quite satisfactory... because these items convey nothing." He suggested reversion to "the previous method of accounting". He was then in frail health and was recuperating at the hill station Matheran as a guest of Sir Cawasji Jehangir.

Twenty years earlier he had watched from a distance how the Khilafat funds disappeared. Nor was he unaware of some scandals surrounding other parties, the Congress included (vide the writer's article "Money politics: The Congress culture"; *Frontline*, April 19, 1996, based on files of the National Archives). The spectacle of a Bombay Khoja instructing a U.P. Nawab in accountancy verges on the hilarious, though.

It is amazing how Jinnah was dragged into organisational matters despite his repeated protests that they be sorted out in the fora set up by the party's Constitution. The subcontinent's feudal culture ordains that all matters be settled by the top leadership. Rising to the challenge, Jinnah stunned everyone by emerging as a mass leader. He also proved to be a good organisation man and constantly reminded his followers that they had to adhere to the League's Constitution.

The squabbles that preoccupied him most were the ones that rocked the League's Ministry in Sindh. *It was Sindh, not Punjab, which blazed the trail for the establishment of Pakistan.* The man who led this movement there was Sir Abdullah Haroon. Orphaned by the death of his father, he hawked knick-knacks in the lanes after school hours. He dropped out from school and educated himself in a public library. Sir Abdullah became a fabulously rich business magnate. For his fine qualities as a human being, contemporaries called him a prince among men. His daughter Doulat's biography is a moving and instructive account of Sir Abdullah's life. He tried to emulate Sir Sikandar Hayat Khan's example in Punjab and floated a secular party but failed.

Sindh's disquiet lay in the unwise opposition to its demand for separation from the Bombay Presidency, which comprised Marathi- and Gujarati-speaking areas. It was separated only in 1937 after a bruising struggle. The demand was opposed on the ground that it was "communal" while it was the opposition to so sensible a demand that exposed the spurious claims to secularism by the opponents. The Congress' refusal to share power after 1937 was another factor.

Jinnah Stunned Everyone by emerging as a mass leader.

Doulat Hidayatullah's book reflects hard labour and deep devotion to her father's memory. It fails dismally on a crucial phase in his political career. He initiated moves for the demand for Pakistan in 1938. Once it was formally adopted by the Muslim League in the famous Lahore Resolution on March 23, 1940, this realist insisted that a common centre, no matter how limited, was necessary, between two otherwise independent states; not least for enforcing safeguards for the minorities.

The author writes "during these days [1939-40] Sir Abdullah Haroon was also busy as chairman of the Foreign Committee". But she refrains from narrating in detail the most important phase in her distinguished father's life. It merits a detailed documented account by a scholar based on archival material. Much has been written about how the Resolution came to be drafted and adopted (vide the writer's review of Mohammed Aslam Malik's book *The Making of the Pakistan Resolution* in *Frontline,* January 4, 2002).

Sir Abdullah Haroon was the first League leader of standing to hint at the partition of India in his welcome address to the Sindh Provincial Muslim League Conference on October 8, 1938: "Unless this [communal] problem is solved to the satisfaction of all it will be impossible for any body to save India from being divided... ." On December 4, 1938, the League's general body, the Council, set up the Foreign Committee with Sir Abdullah as its chairman. Jinnah was, however, non-committal; as was his style. For instance, when E.V. Ramaswami 'Periyar' wrote to him on August 9, 1944, joining his demand for Dravidistan to the demand for Pakistan, for a fight against "our opponents" Jinnah replied on August 17, 1944, to say "it is entirely for you people to decide on this matter [Dravidistan]... ".

The Foreign Committee was only one of the contributors to the Lahore Resolution. However, it set up a Constitution Sub-Committee in February 1940 with a rather lop-sided composition and presented a report on December 23, 1940. It was leaked to the press in March 1941. Jinnah repudiated the subcommittee: "The Muslim League has appointed no such committee." The report opined that the Lahore Resolution envisaged "a common coordinating agency" on defence, foreign affairs, customs, etc. during a "transitional stage". It went further and proposed that it deal also with the enforcement of safeguards for the minorities in both states.

The record reveals that apart from the dubious procedure of its appointment and its odd composition, the subcommittee was hijacked by Dr. S.A. Latif of Hyderabad whom Jinnah called a "busy body". In June 1946, Jinnah did accept an all-India federation under the Cabinet Mission's Plan. The Congress sabotaged it. That was the last chance for preserving the subcontinent's unity. Its partition and the bloodbath that followed on the dawn of its independence from British rule must rank among the 10 greatest tragedies in recorded human history.

Reports by successive Governors of Punjab warned against the bloodbath. Lionel Carter produced two compilations of their Reports to the Viceroy from 1936 to 1943. The latest provided warning enough (*Punjab Politics: 1 January 1944 - 3 March 1947*; Lionel Carter (edited); Manohar, distributed by Foundation Books; pages 392, Rs. 950). Raghuvendra Tandon's collection of press reports and public statements is an invaluable record of the massacre in Punjab (*Reporting the Partition of Punjab 1947*; Manohar, distributed by Foundation Books; pages 622, Rs.1,195). Both India and Pakistan paid a heavy price in overcoming this misfortune of great consequence.

Two scholars of note, Hafeez Malik and Yuri Gankovsky, have edited an extremely informative encyclopaedia on all the significant aspects of Pakistan to which other scholars of note also contributed. Its illustrations are as rich as the text.

Bibliography

Adikaram, E. W.: *Early History of Buddhism in Ceylon,* D. S. Puswella, Migoda, 1946.

Agrawala, V. S.: *Shiva Mahadeva: The Great God,* Veda Academy, Varanasi, 1966.

Ahmad, Imtiaz: *State and Foreign Policy: India's Role in South Asia,* Vikas, New Delhi, 1993.

Ahmad, Jamil-ud-din: *Some Recent Speeches and Writings of Mr. Jinnah,* Lahore, Ashraf, 1952.

Aiyar, R. Krishnaswami: *Outlines of Vedaanta,* Chetana, Bombay, 1978.

Archer, W. G.: *The Kama Sutra,* Unwin Hyman, London, 1990.

Ashton, S.R. : *British Policy Towards the Indian States, 1905-1939,* London, Curzon, 1982.

Aurobindo, Sri: *Vyasa and Valmiki,* Acharya Press, Pondicherry, 1956.

Avalon, Arthur and Ellen: *Hymns to the Goddess,* Ganesh and Co., Madras, 1964.

Aziz, Ashraf: *Light of the Universe: Essays on Hindustani Film Music,* Three Essays Collective, New Delhi, 2003.

Bagchi, P. C.: *Studies in Dharmashastra,* University of Calcutta Press, Calcutta, 1939.

Bahadur, K.P.: *The Wisdom of Vedaanta,* Sterling Publishers Private Limited, New Delhi, 1996.

Banerjea, J. N.: *Pauranic and Vedanta Religion,* University of Calcutta, Calcutta, 1996.

Bankimchandra, C.: *Essentials of Dharma,* Sanskrit Book Depot, Calcutta 1979.

Basu, Manoranjan: *Dharmashastra: A General Study,* Shrimati Mira Basu, Calcutta, 1976.

Beaumont, Roger : *Sword of the Raj: The British Army in India, 1747-1947*, Indianapolis, Bobbs-Merrill, 1977.

Benjamin, Joseph : *Scheduled Castes in Indian Politics and Society*, New Delhi, Ess Ess Publications, 1989.

Bhattacharyya, B.: *Nispannayogavali of Mahapandita Abhyakara Gupta*, Oriental Institute, Baroda, 1949.

Borchert, Bruno: *Mysticism: Its History and Challenge*, Samuel Wiser, York Beach, 1994.

Bose, D. N.: *Dharmashastra: Their Philosophy and Occult Secrets*, Kali Press, Calcutta, 1965.

Bowle, John: *The Imperial Achievement: The Rise and Transformation of the British Empire*, Little, Brown, 1974.

Brockington, J. L.: *Righteous Rama: The Evolution of an Epic*, Oxford, London, 1984.

Bromley, D.: *Krishna Consciousness in the West*, Bucknell University Press, Lewisburg, 1989.

Brooks, E.: *The Original Analects: Sayings of Confucius and His Successors*. Columbia University Press, New York, 1988.

Bruhn, Klaus: *The Jina-Images of Deogarh*, MacMillan, Leiden, 1969.

Burke, Mary Louise: *Swami Vivekananda in America: New Discoveries*, Advaita Ashrama, Calcutta, 1966.

Chaudhary, M.: *Partition and the Curse of Rehabilitation*, Calcutta, Bengal Rehabilitation Organization, 1964.

Chaudhuri, Nirad: *Thy Hand, Great Anarch! India: 1921-1952*, London, Chatto & Windus, 1987.

Coomeraswamy, Ananda K.: *Buddha and the Gospel of Buddhism*, MacMillan, London, 1928.

Crawford, Cromwell S.: *Ram Mohan Roy: His Era and Ethics*, Acharya Press, New Delhi, 1984.

Dalton, Dennis : *Gandhi's Power : Nonviolence in Action*, New Delhi, OUP, 2001.

Danielou, Alain: *The Complete Kama Sutra*, Park Street Press, Rochester, 2000.

Dasgupta, Shahana: *Rani Lakshmibai: The Indian Heroine*, Rupa & Company, Calcutta, 2002.

Datta, V.N.: *Sati: Widow Burning in India*, Manohar, New Delhi, 1990.

David, M. D.: *John Wilson and his Institutions*, Mumbai, 1957.

De Bary: *Self and Society in Ming Thought*, Columbia University Press, New York, 1970.

De, Sushil Kumar: *Ancient Indian Erotics and Erotic Literature*, Firma K. L. Mukhopadhyay, Calcutta, 1959.

Deak, Istvan: *The Lawful Revolution: Louis Kossuth and the Hungarians 1848-1849*, Columbia University Press, 1979.

Dhar, Niranjan: *Vedanta and Bengal Renaissance*, Minerva Associates, Calcutta, 1977.

Dikshit, D.P. *Political History of the Chalukyas of Badami*. New Delhi: Abhinav, 1980.

Donat, K.: *Meditate the Tantric Yoga Way*, George Allen and Unwin, London, 1973.

Doniger, W.: *The Rig Veda: An Anthology*, Penguin, New York, 1981.

Duboi, Abbe: *Hindu Manners, Customs and Ceremonies*, Fifth Indian Impression, CUP, 1985.

Dwivedi, M.: *The Principal Upanishads*, Adyar Library, Madras, 1931.

Eaton, Richard M.: *Sufis of Bijapur, 1300-1700: Social Roles of Sufis in Medieval India*, Princeton University Press, Princeton, 1978.

Edwardes, Michael: *Battles of the Indian Mutiny*, London; B. T. Batsford Ltd., 1963.

Erickson, Erik H.: *Gandhi's Truth: On the Origins of Militant Nonviolence*, Norton, New York, 1970.

Farquhar, J.N.: *Modern Religious Movements in India*, Munshiram, New Delhi, 1967.

Fay, Peter Ward: *The Opium War, 1840-42*, University of North Carolina Press, 1975.

Fisher, Michael H.: *The Politics of British Annexation of India - 1757-1857*, Oxford, 1996.

Frauwallner, E..: *History of Indian Philosophy*, Motilal, Delhi, 1973.

Gambhirananda, S.: *Brahma Sutra Shamkar Bhasya*, Adavita Ashrama, Calcutta, 1977.

Gambhirananda, Swami: *Brahma Sutra Shamkar Bhasya*, Adavita Ashrama, Calcutta, 1977.

Gandhi, M. K.: *The Story of My Experiment With Trust*, Washington, Public Affairs Press, 1948.

Garbe, R.: *The Philosophy of Ancient India,* Chicago University Press, Chicago, 1899.

Goradia, Nayana: *Lord Curzon: The Last of the British Moghuls,* New Delhi, Oxford University Press, 1993.

Goudriaan, T.: *Ritual and Speculation in Early Tantrism,* State University of New York Press, New York, 1992.

Gough, A.E.: *The Philosophy of the Upanisads and Ancient Indian Metaphysics,* MacMillan, London, 1882.

Grant, G. P.: *Philosophy in the Mass Age,* Copp Clark, Toronto, 1959.

Grisenold, H.D.: *Insights into Modern Hinduism,* Oxford, New York, 1934.

Growse, F. S.: *The Ramayana of Tulasidasa,* Motilal Banarsidass, Delhi, 1995.

Gurumurthy, S. : *Hindu Heritage, Assimilative, Not Divisive,* Vigil, Madras 1993.

Haich, E.: *Sexual Energy and Yoga,* Aurora Press, New York, 1982.

Hasan, Murhirul: *Legacy of a Divided Nation: India's Muslims Since Independence,* New Delhi, Oxford, 1997.

Hasan, Mushirul: *India's Partition: Process, Strategy and Mobilization,* New Delhi, Oxford UP, 1993.

Heifetz, Hank: *The Origin of the Young God: Kalidasa's Kumarasambhava,* University of California Press, Berkeley, 1985.

Heimann, Betty: *Facets of Indian Thought,* Geroge Allen & Unwin, London, 1964.

Heinsath, Charles: *Indian Nationalism and Hindu Social Reform,* Princeton University Press, Princeton, 1964.

Heschel, J.: *God in Search of Man: A Philosophy of Judaism,* Noonday Press, New York, 1997.

Hirschman, Edwin: *White Mutiny: The Ilbert Bill Crisis in India and the Genesis of the Indian National Congress,* New Delhi, Heritage, 1980.

Hixon, L.: *Mother of the Universe: Visions of the Goddess, Tantric Hymns of Enlightenment,* Quest Books, Wheaton, 1994.

Hopkins, J.: *Kalachakra Tantra Rite of Initiation,* Wisdom Publications, Boston, 1982.

Hopkirk, Peter: *The Great Game: The Struggle for Empire in Central Asia,* Kodansha, 1992.

Hume, R.E.: *The Thirteen Principle Upanishads*, Oxford University Press, London, 1971.

Hutchins, Francis: *Spontaneous Revolution: The Quit India Movement*, New Delhi, Manohar, 1971.

Irene, S.: *Vedic Heritage Teaching Program*. Arsha Vidya Gurukulam, Coimbatore, 1994.

Iyar, K.: *Vedanta: The Science of Reality*, Ganesh and Co., Mardas, 1930.

Iyengar, B.K.S.: *Light on the Yoga Sutras of Patanjali*, Aquarian Press, London 1993.

Jacob, K.: *Religion and Ethics in Advaita*, C.M.S. Press, Kottayam, 1982.

Jafar, Malik Muhammad: *Jinnah as a Parliamentarian*, Lahore, Afzar Publications, 1977.

Jain, Kailash Chand, *Lord Mahavira and His Times*, Saraswati Press, Delhi, 1974.

James, Lawrence: *The Rise and Fall of the British Empire*, St. Martin's, 1997.

James, Robert Rhodes: *The British Revolution, 1880-1939*, New York, Knopf, 1976.

Jean, M.: *Tantrik Yoga*, The Aquarian Press, Wellingborough, 1970.

John, B.: *Mantras: Sacred Words of Power*, George Allen and Unwin, London, 1977.

John, Elsner: *Pilgrimage: Past and Present in the World Religions*, Harvard University Press, Cambridge, 1995.

John, K.: *The Origin and Development of the State Cult of Confucius*, Paragon Book, New York, 1966.

Karmarkar, D.: *Sankara's Advaita*, Karnatak University, Dharwar, 1976.

Kaushik, Asha : *Globalization, Democracy and Culture : Situating Gandhian Alternatives*, Jaipur, Pointer, 2002.

Kaviraj, G.: *Aspects of Indian Thought*, University of Burdwan, Calcutta, 1966.

Kavlekar, K.K. : *Non-Brahmin Movement in Southern India, 1873-1949*, Kolhapur, Shivaji University, 19790

Keith, A.B. : *Rigveda Brahmanas*, Harvard University Press, Cambridge, 1920.

Keith, Arthur Berriedale: *The Religion and Philosophy of the Veda and Upanishads*, MacMillan, Delhi, 1925.

Kishwar, Madhu : *Religion at the Service of Nationalism, and Other Essays*, OUP, Delhi, 1998.

Klaus, K.: *A Survey of Hinduism*, State University of New York Press, Albany, 1989.

Knipe, M.: *Hinduism: Experiments in the Sacred*, Harper, San Francisco, 1991.

Knott, K.: *Hinduism, A Very Short Introduction*, Oxford University Press, New York, 1998.

Kosambi, D. D. : *The Culture and Civilisation of Ancient India in Historical Outline*, London, Routledge and Kegan Paul, 1956.

Kottackal, Jacob: *Religion and Ethics in Advaita*, C.M.S. Press, Kottayam, 1982.

Kuiper, F.B.J. : *Aryans in the Rigveda*, Rodopi, Amsterdam, 1991.

Kuppuswamy, Sastri S.: *Compromises in the History of Advaitic Thought*, Kalyani Press, Madras, 1940.

Louis, Fischer: *Essential Gandhi: An Anthology of His Writings*, Vintage, New York, 1983.

Low, D. A. and Brasted, Howard: *Freedom, Trauma, Continuities: Northern India and Independence*, New Delhi, Sage Publications, 1998.

Maheshwari, Shriram: *Rural Development in India: A Public Policy Approach*, New Delhi, Sage, 1995.

Makhan, L.: *The Ramayana of Valmiki*, Munshiram Manoharlal, New Delhi, 1978.

Mathew, Arnold: *Culture and Anarchy*, The University Press, Cambridge, 1935.

Mayer, A. : *Caste in an Indian Village: Change and Continuity 1954-1992*, Delhi, OUP, 1996.

Mazumder, Sukhendu : *Politico-Economic Ideas of Mahatma Gandhi: Their Relevance in the Present Day*, New Delhi, Concept Pub., 2004.

Mearns, David J.: *Shiva's Other Children: Religion and Social Identity amongst Overseas Indians*, Sage, Walnut Creek, 1995.

Mearns, J.: *Shiva's Other Children: Religion and Social Identity amongst Overseas Indians*, Sage, Walnut Creek, 1995.

Mehra, Parshotam: *A Dictionary of Modern Indian History, 1707-1947*, New Delhi, Oxford University Press, 1985.

Metcalf, Thomas R.: *The Aftermath of the Revolt: India, 1857-1870*, Princeton, Princeton University, 1964.

Mohan, K.: *The Mahabharata*, Munshiram Manoharlal, Delhi 1997.

Mookerjee, Ajit: *Kali The Feminine Force*, Thames and Hudson, London, 1988.

Mookerji, Satkari: *Modern Polity and Vedanta*, Sanskrit College, Calcutta, 1972.

Moon, Penderel: *The British Conquest and Dominion of India*, London, Duckworth, 1989.

Morris-Jones, W.H.: *The Government and Politics of India*, London, Hutchinson, 1971.

Nanda, B. R. : *Gandhi and His Critics*, Oxford University Press, Delhi, 1993.

Neale, Walter C.: *Economic Change in Rural India: Land Tenure and Reform in the United Provinces, 1800-1955*, New Haven, 1962.

Nevile, P.: *Lahore: A Sentimental Journey*, New Delhi, Penguin, 1993.

Oddie, G.A. : *Hindu and Christian in South-East India*, London, Curzon Press, 1991.

Pathak, Dr S.P.: *Jhansi during the British Rule*, Ramanand Vidya Bhawan, Delhi, 1987.

Preston, Diana: *The Boxer Rebellion*, Berkley Books, 2000.

Raimundo Panikkar: *The Vedic Experience: Mantramanjari*, Longman Todd, London, 1977.

Raja, C. Kunhan : *The Taittiriya Sarvanukramani of Yaska*, Madras, 1931.

Ramamurti, A.: *Advaitic Mysticism of Sankara*, Visvabharati, Santiniketan, 1974.

Ranajit Guha: *A Construction of Humanism in Colonial India*, CASA, Amsterdam, 1993.

Renou, Louis: *The Nature of Dharmashastra*, Walker and Co., New York, 1997.

Robson, Brian: *Sir Hugh Rose and the Central India Campaign*, Sutton Publishing Ltd for the Army Records Society, UK, 2000.

Satyapal Verma: *Role of Reason in Sankara Vedanta*, Parimal Publication, Delhi, 1992.

Savarkar, Vinayak Damodar : *The Indian War of Independence* 1857 Rajdhani Granthagar, Delhi, 1988.

Scheftelowitz, Isidor : *Die Kasmirische Rezension von Katyayanas Sarvanukramani,* Zeitschrift fur Indologie und Iranistik, 1922.

Shukla, D. N.: *Vastu-Shastra,* Motilal Banarsidass, Delhi, 1966.

Singh, Birendra Kumar: *Early Chalukyas of Vatapi, circa A.D. 500 to 757,* Delhi, Eastern Book Linkers, 1991.

Smith, Col. J. T. : *Silver and the India Exchanges,* Effingham Wilson, London, 1876.

Strauss, L.: *Political Philosophy,* The Bobbs Merrill Co., New York, 1975.

Swami Vishnu Tirtha: *Devatma Shakti,* Swami Shivom Tirth, Rishikesh, 1962.

Talageri, Shrikant : *Aryan Invasion Theory and Indian Nationalism,* Voice of India, Delhi, 1993.

Tejomayananda, Swami: *Hindu Culture: An Introduction,* Chinmaya Publications, Piercy, 1993.

Thapar, Romila : *Ashoka and the Decline of the Mauryas,* London, Oxford University Press, 1961.

Thompson, Edward: *The Making of the Indian Princes,* Oxford University Press, London, 1943.

Trautmann, Thomas R.: *Kautilya and the Arthasastra: A Statistical Study,* Leiden, Brill, 1971.

Trimingham, J.: *Sufi Orders in Islam,* Oxford University Press, New York, 1998.

Utpat, V.N.: *Riddles of Buddha and Ambedkar,* Itihas Patrika Prakashan, Thane 1988.

Vable, D.: *The Arya Samaj. Hindu without Hinduism.* Vikas Publ., Delhi, 1983.

Vedalankar, Pandit Nardev : *Basic Teachings of Hinduism,* Veda Niketan, Durban, 1978.

Visvantha, K.: *Essentials of Hinduism,* Narosa Pub. House, New Delhi, 1989.

Wendy Doniger: *Siva: The Erotic Ascetic,* Oxford University Press, Delhi, 1998.

Zaidi, A. Moin: *Evolution of Muslim Political Thought in India,* New Delhi: S. Chand, 1975.

Index

D

E

F

G

H

I

J

K

L

M

N

O

P

Q

R

S

T

V

W

□□□